The
Social
Psychologists

RESEARCH ADVENTURES

McGRAW-HILL SERIES IN SOCIAL PSYCHOLOGY

CONSULTING EDITOR
Philip G. Zimbardo

The Social Psychologists

RESEARCH ADVENTURES

❖

EDITED BY

Gary G. Brannigan
Matthew R. Merrens
State University of New York–Plattsburgh

McGraw-Hill, Inc.

New York   St. Louis   San Francisco   Auckland   Bogotá   Caracas   Lisbon
London   Madrid   Mexico City   Milan   Montreal   New Delhi   San Juan
Singapore   Sydney   Tokyo   Toronto

THE SOCIAL PSYCHOLOGISTS
Research Adventures

 This book is printed on recycled, acid-free paper containing
10% postconsumer waste.

1 2 3 4 5 6 7 8 9 0 DOC DOC 9 0 9 8 7 6 5 4

ISBN 0-07-007234-5

This book was set in Palatino by The Clarinda Company.
The editors were Jane Vaicunas, Laura Lynch, and Fred H. Burns;
the production supervisor was Louise Karam.
The cover was designed by Carol A. Couch;
the cover illustration was painted by Gary Kelley.
R. R. Donnelley & Sons Company was printer and binder.

Photo Credits
Page v, top and bottom: photos by Robin Brown; *page 74:* photo by
Doug Detterman; *page 264:* photo by John Sheretz.

Library of Congress Cataloging-in-Publication Data

The Social psychologists: research adventures / edited by Gary G.
    Brannigan, Matthew R. Merrens.
        p.   cm. — (McGraw-Hill series in social psychology)
    Includes bibliographical references.
    ISBN 0-07-007234-5
    1. Social psychology—Research—Case studies.   I. Brannigan, Gary
G.   II. Merrens, Matthew R.   III. Series.
HM251.S67145   1995
302'.072—dc20   94-16599

About the Editors

❖

Gary G. Brannigan (Ph.D., University of Delaware) is Professor of Psychology at SUNY–Plattsburgh and a Fellow of the Society for Personality Assessment. His research is primarily on psychological assessment and therapy with children. He served as director of the Psychological Services Clinic at SUNY–Plattsburgh and is currently a consultant to the Clinton County Association for Retarded Citizens' Early Education Program. He is also serving on the editorial boards of three journals. In addition to coediting *The Undaunted Psychologist: Adventures in Research*, he has published numerous articles, chapters, books, and tests, including (with A. Tolor) *Research and Clinical Applications of the Bender Gestalt Test* and (with N. Brunner) *The Modified Version of the Bender Gestalt Test*. His interests include sports, art, music, and fine dining.

Matthew R. Merrens (Ph.D., University of Montana) is Professor and Chairperson of the Department of Psychology at SUNY–Plattsburgh. His research has focused on personality assessment and behavior modification. He has coordinated a large innovative introductory psychology course and has authored several general psychology handbooks. He is the coeditor of *The Undaunted Psychologist: Adventures in Research*. Dr. Merrens received the SUNY Chancellor's Award for Excellence in Teaching. He and his family enjoy outdoor activities in the Lake Champlain–Adirondack region of New York.

To my wife, Linda, and my sons, Marc and Michael
GGB

To my mother and father, Helen and Eddie, and my sister, Fran
MRM

Contents

———— ❖ ————

Foreword

———— ❖ ————

My uncle Gino, a Sicilian farmer from Palermo, believed that it was possible to develop a new kind of sweet cucumber to replace its sour-pickled cousin. He planted it in special soil, watered it ever so carefully, cross-bred it with varieties of vegetables renowned for their sweetness, and gently harvested it while singing soothing operatic arias. Even this sturdy young specimen knew in its heart that it was unique, different from others that merely looked comparable. It had been given a special head start in life and would do its best to make the farmer proud of his innovative techniques. Then Gino put his intervention to the ultimate test—by placing that sweet, some might say charming, young cucumber into the vinegar vat, all the while urging it to resist the conformity influences of its peers. But sad to tell, that sweet, distinctive cucumber came out a sour pickle, just like all the other less-privileged cucumbers. Gino had learned a powerful lesson that his nephew could have told him, saving him from much effort and soul-searching grief: Situations matter. Situations matter more than we acknowledge and more than most people even recognize. Situations can exert powerful influences on the behavior of individuals and groups, sometimes transforming them in ways that seem to violate basic conceptions of human nature.

The power of the situation has been considered the first lesson of social psychology. It is often posed as an antidote to the excessive preoccupation of those from individualistic cultures for whom dispositions, traits, and individual differences are seen as the central determinant of behavioral variability. Of course, situations are constructed by people, by their expectations and the normative standards they create. And yes, most behavioral outcomes are the product of interactions between dispositional proneness and situational forces. But what strikes the student of social behavior as surprising and curious is the unexpectedly strong impact of subtle, sometimes seemingly trivial, interventions that ought not to make such a difference in how people think, feel, and act. And yet, in research study after study, they do. That is one of the fascinations inherent in the study of social psychology, revealing the myriad ways in which smart people can be induced to act stupidly, good people recruited into evil, rational men to behave irrationally, passive women to take control of their lives by the simplest acts of choice, and throughout, mere words creating new realms of social reality.

To these intriguing demonstrations of the principles of situational power and the subjective construction of social reality, other social psychologists have added several more that give greater depth and breadth to our field. Some have shown the fallibility of human inference and the biases inherent in our decision-making processes; we are more self-justifying and rationalizing creatures than we are rational or objective in our self-evaluations. Other researchers add the dynamic power of groups over individual actions as a key contribution to knowledge made by social psychology. But for what, others ask. For a considerable number of our kin-folk, social psychology is special among all the areas of psychology because of the continuing legacy of concern for using its knowledge to help improve the human condition. It does so by choosing to study issues of social significance, by translating its findings into recommendations for public and social policy. And some of its scholars often change hats to become advocates of social change in areas as diverse as peace, health, law, criminal justice, education, business, environment, and many more.

So Uncle Gino's somewhat apocryphal story is but one of the host of tales whose message is part of the wisdom forming the foundation of social psychology. Indeed, there are interesting stories behind many of these general lessons that are passed along in our scholarly journals and college textbooks. What is missing from these objectively presented accounts is a human voice, a storyteller who goes beyond the description of facts to create the context of discovery which captured her imagination, or which compelled him to spend the next years of life tracking down that elusive social truth. Students know the *what* of our research, sometimes they also get the *how* of it. But rarely are they privileged to understand the *why* of it, or the *by whom* of it—unless their instructor is one of those original thinkers or among the family of his or her students.

Gary Brannigan and Matthew Merrens have opened up that family album of social psychology to everyone's benefit. Those in the close family circle will be pleased to recall some familiar stories, while being surprised to learn so many new details that were misconstrued in their second-hand retelling. New students of social psychology will be brought into the fold by getting the original tales—of what was done, by whom, for what reasons—told by each of sixteen delightful storytellers who have helped to write the book of lessons of social psychology. Their accounts cover a wide path that our field has explored in the past fifty years of its post-World

War II existence. Women and men, young and senior, from the United States, Europe, and Asia, basic researchers and practical policy advocates, theorists and empiricists, all tell instructively entertaining stories about how they came to do what they are doing, or have done, to shape the direction of modern social psychology. In the process, we learn about them as people and how their values and perspectives, choices and serendipity shaped their intellectual contributions. As we do, their tales become memorable since we encode this autobiographical information about the storytellers along with the content of their stories. By humanizing the research process in this way, it is my hope that today's graduate and undergraduate students will read these tales and come away saying, "I could have done that," or "I can do that," and perhaps, "I will do even better than that."

The **McGraw-Hill Series in Social Psychology** has been designed as a celebration of the fundamental contributions being made by researchers, theorists, and practitioners of social psychology to our understanding of human nature and to the potential for enriching the quality of our lives through wise applications of their knowledge. It has become a showcase for presenting new theories, original syntheses, analyses, and current methodologies by distinguished scholars and promising young writer-researchers. Our authors reveal a common commitment to sharing their vision with a broad audience, starting with their colleagues and extending out to graduate students, but especially to undergraduates with an interest in social psychology. Some of our titles convey ideas that are of sufficient general interest that their message needs to be carried out into the world of practical application to those who may translate some of them into public action and public policy. Although each text in our series is created to stand alone as the best representative of its area of scholarship, taken as a whole they represent the core of social psychology. Teachers may elect to use any of them as "in-depth" supplements to a basic, general textbook, while others may choose to organize their course entirely around a set of these monographs. Each of our authors has been guided by the objective of conveying the essential lessons and principles of his or her area of expertise in an interesting style, one that informs without resort to technical jargon, and that inspires others to utilize these ideas at conceptual or practical levels.

Please now enjoy the tales in this storybook, edited so superbly by Gary Brannigan and Matthew Merrens, and later on make some time to browse through the rest of the dozen or so intriguing titles in our family store. But if you run into Uncle Gino please don't ask if he wants cucumbers in his salad or pickles with his American hot dog. I am told that he is still sensitive about his failed experiment. However, he does make terrific pasta with prawns and, if you supply the wine and unlimited attention, he will share a new story. He might even tell you a provocative tale about how he used the principles of social influence, adapted and culturally modified from the storybook of paisan Roberto Cialdini, to induce his townsfolk to mobilize against the mafia. But that's another story, for another time, maybe after you first turn to the feast before us with its enticing presentation by our editor-chefs.

Philip G. Zimbardo
Consulting Editor

Preface

❖

The impetus for this book came from our dissatisfaction with many textbooks that characterize research as a dull, routine, lifeless process. In our first book, *The Undaunted Psychologist: Adventures in Research,* we provided readers with in-depth, first-person accounts of research in major areas of psychology. It was designed to complement texts in introductory psychology and psychological research methods courses as well as to serve as a primary text in advanced seminars. *The Undaunted Psychologist* has proved to be very successful, and we felt the approach would be of value in major discipline areas of psychology. *The Social Psychologists: Research Adventures* follows the same strategy and approach as *The Undaunted Psychologist,* but with a greater emphasis on the "nitty-gritty" aspects of research—planning, design, and methodology.

It seems natural to begin with social psychology. Research in this area contributes greatly to our understanding of the people and situations we encounter in our day-to-day lives. Furthermore, the research often concerns major social issues such as violence, racial prejudice, health care, overcrowding, and sex discrimination. These are issues that we read about in the newspaper, see on the evening news, and talk about in the workplace.

If, as we believe, we learn more from people than from textbooks, this collection of personal research stories will be enlightening, informative, and enriching. Our contributors provide lively narrative accounts covering a broad range of topics that closely parallel those found in most social psychology textbooks. The topics include

> Psychology of the self
> Social cognition
> Personality and behavior
> Social influence
> Interpersonal processes

Prosocial behavior
Attraction
Love
Relationships
Aggression
Prejudice and discrimination
Cross-cultural psychology

We also have included chapters in the applied social areas of

Health
The environment
The legal system
Politics

As you read about the personal experiences of the contributors, you will see how they approached significant problems and developed strategies to deal with, understand, and explore those issues. Finally, you will get to know some of the important figures whose names and areas of study appear in social psychology texts and journals. We hope you enjoy their stories.

ACKNOWLEDGMENTS

The Social Psychologists: Research Adventures tells about the experiences of sixteen distinguished researchers. The chapters genuinely communicate the excitement and enthusiasm of their search for knowledge and understanding. We are very appreciative of their efforts and thank them for their commitment to this book.

We owe a significant debt of gratitude to Chris Rogers, former editor at McGraw-Hill. Chris's foresight, as well as his support and friendship, made this book a reality. We also appreciate the ongoing support and counsel of Jane Vaicunas, executive editor, and Laura Lynch, assistant editor, as well as the superb job of final editing by Fred Burns, senior editing supervisor, and Eric Lowenkron, copyeditor. In addition, the guidance of our counsulting editor, Phil Zimbardo, helped shape the quality of the final product. The reviewers of this book also provided many insightful suggestions for refining and improving the chapters. We thank Michael Leippe, Adelphi University; David Myers, Hope College; David Schroeder, University of Arkansas; and Ann Weber, University of North Carolina–Asheville.

We are grateful to the State University of New York–Plattsburgh for providing a supportive environment that enabled us to pursue this project. The advice and help of our colleagues, especially Bill Tooke, Dave Dustin, and Naomi McCormick, were also invaluable. In addition, the assistance of the following students, who critiqued the chapters, was also very important to the final outcome: Josh Duntley, Marc Brannigan, Amanda Jankowski, Carole Cruse, Michael Brannigan, and Lynn Mintz. Their suggestions helped make this book more reader-focused and accessible.

Our secretary, Judy Dashnaw, is deserving of special commendation. Her superior editorial and word processing skills were absolutely vital to the timely and successful completion of this project.

Finally, we would like to thank our wives, Linda Brannigan and Roberta Merrens, for their efforts in reading and proofing the chapters in this book. Their comments, thoughts, and ongoing support contributed greatly to the quality of this volume.

Gary G. Brannigan
Matthew R. Merrens

Introduction

❖

Since our days in graduate school we have been fascinated with social psychology research, both as participants (e.g., investigating topics such as the Barnum effect and the approval motive) and as observers. The problems and issues explored, the interesting methodologies, and the ability to focus on "real-world" concerns made social psychology seem relevant and challenging, a field that is constantly reinventing itself.

In this book we hear the voices of sixteen prominent social psychologists who describe their personal encounters with interesting and meaningful social issues. Through their encounters we are able to see these psychologists as people who struggle with doubts, benefit from serendipity, encounter frustration, and enjoy success; that is, they experience all the ups and downs that characterize the process of psychological investigation.

We feel strongly that it is important for you to experience these research adventures firsthand, and so we refrained from using a heavy editorial style that promotes the kind of sameness one sees in textbooks. We want you to hear the unique voices and perspectives of the contributors as they relate their individual stories. In this way we have eliminated the "middleman" so that you can experience for yourself what social psychological research is all about.

We have chosen selectively among the varied topics social psychologists study to give you a cross section of their work. Thus, some topics are featured under specific headings in specific chapters (e.g., helping, aggression, prejudice), while others (most notably, attitudes) are not featured but appear in a variety of ways throughout the book. Also, we have avoided chapter introductions and summaries in favor of letting the stories "unfold like good mystery novels." However, we want to give you a taste of what's to come. We hope this sampler of the research tales (gleaned from reviewers' observations) will whet your appetite for more.

In the opening chapter Tony Greenwald describes the gradual development of his ideas about the "self" that ultimately found their expression in his well-known "totalitarian-ego" article. In turn, he discusses the consequences those ideas have had for his research life, teaching life, and personal life. Next, Susan Fiske recounts her experience giving expert testimony before the U.S. Supreme Court on a famous sex discrimination case while weaving in personal and professional experiences from her undergraduate days to the present involving her research on the social cognitive view of stereotyping. In a clear, well-delineated chronology, Mark Snyder details how the concept of self-monitoring began as an idea and a set of personal observations and evolved into an important line of research. Bob Cialdini provides an absorbing glimpse into his research on social influence and the serendipitous beginning of his psychology career in college. Through his poignantly personal look at the development of a social psychologist, Roy Baumeister guides us through a flowing description of his youth, college years, graduate training, and job search as well as his attempts to publish his research on the social aspects of self. Jack Dovidio presents a very engaging account of the turning points and influential experiences in his life that led him to his research on pro-social behavior. Karen and Ken Dion relate two stories in one chapter, describing their exciting research experiences on the power of physical attractiveness and love. In tracing her long research career, Elaine Hatfield gives readers a behind-the-scenes look at how her ideas developed, persevered, and translated into significant research on self-esteem and relationships. Leonard Berkowitz weaves general, all-encompassing theories of psychology into a personal discussion of his diverse research studies on aggression. Patricia Devine presents a detailed discussion of her development as a social psychologist through her research experiences in eyewitness identification and prejudice. With special emphasis on the impact of collectivism on Chinese and Americans, Michael Bond provides unique insights into the ins and outs of doing cross-cultural research. Robin DiMatteo presents an intriguing, touching account of her work in medical settings that examines the nature of the physician-patient relationship. Paul Paulus's engaging, up-close look at research on crowding in prisons is loaded with anecdotes and personal contemplation. Norbert Kerr "thinks out loud" about the design of and procedural considerations in setting up an intriguing research study of the effects of pretrial publicity on jury behavior. And last but not least, Phil Tetlock takes us on an absorbing intellectual journey into his research program on integrative complexity and its implications for political decision making.

The
Social
Psychologists

RESEARCH ADVENTURES

*A*NTHONY *G*REENWALD *(Ph.D., Harvard University) has been Professor of Psychology at the University of Washington since 1986 and was previously a member of the psychology faculty at Ohio State University for twenty-one years. Greenwald was editor of the* Journal of Personality and Social Psychology, *has coedited five books, and has authored or coauthored about ninety published articles and chapters on the topics of attitude, self, unconscious cognition, and research methodology.*

1

Getting (My) Self into Social Psychology

————————— ❖ —————————

*I*t's supposed to happen like this: First you get a great, original theoretical idea. You proceed to devise and construct an ingenious experiment, confirming a prediction that runs counter to virtually every intelligent person's expectations. Then, in an inevitable progression, your first dramatic finding leads to a succession of studies and publications that eventually demonstrate completely unexpected applications that prove to be of immense value. Not to mention that along the way you accumulate research grants, academic promotions, scientific awards, and of course romantic admirers as you are chauffeur-driven off into the sunset.

Of course, it never happens that way. A careful analysis of actual research might even show that for each step of a typical research program, the opposite is more likely to be true. The research described in this chapter may, however, exceed most in its deviation from the Hollywood script.

There is another aspect of this chapter that does not follow the Hollywood story line, one that is very familiar to researchers but not to those inexperienced in research. Hollywood stories have the standard beginning, middle, and end. Research stories, however, typically have a beginning and a middle but no end. Don't take my word for it—instead, do something that I won't have had a chance to do as I'm writing this: Read the other chapters in this book and see if you can find one that, somewhere near the end, declares that a final conclusion has been reached on the problem that prompted the research. And while you're at it, you might see if you can find one that comes anywhere close to the Hollywood script.

Going beyond the endless character of research stories, this story also lacks a clear beginning, so I'll go directly to the middle: Sometime around 1975 it dawned on me that things I had been thinking about for some time were pieces that fit together to make a surprising picture of the way one's self works. The picture was surprising in part because it had already been described in an unlikely place, George Orwell's famous political fiction, *1984*. It was surprising also because Orwell had presented it not as the way the self works but rather as the workings of thought control and propaganda in a totalitarian state.

One other unusual aspect of this story is that I had not done research on any topic that was even close to the question of what the self is and how it works. So I should explain how I came to spend a lot of time thinking about a topic on which I was doing no research.

EDUCATION OF AN EDITOR (I): READ

In the early 1970s, as a young faculty member at Ohio State University, I had become a very active manuscript reviewer; that is, editors regularly asked me to evaluate scientific papers that had been submitted for publication in their journals. I liked reviewing manuscripts. Not only did it give me a feeling of privilege to learn about new research developments before they were published, it also gave me a sense of power—after all, the editor might be persuaded by my recommendation to publish or not publish the manuscript. Reviewing manuscripts was also work. It typically took at least three hours to read a manuscript (carefully) and write an evaluation that was then mailed back to the editor.

I had reached a high level of reviewing activity because in addition to any other qualities my reviews had, they were done promptly, and editors liked that. As a reward for this professional good behavior, in 1972 I was invited to become an associate editor of the *Journal of Personality and Social Psychology* and, in 1976, its editor. (Alas, this lofty position included no chauffeur.)

Holding an editorship severely affects one's reading diet. Ordinarily a scientist's professional reading focuses on the latest published work in his or her areas of research, along with prepublication manuscripts exchanged with colleagues working in those areas, supplemented (for variety) by browsing through the new issues of major journals. The operative principle in this reading diet of the active researcher is *choice*—your reading is guided primarily by your interests.

There is also a principle of choice operating in a journal editor's reading diet, but it is slightly different: It is what *others* choose to send to you as manuscript submissions. *Journal of Personality and Social Psychology* was then receiving about 1,000 manuscripts a year. As an associate editor, I supervised the review of about 100 manuscripts that the editor *chose* to send to me for evaluation. Later, as the editor, I supervised the review of almost twice that number, my reward being that I could *choose* those manuscripts from the total, sending the rest to associate editors.

Perhaps this will better give the flavor of the work of editorship: Imagine that you have a full-time day job but have decided to advance your education by devoting your evenings to a correspondence course. But it's an unusual correspondence course: It has no consistent topic and has a homework assignment due every day (two on Sunday!). Each lesson is taught by a new teacher who has provided a reading assignment of twenty to sixty double-spaced pages. This may sound like the nightmare in which you show up naked (and perhaps otherwise unprepared) for final exams. But this isn't a nightmare—it really resembles what an editor does. And likening it to being a student is exactly on target, because an editor cannot help but learn from all this reading.

*E*DUCATION OF AN EDITOR (II): LEARN

Here are a few of the articles I got to read during the period of my editorship. One was by Michael Ross and Fiore Sicoly, showing that when the two members of each of a sample of married couples were separately asked to report their percentage contribution to each of twenty ordinary household chores (cooking, child care, dishwashing, etc.), the averaged sum of each pair's responses reliably *exceeded* 100 percent. A set of survey studies conducted by Philip Brickman, Dan Coates, and Ronnie Janoff-Bulman demonstrated that on average respondents believed themselves to be better off than they had been five years previously and also believed that they would be even better off five years in the future. A field experiment by Ellen Langer showed that purchasers of lottery tickets placed monetary values on their tickets that were considerably greater than the price they paid for the tickets and did this especially when each purchaser had been able to choose a ticket from a set of distinctive available alternative tickets. A laboratory experiment by Timothy Rogers, Nicholas Kuiper, and W. S. Kirker showed that college students remembered words that named traits (such as *sincere, intelligent, stubborn*) better after judging whether each word was self-descriptive than they did after making other yes-no judgments concerning the trait words. And a study by Baruch Fischhoff showed that after being shown the correct answer to a trivia question, students overestimated the likelihood that prior to learning the correct answer they would have given that answer. For example, if I tell you that *absinthe* is the name of a type of drink and then ask you to estimate your likelihood of having guessed "a type of drink" rather than "a type of stone," you are likely to give a higher estimate than you would have if I hadn't first told you which answer was correct.

These studies were all interesting, well written, and original. However, I doubt that it's obvious (is it?) that they call for any major adjustment of thinking about the self-concept. But beware—we often fail to notice the extent to which new findings extend what we already know. Indeed, that was just what was shown by Fischhoff's study of the "knew-it-all-along effect." As it turned out, these findings, along with others that were accumulating during the 1970s, were pointing toward conclusions that were surprisingly different from what I already knew. By perhaps eighteen to twenty-four months after encountering the first of these findings, I had become convinced that the accumulating findings displayed three themes that could be stated as generalizations about the self. Here are the three themes, together with shorthand names for each:

First, *perception and memory revolve around self (egocentricity)*. The accumulated findings showed that we remember things associated with ourselves better than things associated with other people; that in observing others, we most easily notice characteristics that are central to our own personalities; and that in interpreting our own and others' actions, we are biased toward seeing others' actions as being caused by, or aimed at influencing, our own behavior.

Second, *charity begins with self (beneffectance)*. In judging the self compared to others, we see ourselves as having more than our fair share of good qualities and also more than others are inclined to credit us with; in judging our own performances, we readily believe that successes fairly reflect our abilities at the same time that we avoid taking responsibility for failures, chalking them up instead to uncontrollable circumstances.

Third, *self is perceived as rocklike in stability (cognitive conservatism)*. We resist acknowledging changes in our political opinions even when objective measures show that they have changed dramatically; we resist admitting previous ignorance of informally acquired knowledge; and, above all, we smoothly reconstruct memories of our past behavior to make it—at least in the retelling—consistent with our present self-image.

The labels for these three themes (egocentricity, beneffectance, and cognitive conservatism), even though captured as single words, are still cumbersome, so I will go further and use the three labels' initials (EBC) as a shorthand for the set. The EBC principles have some value in themselves as summaries of research findings, but it was also clear that their significance would be greater if I could find an effective way to interconnect them. And that seemed possible, because they already had a common ingredient: Each had a connection to the notion of the self.

Unfortunately, in the mid-1970s my knowledge of psychological theory concerning the self was very limited. The concept of the self had been actively used in psychoanalytic theory (for example, in Freud's concepts of the ego and superego) and was also used in some approaches to personality theory and clinical psychology (for example, in Carl Rogers's client-centered therapy and Abraham Maslow's concept of self-actualization as the pinnacle of human motivation). But in my domain of social psychology the self was little more than a wispy ghost from the past.

The self had played a prominent role in William James's major work, *Principles of Psychology* (1890), and had received renewed attention in the mid-1940s when Gordon Allport predicted (incorrectly or perhaps just very prematurely) that academic psychology was on the verge of vigorously embracing the concept of the self. (A parenthetical comment: It is both ironic and embarrassing for me to observe that some thirty years ago I failed to appreciate the scope of Gordon Allport's intellect. Allport, who died in 1967 after a long and bright career, was my Ph.D. adviser. Three topics that have been important in my career—attitudes, the self, and prejudice—were central to Allport's work. Unfortunately, while I was in graduate school, Allport was no longer actively involved with those topics and I had not yet become interested in them.)

ORWELL'S 1984

Perhaps I would have discovered no effective relation among the EBC principles if I had not previously read, and been fascinated enough to read a few times, George Orwell's 1949 poli-sci-fi novel, *1984*. Orwell's *1984* marvelously mixes a dramatic plot with a biting and far-ranging analysis of the effects of totalitarian government on the human psyche. It was on (perhaps) my fourth reading of *1984*—this one prompted by a suspicion that the book held a key to integrating the EBC principles—that I discovered many passages that expressed thoughts related to those three principles. The following quotations from *1984* may begin to suggest my growing sense of excitement as I happened upon, one after another, passages that were saturated with the EBC principles.

> "Who controls the past," ran the Party slogan, "controls the future: who controls the present controls the past." [p. 32]

Orwell was referring mainly to the written history of the totalitarian society, which could be controlled from the present by rewriting it whenever desired. This written history was (like the egocentricity of normal memory) centered on the ruling organization (the Party) and its leader, and (like beneffectance) it contained distortions in the form of recording that the leader generally produced good effects. But Orwell was also interested in the memories carried in the minds of citizens:

> The Party member . . . tolerates present-day conditions partly because he has no standards of comparison. He must be cut off from the past . . . because it is necessary for him to believe that he is better off than his ancestors and that the average level of material comfort is constantly rising. [p. 175]

Doesn't that sound just like the survey finding by Brickman, Coates, and Janoff-Bulman that I mentioned a few pages back? (They found that people believe they are now better off than they were five years ago and expect to be even better off another five years in the future.) Perhaps no passage was more relevant than the following one, which managed to merge the three principles and thus suggested how to interconnect them:

> The reason for the readjustment of the past is the need to safeguard the infallibility of the Party. . . . No change of doctrine or in political alignment can ever be admitted. For to change one's mind, or even one's policy, is a confession of weakness. [p. 175]

In this quote the centrality and infallibility of the Party (which are like egocentricity and beneffectance) are mentioned, and the importance of preserving the appearance of constancy (which is like cognitive conservatism) is also incorporated. Orwell understood that these distortions of the past and present served to maintain the Party's ruling position—its ability to "control the future."

While engaged in this intense rereading of Orwell, I at last became convinced that I had happened on an idea that was powerful enough to do more than just shift my intellectual interests. It would also change the way I understood myself, and if I could manage to communicate it effectively, it might also change the ways in which many other psychologists conceived of the operation of the self.

A PUZZLE TO SOLVE

Those familiar with *1984* know that Orwell was describing the operation not of an individual human mind but of a totalitarian state. In particular, Orwell was describing the totalitarian state's propaganda ministry (the Ministry of Truth in *1984*'s fictional Oceania). Why should there be an apparently close relation between Orwell's analysis of totalitarian information control and the EBC principles (which, you recall, were found in social psychological research to be characteristic of average, normal adults of the *non*totalitarian American society)? How can the most ordinary operations of human thought possibly be like the thought-control operations of a totalitarian state?

It seems grossly insulting—to you, to me, and to other presumably ordinary humans—to liken our routine mental functioning to the fabrications and distortions of a totalitarian propaganda apparatus. This poses a puzzle: Can one accept the EBC principles as valid *and* maintain self-respect in regard to one's own mental functioning? We could solve this puzzle by deciding that the EBC principles must be wrong. However, the research evidence for them was so strong as to be for all practical purposes irrefutable. And research since 1980 has provided further support and made the even stronger point that the ego's biases and illusions are *essential* to mental health (see the article by Shelley Taylor and Jonathan Brown and the book by Martin Seligman listed in this chapter's Suggested Readings).

To restate the puzzle: How can principles that are central to what appears to be a very *dys*functional organization (a totalitarian society) also describe the presumably successful functioning of an ordinary ("normal") human psyche? Finding the answer to that question put the final piece into the picture that I then proceeded to call "the totalitarian ego," which is, I hope, a more attention-grabbing shorthand than "EBC principles."

One way to establish the fact that the EBC principles serve useful functions in my psyche and yours would be to find some outside-the-head domain in which we could see the same or similar principles operating effectively. I already had a good hunch about a place to look. In a book, *The Structure of Scientific Revolutions*, that created a major stir when it was published in 1960, historian of science Thomas Kuhn pointed out that scientists often display strange patterns of thought—appearing to function irrationally—in their efforts to maintain the good reputation of a theory (or "paradigm") with which they are associated. Some quotes from Kuhn can illustrate this point.

In reading the following quotes, please be patient with Kuhn's language. Kuhn was writing for philosophers, who are notorious for believing that a scholarly argument is convincing to the extent that it is difficult to understand. Even so, I hope you can see that these quotes identify in the behavior of ordinary ("normal") scientists parallels to the EBC principles.

> To scientists . . . the results gained in normal research are significant because they add to the scope and precision with which the paradigm can be applied. [p. 56]

Gathering knowledge into the paradigm (adding to "the scope and precision with which [it] can be applied") parallels egocentricity: New knowledge is of interest and value to normal scientists primarily to the extent that it can be related to (centers on) the paradigm, just as new knowledge is of interest to you and me primarily to the extent that we can see its relation to our selves.

> [Normal science's] object is to solve a puzzle for whose very existence the validity of the paradigm must be assumed. Failure to achieve a solution discredits only the scientist and not the theory. [p. 80]

When scientists protect the paradigm from being discredited (by labeling another scientist's apparently theory-disconfirming findings as failures of "the scientist and not the theory"), their efforts are like the ego's beneffectance: The theory is credited with responsibility only for research findings that it correctly predicted and not for findings that may appear to disconfirm its predictions. Much as we, in perceiving our social worlds, find ways to blame situations or other people for our misfortunes and much as the Party in Orwell's *1984* is ready to sacrifice its members to maintain its appearance of power and goodness, so also may the reputations of individual scientists be sacrificed to sustain the illusion of the paradigm's correctness.

> [Normal science] seems an attempt to force nature into the preformed and relatively inflexible box that the paradigm supplies. [p. 24]

Scientists' forcing nature into the paradigm's "inflexible box" is a direct parallel of the ego's cognitive conservatism: The theory's central principles remain rocklike in their stability even in the face of new and unexpected findings.

Kuhn's conclusion was that this "normal" behavior of scientists serves to *protect* and *preserve* the underlying theory ("paradigm") on which their research rests.

> By ensuring that the paradigm will not be too easily surrendered resistance guarantees that scientists will not be lightly distracted and that the anomalies that lead to paradigm change will penetrate existing knowledge to the core. [p. 65]

Allow me to translate: Kuhn observes that it is a good thing that as science normally operates, occasional findings that are embarrassing to a theory ("anomalies") will not cause the entire established theoretical structure (the paradigm) to be abandoned ("easily surrendered"). The paradigm should be abandoned only when the force of embarrassing findings is so great as to question its most central assumptions (its "core"). Although some modifications of Kuhn's views have been suggested by other philosophers of science, Kuhn's central observations continue to be widely accepted. In other words, the "normal" activities of a group of scientists provide a context in which the EBC principles operate with apparently good effect.

A RESTING POINT

The EBC biases had been identified in totalitarian thought control, in scientific theory, and in the normal self. With the identification of these three domains which shared the EBC (or totalitarian-ego) principles, I was confident that the intellectual odyssey started by my editorship was near a resting point (recall that it has no end!). Nevertheless, before I could feel ready to explain these ideas to others in print, I still needed to explain to myself how and why the self could function well with these biases.

If the trio of domains showing the biases had not included scientific theory, I might not have found the answer. Fortunately, the writings of Kuhn and other philosophers of science had identified a beneficial aspect of the normal scientist's biases. As indicated most clearly by the last quote from Kuhn (about not being "lightly distracted"), the set of biases works to preserve and protect a theory, allowing it to have a long life of explaining many phenomena and generating useful applications. That observation provided the core of the explanation of why biases work. The totalitarian-ego biases protect the structure and individuality of an organization of knowledge such as a scientific theory and the totalitarian society and even the human self. (It may seem unusual to regard your self as an "organization of knowledge." Nevertheless, what constitutes you and your individuality is just that—an organization of knowledge that includes things such as your memories of the past, your present perceptions of self and environment, and your expectations for the future.)

SIDE EFFECTS

Early in the writing of "The totalitarian ego: Fabrication and revision of personal history," I could not avoid trying to judge the extent to which I possessed the totalitarian-ego biases: Did I function in the "normal" biased fashion, or was I capable of operating bias-free? A possible answer that was very consistent with the totalitarian-ego conception would be for me to consider myself free of the biases and thus better than average, even though I might possess the biases full-blown. It would just be the operation of the beneffectance bias, in particular, that would prevent me from seeing it and the other biases in myself. However, I had no doubt that I possessed all three. I knew that if I didn't possess them, it would not have been nearly so easy for me to discover illustrations of them in my own experience. Also, if I lacked them, I probably would not have been nearly so ready to conceive of them as part of normal cognitive functioning.

After having diagnosed myself as a walking case of the totalitarian-ego biases, I assumed that it was likely that my understanding of these biases would gradually reduce or eliminate them. How could I maintain, for example, the inflated self-image associated with beneffectance after I became aware that I was perceiving myself more favorably than could be objectively justified?

Fifteen years later I can say with confidence that for the most part I was wrong in expecting that I would lose these biases. This is an interesting situation. I continue to engage in biased memory and self-perception despite knowing about the existence and nature of those biases. It sounds a bit like what Orwell had in mind in creating the idea of double-think:

> The control of the past depends above all on the training of memory. . . . [It is] necessary to remember that events happened in the desired manner. And if it is necessary to rearrange one's memories or to tamper with written records, then it is necessary to forget that one has done so. The trick of doing this can be learned like any other mental technique. . . . It is called double-think. [p. 176]

However, there may be a simpler explanation than Orwell supposed. Maintaining beneffectance despite knowing about it may have something in common with smokers being unable to abandon their addictive habit despite understanding that it is fatal. As another example, it may have something in common with my being unable to offer a mathematical description of Einstein's theory of relativity despite knowing that such a description is possible. The explanation lies in inability: I don't know *how* to mathematically describe Einstein's theory, the habitual smoker doesn't know *how* to stop smoking, and apparently I also don't know *how* to operate other than by using my ego's ingrained biases.

If there is one area in which I may have managed to reduce biases, it is memory. It's not that I have improved in memory ability but rather that I have become consciously distrustful of my memory. I have had significant help in this. Ever since 1980, when I offered my wife a preliminary copy of the totalitarian-ego article to read, we have both understood that we tread on thin ice when we find ourselves in a conversation that includes the following: "Don't you remember? I said [such and such], and then you said [whatever]." "No," she replies. "You're reconstructing personal history again! *I* said [such and such], and then *you* said [whatever]." Our totalitarian egos notwithstanding, this distrust of our own and each other's memory seems to have been a healthy development.

*A*FTEREFFECTS (I): PROFESSIONAL

The decision, if it was that, to let my scholarly interests be shaped by the apparent happenstance of what colleagues chose to submit to the *Journal of Personality and Social Psychology* in the mid-1970s seems in retrospect to have been fortunate. The easier professional path is usually to remain in the specialized area in which you have already had the good fortune to establish some expertise. Colleagues and editors send you prepublication manuscripts that make it easy to maintain your edge over those who will not have a chance to see the same material until it appears in print at least a few years later. You are probably also actively teaching the topic to graduate students, who keep you sharp by raising embarrassing questions and suggesting research ideas. Nevertheless, one scientist's established area of expertise is another's rut.

Trying not to let the ruts grow too deep in any topic, I have progressed through the development of a few new research interests since writing the totalitarian-ego article. However, the self's cognitive biases continue to occupy me. As an illustration, I recently became involved with a problem that, as I eventually interpreted it, pitted my totalitarian-ego biases against those of my students—with no victor yet.

After several years of teaching undergraduate social psychology only to small groups of honors students and receiving very favorable evaluations by students, I resumed lecturing to a large class a few years ago. At the end of the term I was surprised to discover that the student ratings were quite low. I was not only surprised but distressed. Either I was a poor teacher or there was another reasonable explanation for the low ratings. Now that you've learned what beneffectance is, you won't be surprised to learn that I formed some hypotheses in the "other reasonable explanation" category. One possibility was that my course might have violated students' expectations about the amount of assigned work and difficulty, with the result that many students got lower grades than they expected or had to work unexpectedly hard for their grades, leading to displeasure that was reflected in their ratings. As a social psychologist, however, I wasn't content just to have this hypothesis; I wanted evidence.

So, a few years ago I started doing research on course evaluations. Data collected from student evaluations for a large number of courses at the University of Washington have now confirmed a powerful relationship between instructors' grading policies and students' evaluations. Courses that give higher grades get more favorable evaluations. Although this research hasn't yet solidified to the point of publication, I now believe that the grade-evaluation relationship involves a phenomenon of *displaced self-esteem* and that this also reflects the operation of students' totalitarian egos.

Self-esteem may be involved in course ratings because students can indirectly assert their own self-worth by perceiving either high quality in a course that has evaluated them highly or low quality in one that has not. To explain this a bit further, try this thought experiment: If you receive two evaluations, one very positive and the other very negative, with one of them coming from someone you greatly admire and the other coming from someone you dislike, would it make a difference which person gave you which evaluation? Of course it would. You would much prefer to believe that the person you admire considers you worthy. To say this another way, you can feel better about yourself either by reducing your opinion of someone who has a low opinion of you or by raising your opinion of someone who has a high opinion of you. All other things being equal (which we can assume in a thought experiment), should this affect your judgment of a teacher who gives you a high grade? If it does, then the effect deserves to be called displaced self-esteem—you are indirectly seeing your own self-worth as a quality of the other.

The discovery of apparent displaced self-esteem in course evaluations has prompted me to pursue this new line of research. I have learned enough already to become convinced of the need to change the methods by which instruction is routinely evaluated in most colleges and universities. Although it is too early to predict confidently what will come of this research, a proposal for an altered evaluation procedure is likely to specify the following two goals: (1) statistical correction for the effect of an instructor's grading policy on evaluations (to avoid distortions due to displaced self-esteem) and (2) attempts to evaluate the amount of student learning independently of student survey responses. (The second goal is much more easily said than done.) The ideal course should be one in which students not only enjoy the experience but also learn a lot.

*A*FTEREFFECTS (II): PERSONAL

My understanding of daily events in almost all contexts has been sharply altered by absorbing the idea of the totalitarian ego. Two of the strongest lessons of the totalitarian-ego conception concern the importance of persevering toward goals and learning from failure.

I now understand that perseverance, which is related to the beneffectance bias of the totalitarian ego, is one of life's major virtues. Optimistic expectations for success that are rooted in a beneffectance-biased positive self-image can encourage repeated attempts when initial efforts don't succeed. I see all around me the successes of colleagues who, confident in the quality of their work—and, not so incidentally, confident in the folly of those who disagree with that estimate—revise and resubmit, perhaps several times, an initially rejected journal manuscript or research grant proposal. And I see others who abandon such projects after a single experience of rejection. It is clear that the successes of the first group may be better explained by their perseverance than by the raw quality of their work. It's not that all projects succeed if you persist at them; rather, it's that except for those gifted few who usually *do* succeed on the first try, virtually nothing succeeds if you *don't* persist.

Another major virtue is discovering how to be receptive enough to experiences of failure to be able to improve yourself while at the same time not concluding that you are a dunce. I don't think this point can be put more effectively than with George Orwell's words from *1984*:

> The secret of [self-rule] is to combine a belief in one's own infallibility with the power to learn from past mistakes. [Orwell had written "rulership" where I put "self-rule."]

Orwell's advice easily finds its way into practice in the activities of scientists. Recall the situation of those who respond to rejection of their manuscripts and grant proposals by resubmitting them. Some resubmit by taking the manuscript or proposal out of one envelope, contemptuously discarding the accompanying reviewers' comments, and putting it into another envelope, addressed to a different journal or granting agency. My preferred variant is to read the reviewers' comments and, although regarding them (as seen by my totalitarian ego) as basically foolish opinions, nevertheless to put them to use in revising the manuscript or proposal. After all (my totalitarian-ego reasons), I may be unfortunate enough to encounter other like-minded reviewers, and I had best not give those others the occasion to make the same criticisms. Similarly, my suspicion that students' displaced self-esteem is a possible explanation of low teaching evaluations does not prevent me from suspecting that I can effectively change some aspects of my teaching. Although I don't want to reduce assigned reading or make exams so easy that students won't need to read the assignments, I would also like to find ways of producing greater enjoyment of this arduous experience. (Please send suggestions.)

EPILOGUE

A very pleasing aftereffect of having written the totalitarian-ego article is to see that in a relatively short period of time basic features of the view of the self that it described have now been incorporated widely into psychological thinking and writing about the self. The main features of this view are, first, conceiving the self as an organization of knowledge and, second, recognizing that the self's biases and illusions work toward preserving that organization and making it adaptive. I know that the component ideas of this view are not original to me. The most I can claim is to have seen a connection among ideas that were afloat within the discipline of social psychology. And my ability to see that connection was possible only because that same discipline had given me a privileged observer's position—a rather flattering way, you may agree, to describe the editor's role that started me on a path toward the totalitarian ego.

Acknowledgments

References to works by writers and researchers who are named in this chapter as well as citations for the chapter's quotations from George Orwell and others will be found in my 1980 article listed as one of the suggested readings. The preparation of this chapter was assisted by support from the National Institutes of Mental Health (Grant MH41328) and the National Science Foundation (Grant DBC-9205890).

SUGGESTED READINGS

ARENDT, H. (1966). *The origins of totalitarianism* (3d ed.). New York: Harcourt, Brace & World.

GREENWALD, A. G. (1980). The totalitarian ego: Fabrication and revision of personal history. *American Psychologist, 35,* 603–618.

JAMES, W. (1890). *Principles of psychology* (2 vols.). New York: Holt (James's famous chapter on the self is in vol. 1).

ORWELL, G. (1949). *1984.* New York: Harcourt Brace.

SELIGMAN, M. E. P. (1991). *Learned optimism.* New York: Knopf.

TAYLOR, S. E., & BROWN, J. D. (1988). Illusion and well-being: A social psychological perspective on mental health. *Psychological Bulletin, 103,* 193–210.

*S*USAN *T. FISKE (Ph.D., Harvard University) is Distinguished University
Professor of Psychology at the University of Massachusetts at Amherst.
She received a B.A. in social relations and a Ph.D. in social psychology.
Her federally funded social cognition research is focused on motivation and
stereotyping. Fiske has authored over eighty professional articles and chapters
and coauthored* Social Cognition *with Shelley E. Taylor (1984; 2d ed., 1991).
Fiske is the 1991 winner of the American Psychological Association Award for
Distinguished Contributions to Psychology in the Public Interest, Early Career;
the 1994 President of the Society for Personality and Social Psychology; and the
editor, with Daniel Gilbert and Gardner Lindzey, of the forthcoming fourth edition of the* Handbook of Social Psychology.

2

From the Still Small Voice of Discontent to the Supreme Court: How I Learned to Stop Worrying and Love Social Cognition

❖

The great hall of the Supreme Court was packed. Silence fell as the justices settled themselves. The attorney for the Big Eight accounting firm Price Waterhouse started to present the case by explaining why that corporate giant had nixed the partnership bid of a candidate with more billable hours than the eighty-seven other people who had come up that year, a senior manager who had garnered millions of dollars in contracts and was described as hard-driving, exacting, and successful with clients. Criticized for "interpersonal skills problems," this "lady partner candidate" was counseled that she should walk, talk, and dress in a more feminine fashion. Before the attorney could explain the firm's view that Ms. Hopkins really was obnoxious and not primarily a victim of sex discrimination, the justices commenced their grueling questions for the remainder of the firm's allotted time. Next, the Price Waterhouse presentation was countered by Ms. Hopkins's attorney, who, among other things, tried to argue that she was the victim of stereotyped expectations, "as Dr. Fiske testified." However, he was cut off by the justices before he could elaborate. Sitting in the crowded courtroom, I was thrilled, frankly, to have my nanosecond in history even if the justices were not interested in the end of the attorney's sentence. How had this all come about?

*H*OW I GOT INTO SOCIAL PSYCHOLOGY

Well, in hindsight it all seems overdetermined, but I think the main thing was that I was a confused child of the 1960s at a crucial time and felt that it was really important to try to make the world a better place. I was casting around for things to do, and I did a senior honors thesis that was actually a waste of time. Halfway through, I realized that although it was well intentioned, it was not working and was no good. It concerned therapeutic tutoring of children, comparing behavior modification efforts with more in-depth psychodynamic approaches, but it included only two cases, and so it was not exactly a reliable sample of anything except my efforts to find a career.

I was essentially on my own. I had no adviser because I had not had the foresight to realize that you have to get to know professors or at least graduate students by working with them before they are willing to spend time advising you and helping you. And I had been out of the country during my junior year, so I knew no one in the department. I was lost.

I had actually resisted majoring in psychology in the first place, partly because my father is a prominent psychologist and my brother is moving in that direction very rapidly; it seemed too obvious. When I was growing up, psychological ideas were kicking around the house a lot. And when I went to college, I kept taking psychology courses and doing well in them, and taking other courses and doing okay but not as well. I didn't actually know what any of my grades were until I was about to graduate, and I thought, Gee, I'd better get serious about this. I wonder what my grades have been like. So I got my transcript and, in a true Daryl Bem fashion (i.e., observing my behavior to infer my attitudes), looked back at my transcript and said, "Oh, look at this. I'm doing great in psychology classes. I must really like it." It's true—that's exactly how it happened. But I still was stuck in the middle of my senior year with a thesis that was going to be a flop and no prospects except the midnight shift at the downtown record mart.

At that point a vague mix of ideas were all going around and around in my head. Part of it was that I wanted to do something to help the world be a better place, and part of it was that I just wanted to do something that would make me employable. I had considered dropping out of college until I realized that I had no salable skills. It was pretty dicey. But I had the good fortune to be living in a group house (this was the early 1970s, and yes, it was a commune), and I was moaning to one of my roommates, who suggested, "Well, why don't you do some research?" I said, "Research?" He said, "Yeah, you could work with a faculty member." I said, "Really? Me, an undergraduate; why would they want me?" And he said, "Because it's free labor." "Well," I said, "I can understand that. Who should I work with?" So he reeled off a list of names, and one of them was Shelley Taylor. I thought, Gee, that sounds like a woman. I'll go talk to her; maybe I'll be able to relate to her. (Not that I couldn't have worked with a man, but since she was the only woman on the faculty at the time, she stood out. More about this later.)

Shelley Taylor was a first-year assistant professor at the time. When I walked into her office, I said, "I'd like to work on your research." She put down the journal she had been reading, clearly a little surprised. (It turned out that I was the first person to approach her, and she was not fully prepared.) She said, "Oh, well, um, why don't you come back tomorrow." Because she had spent the whole semester preparing her classes, she did not have research going on at the moment, although she had lots of ideas. So I came back the next day, and we discussed some great ideas.

She and many others were interested in how people make sense of other people. At that time researchers were trying to unravel the actor-observer effect. That is, when people explain other people's behavior, they tend to use personality descriptions, or *dispositional* attributions. Why did your friend fail the exam? Because he is a chronic procrastinator and tried to do the whole course the night before the exam. By contrast, when people explain their own behavior, they tend to see *situational* causes for that behavior. Why did you (nearly) fail the exam? Because the professor expected an unreasonable amount, the teaching assistant never reviewed the material properly, and your roommate kept distracting you whenever you tried to study. Edward Jones and Richard Nisbett had suggested, among other potential explanations, the possibility that the actor-observer effect is due to people's visual orientation. When people observe other people, the actor stands out against the background and seems salient in comparison, and so people seize on the person as a plausible explanation; in other words, they make dispositional attributions. But people do not see themselves behaving; they see the situation, and so the situation seems like the most salient explanation for their behavior.

Shelley suggested the idea of isolating this salience factor in terms of visual orientation to see if people's explanations tend to rely on whatever dominates the visual field. She designed a study in which two subjects would have a face-to-face conversation, with other subjects seated in an observer's circle around them. This would naturally make some people take the visual perspective of focusing on one person and looking over the shoulder of the other, while those on the opposite side of the circle would do the reverse. We would then ask these people who had the most impact on the conversation. We predicted that the person in one's direct line of sight would be seen as the most important. This would support the reasoning behind the attentional explanation for the actor-observer effect.

Without exactly understanding all the details (as I recall, I thought attribution theory was rather dry stuff), I dutifully helped run scores of subjects through the procedure, coded and entered data, and came to Shelley's office to find out what the results meant. The very first study confirmed our predictions: Subjects thought that whoever was facing the observers was causal (the person who contributed the most to the conversation, determined its course, and had the greatest impact). I was hooked. In effect, I thought, Wow! This is great! You can make predictions about people, you can set up a situation to test them, and it works! They do what you think they're going to do!

It was not quite as simple as that in several respects; in fact, only some of our predictions were confirmed. Moreover, the thing that got us into the scenario in the first place—the actor-observer difference—was not precisely tested by this study. (The actors' own perceptions were not assessed because the conversational actors were confederates, not real subjects. We made this choice to standardize the conversation.) Moreover, we obtained no results on what was at that time thought to be a key measure, a direct comparison of dispositional and situational inferences. (Subsequent research demonstrated the weakness of this measure.) But the basic mechanism was supported: Salience encourages perceived causality. The paper was later published, but not before we had conceptually replicated the study and dealt with reviewers' objections and I had applied to graduate school.

Applying to graduate school was not an easy decision either, but I was lucky enough to work for Shelley as a research assistant for a few months after graduating and got to know her and some other bright young assistant professors, who struck me as the kind of people I could imagine becoming. They worked hard, they played hard, they used their intellect to its full capacity, the problems they tackled were truly challenging, and they knew all the oldies on the jukebox at Falcon's Grill. There were also some inspiring older professors who were doing really interesting research, but their careers were so well established that I could not imagine how they had gotten from where I was to where they were. The assistant professors seemed more accessible.

Besides the thrill of my first research results and the charm of the people, there was my 1960s social conscience. In taking courses during the end of my senior year and auditing courses the year after that, I noticed that a lot of ideas were being studied from a particular point of view; the researchers studying a particular topic often had a hidden ax to grind. It seemed to me that they had a particular ideological perspective or a particular set of values that they were pushing. It seemed to me that a lot of disadvantaged groups were being put in an unfavorable light by some of the research that was being done. You could see it in the language researchers were using to describe their findings.

As an example, when I took a course on sex differences, the teacher described women and blacks as being field-dependent. That basically means that when there is a conflict between internal cues and external cues, women and blacks tend to rely on the external cues. I thought, "Field-dependent"; that doesn't sound good. That sounds like a disorder. Then it occurred to me, Well, why not call it field-sensitive? Maybe people who are field-independent should be field-insensitive. Suddenly it sounded less like a disorder and more like an asset. Because the researcher who had discovered this phenomenon was presumably neither black nor female, it seemed to me that values were guiding the very labels researchers used.

Thinking about that and some related ideas made me realize that it was probably hopeless to expect researchers ever to be value free, but at the very least, there needed to be some researchers who had different kinds of values. Essentially, I felt there has to be a mix of different people with different values doing research, all according to the agreed-on rules of evidence (so they can all play the same game). If I wanted my values to be represented, I had to be just as methodologically precise and scientifically rigorous or no one would listen to me. So that really was what propelled me into social psychology. I saw a chance to work on social problems in a way that was intellectually challenging and scientifically respectable.

WHY SOCIAL COGNITION?

Of course, I had not completely committed myself to a specific area yet. At that point I had a vague social conscience and was looking around to be, or at least to have the opportunity to be, gainfully employed while being useful. I had a notion that I might have something different to say, but unless I represented it and represented it well, it might not get heard. And all this was guided by my interaction with my adviser, who was in the area that became known as social cognition.

But it was not as if there were something about the work in social cognition that resonated right away. I remember that I met Shelley in January of my senior year, and at spring break she gave me the orange *Attribution* book (*Attribution: Perceiving the Causes of Behavior* by Edward Jones and colleagues) to read. I took it to Martha's Vineyard on my break. Sitting by the wood stove in the gray spring, I read the book cover to cover, thinking, I can't believe people are studying this. They're thinking about how people think about people? It just seemed so removed, so obscure, so complicated. But I stayed with it. And it was not until I began to see how these rather dry-seeming processes affect real social interactions and politically important situations that I began to get intrigued by it.

For example, shortly after the initial studies, Shelley and I developed the idea that individual people who attract attention may be seen as particularly causal and impactful. As the only woman at Harvard in her area, she was probably acutely aware that everyone else at area meetings was male. There was soon a single black faculty member, and he doubtless had a similar experience. Everything they did stood out compared to the actions of a comparable white male, who tended to blend in. Being a focus of attention because you are different was later identified as the solo phenomenon. Shelley pointed out that solos should capture attention and that their salience should make them seem particularly causal. But at the same time, their exaggerated impact will be interpreted in stereotypic terms because their category (gender, race, or the like) is the very dimension that made them stand out in the first place.

We designed some studies in which six people were tape-recorded having a conversation, each contributing the same number and quality of ideas (supplied by us). I then photographed individually six whites and six blacks posed to look as if they were talking. That way, we could present a slide and tape show in which the discussion itself was held constant but the apparent race of the speakers could be varied. We set up conditions in which the target person was a member of an all-white group, a solo black in an otherwise homogeneously white group, or a black member of a fully integrated (three whites and three blacks) group. We decided not to set up a group in which there was a solo white and five blacks because it seemed unlikely for Harvard at that time and we were sure it would arouse suspicion.

We also designed a conceptual replication, using a different conversation, in which we varied the apparent gender of the speakers. You might wonder what we did about the voices in that version. I actually invested a lot of time visiting electronic speech generation specialists, who were then only just developing a machine that could switch the apparent gender of a person's voice (as I recall, there were three main parameters; it wasn't just pitch). This high-tech solution was fun but far too expensive at the time (now you can buy such a gadget for your home phone). So we picked a labor-intensive solution in which opposite-gender people would imitate phrase by phrase the comments of the original discussants, half of whom had been male and half had been female. I then spliced the conversation back together phrase by phrase, so we ended up with an all-male version, an all-female version, solo male and solo female versions, and a three-three version.

In both studies we found that solos are perceived as more prominent (rated as talking more, having more influence on group interaction, and yielding a clearer impression), evaluated more extremely (more positively or negatively on warmth and on usefulness and originality of contributions), and cast in special, often stereotyped roles (e.g., for women, "the motherly type"; for men, "giving the male point of view"; for blacks, "organizational backup person but never the leader"). All this constituted a rather nice confirmation of the basic theory (salience polarizes judgments and makes people seem more impactful than they are) and its application (solos are seen in exaggerated ways, along stereotypic dimensions). We submitted the paper to two leading journals, both of which rejected it for what Shelley considered the wrong reasons, and she refused to submit it to lesser journals. To this day I still think it was one of the better projects I have worked on, and it is probably one of the most frequently cited unpublished papers. Subsequently, it was published in chapter form and confirmed by others. It also contributed to the testimony that ended up before the Supreme Court. But I am getting ahead of myself.

So, realizing that where one directs one's attention may be determined by something as trivial as who's the only woman in the room or who's the only black in the room made me aware that social cognition research can say something significant about the world. Hence, in shaping my interests, as is true for many people, it was an interaction between some values I had and the mentor I had. My mentor actually played a very important role in developing these interests. I think there are times in life when you are receptive and ready to be influenced, when you are open to finding someone or some area that is going to grab you.

Now, when students come and ask what to work on, I'm actually conservative. It's helpful for beginning students to work on projects that are quite closely related to what one's adviser is doing, because the adviser is usually more excited about it and the students thus get more attention. Also, I think it is ridiculous to expect someone to come up with something totally new and unprecedented at the beginning. It simply puts too much of a burden on the student.

Partly it is a matter of training advanced undergraduate and graduate students to recognize what their goals should be. If you think, I have to have a *new idea* (in neon), it becomes too frightening and too overwhelming. But if you say, "Well, what I would like to do is take something in the general area that my adviser's working on and put a little twist on it, and then I can call it my own," I think that's the best place to start. Often those ideas come from thinking about what seems to be missing or lacking in the kind of work one's adviser is doing. This is not to say that what the adviser is doing is wrong, just that the student can add something to it. My own dissertation, for example, took the idea of attention and predicted that it would be directed at salient behavior, not just salient people, and that those behaviors would carry added weight in terms of impressions. From a thorough literature review, I hypothesized that negative and extreme behavior would capture attention and weight in impressions. It was supported. Thus I took my adviser's salience work and ran with it to make my own statements.

It was not only Shelley Taylor who got me excited about what I was doing. There was also a nice student culture there at that time, a good cohort of people. And I think that is very important in convincing a person that some area is exciting. Students need to have a sense of other people being active and involved. Jenny Crocker, Bella DePaulo, Judy (Koivumaki) Hall, Judy Harakiewicz, John Jemmott, Joanne Martin, Mike Milburn, Steve Penrod, Eliot Smith, and Janet Weiss were also graduate students at that time, so there were lots of people who were busy doing research and were excited about what they were doing. We tried our ideas out on each other, we were pilot subjects in each other's experiments, we practiced our conference presentations on each other, we drove all night to go to conventions together, we slept on cots once we arrived, and it all created a sense of activity and excitement.

As a result of this experience, I'm committed to education and to building a student culture. I think that that's crucial. And I think that the student-adviser relationship can be very intense. It's really like family in a lot of ways for me. My expectations are that students will take the research seriously and will come to a meeting having done more than I expected them to do. But I also expect them to be open about things they don't understand, or don't know, or want help on or advice on and not feel that that means they're stupid but that inevitably there are questions that they have. I like a good argument. I like it when students disagree with me, but I think that we all have to be open to logic and discussion and not be so emotionally invested in a particular viewpoint that we can't back down if that seems to be more constructive. It's an intellectual exchange against a background of mutual support and trust.

I see in the community of social psychologists more generally an extended family that endures for one's lifetime. But the family idea has cons, too. By that I mean that you can be so involved in it that you can't stand back from your work, which can be a problem. So when I say "almost like a family," I mean that you have to be able to stand back from the adviser-student relationship, or from the research you're doing, or from whatever else and say, "How would someone else see this?" One must develop an internal critic who will say, "What's going on here?" and "How good is it?" So that's why I don't want to overdo this family business too much.

NOTHING SO PRACTICAL AS A GOOD THEORY

A few years and several (successful and unsuccessful) studies later, I was an assistant professor sitting alone in my office, when I received a phone call from someone who had read some of my work. This may seem like a small point, but to a person who has just finished a Ph.D., it is a major thrill. Moreover, she was not even a psychologist. Sarah Burns was a lawyer litigating sex discrimination cases, and she had taken just enough social psychology (a master's degree in sociology at Stanford) to be truly dangerous. She knew quite a lot about social cognition approaches to stereotyping, which argue that people categorize other people just as spontaneously as people call a chair a chair. People can discriminate (behave) on the basis of stereotyping (thoughts or beliefs) without necessarily having strong prejudices (feelings or emotions). She thought that the cognitive approach would lend itself to the courtroom because it made the telling point that people can discriminate against other people without hating them.

As it happened, Sarah Burns's case was settled out of court the night before the trial, but I was soon contacted by another discrimination lawyer. Douglas Huron independently had the hunch that there must be some link between discrimination and comments such as "lady partner candidate," "overcompensated for being a woman," "macho," and "needs a course at charm school" (i.e., stereotypic but not intrinsically illegal comments); he also picked up on the idea that current social psychology might have a contribution to make. Social science evidence had been involved in race discrimination cases since the landmark 1954 *Brown v. Board of Education* decision ending school segregation, but it had not been used before in a gender discrimination case. All this eventually led to my testifying in *Hopkins v. Price Waterhouse,* in which I argued that social factors (her solo status, the nontraditional job, the vague criteria for evaluation, the reliance on casual contacts) had paved the way for stereotype-tainted judgments (revealed by the sexist comments), which could account for her failed partnership bid (discrimination).

My colleagues took a dim view of my involvement in the case because it was not research and, as an assistant professor, I needed to do all the research I could. But I had been told it could be an important case and was convinced that social psychological research had something to say about it. I followed my heart and spent the time on it anyway. It was enormously time-consuming reading all the depositions (each one the thickness of a telephone book) and preparing the explanations of social psychology and the links to the case, all to be presented without notes, lest the opposition use them against me. It was nerve-racking to contribute to the possible course of someone's life, to try to represent the research fairly, to try to explain it in a way that would make sense to a skeptical judge, and to know that there were bright, hostile cross-examining attorneys just waiting to pounce. The cross-examining attorneys turned out to be the least of our problems; they did not know what hit them. It was the judge who conducted a relentless cross-examination. As a result, it was not at all clear how the testimony had come across to him. Afterward, I met Ann Hopkins for the first time, and she said that she had thought she was playing by the rules but that it had never occurred to her that her appropriately aggressive managerial behavior might conflict with the partners' stereotypic prescriptions for feminine behavior. Now, for the first time, she said, she finally understood what had happened to her.

Judges take a long time to make decisions, and I went back to my research. I was starting to think about what could have motivated the partners at Price Waterhouse to be more careful in their judgments, and this began to make me think about the way situations (such as organizations) are structured. Under some circumstances people clearly are more careful than under others, and the direct application of stereotyping research was making me realize that there were a lot of questions we could not yet answer.

At about the same time, at a convention, a colleague and I were disputing the latest findings in person memory research, with both of us feeling that its dominant result—better recall of expectancy-inconsistent information—did not make sense, given the amount of stereotyping and expectancy confirmation that we both saw in people's thinking about other people. We had the hunch that people might rely more on expectancy-consistent (i.e., stereotypic, expectancy-confirming) information when they were more emotionally involved than in the typical person memory study. Early in my career I felt that the social cognitive approach, by excluding affect, was going too far and that there must be some constructive way to reintroduce emotions, feelings, and evaluations. This could be an opportunity to do that.

To make people more involved, in the first studies a student and I used a simple manipulation: making a cash prize dependent on one's joint performance with one's partner. People expected to make up educational games for children, using colorful wind-up toys displayed on the table. We gave people an expectation about the partner's competence, either high (the partner had been a camp counselor, had won prizes for short stories, had experience at this kind of thing, and expected to be good at it) or low (the partner did not expect to be good at it and in fact knew less than the average student). Then everyone received a mixture of consistent and inconsistent information about the partner, comments supposedly written by the partner's peers, such as "I think what impressed me most about your teaching style is that you presented the material quite thoroughly" and "I found the technique used by you to be an inefficient means of conveying important concepts of the subject." Half the subjects were outcome-dependent, and half merely expected to meet the partner but were eligible for the prize as individuals (but were not in competition with the partner).

We predicted that interdependence (motivated involvement) would reverse the usual person memory result, but we obtained no effects on recall. None. Nothing even close. Instead, we discovered interesting effects on looking time; we had thrown in a measure of attention to the consistent and inconsistent information mainly because I continued to be interested in attention, and the more measures, the merrier. We literally timed with a stopwatch in the experimenter's pocket the subjects' attention to consistent comments (blue ink) and inconsistent comments (black ink). To make sure that the experimenter-timer couldn't inadvertently bias the results, the ink colors were reversed for half the subjects and the experimenter was blind to which ink color was which for any given person. We found that outcome dependency dramatically increased people's attention to expectancy-*in*consistent information but not to consistent information. This was not the direction we had expected or on the measure we had expected.

We started thinking more about why people would behave that way, and we realized that involvement was making them search for the most informative information, in this case, the expectancy-inconsistent information. We replicated the effect in a second experiment to make sure it wasn't a fluke. It wasn't. Then we started to wonder what the outcome-dependent subjects were doing as they looked longer at the inconsistent information. We tried asking them to list their thoughts after reading the material, but that yielded nothing. We tried asking them to write a comment on each piece of paper containing an item of information, but that also yielded nothing. Finally, because a number of cognitive colleagues were enthusiastic about think-aloud protocols, we decided to tape-record people as they thought aloud about the material. This was risky because no one had ever used think-aloud protocols in a social situation. But it seemed to work; people could do it. Moreover, when we compared the think-aloud subjects with silent subjects, there were no differences in their attentional patterns under interdependence. We were optimistic.

My student colleague Ralph Erber transcribed and coded the protocols, which were delightful. Here is an example:

> (Reads) "I think your teaching style is best described by saying you are a careful teacher." This is definitely in keeping with the previous statement/ and somewhat with my previous first impression,/ which is that she is conscientious./ Conscientious and careful are related qualities./ So that's probably true./ Somebody who is careful in making appointments on time,/ then they are probably careful in other activities./ And this also goes with the previous statement of her being thorough,/ so it's probably in keeping with the general impression. [Subject 39]

The protocols seemed like a window into people's minds: rich, spontaneous, inspiring . . . and useless. The initial coding yielded nothing. As a veteran of other open-ended coding studies, I was convinced there must be something there to give us a clue about what subjects were doing. I took the protocols home and tried to discern differences between those who were outcome-dependent and those who were not. It seemed to me that the outcome-dependent subjects were making more dispositional inferences, which again would fit with basic attribution theory ideas about prediction and control. But of course we couldn't use my biased coding when I was anything but blind to condition. So I wrote down some simple and objective coding criteria for dispositional and other inferences, scrambled the protocols, and gave them back to my collaborator. When he coded them with the new scheme, he found the same pattern I had, but of course he was blind and so could not have biased the outcome. (Moreover, the result has been replicated in subsequent studies with other coders.)

We presented the results to my colleagues, who were ruthless in their criticisms. We revised our work completely and sent it off to a journal. It was accepted practically without revision. Since that time Steve Neuberg and I have found that outcome dependency motivates people to try to be accurate about their partners, making their judgments more responsive to the information available to them and less expectancy-driven. Subsequently, Janet Ruscher and I found that competitive outcome dependency also makes people try to be accurate about their opponents, because in both cooperation and competition people's outcomes are correlated, although positively in one and negatively in the other. Janet's effect held only in one-on-one competition, not in groups that become stereotypic us-versus-them encounters.

The interdependence research began by addressing a shared discontent regarding uninvolved subjects in a dominant line of research, but we ended up somewhere else. The manipulations and measures we chose depended on enduring interests, and they came full circle to the applied settings that have always been of interest to me. The structure of interdependence seemed relevant to the Hopkins case and other organizational settings in which people may depend on their colleagues for rewards. If they do, they are likely to pay more attention to them and make fewer stereotypic judgments. Thus this work came from both empirical discontent and applied needs, and it fed back into both, although not always in the expected ways.

WHERE DO IDEAS COME FROM?

Besides the gaps revealed by applied settings, as I've noted, the most important source of ideas is that certain nagging discontent. It is a subtle process, but the best ideas come from listening to the still, small voice in the back of one's head that says, "Something's missing, something's wrong here," and really training oneself to pay attention to it. It is important to teach yourself to listen to the brief thought "Why isn't someone

studying this?" or "Why are they doing it this odd way? It doesn't res-
onate with my experience." This is not to say that social psychology is all
intuition, because I do not believe that it is. But I think there is a crucial
component of listening to your own human experience and trying to get
the field to represent better your human experience and that of other people whom you know well enough to know what is going on with them.

Three other sources of ideas are clear. One is the questions and criticisms of colleagues and reviewers. This is not a matter of just suggestions
for revision of a paper, which can save six months of reviewing lag, but
also the thoughtful questions that come from colloquiums or even dissertation defenses, which can lead to years of research. The first year after
my Ph.D. a graduate student's comment at a colloquium pointed out that
two of my interests (schemas and data-driven processes) seemed entirely
at odds. That is, my dissertation (as described earlier) looked at people's
attention to and weighting of information in a piecemeal, attribute-by-
attribute fashion described as data-driven because the information was
not interacting or linking within a larger framework of expectation,
stereotype, or "schema." In apparent contrast, my work on stereotypes
relied on such frameworks or laypersons' theories. I pondered this and,
ten years and several studies later, came out with a model suggesting
that they are two contrasting modes of thinking about people, both valid
and each occurring under predictable circumstances. Another time an
attorney was role-playing a cross-examination and asked me a particularly unanswerable question about intent that I spent my subsequent
sabbatical trying to answer.

And then, of course, there's your basic lit review. Lots of ideas come
from reviewing the literature on a topic and forming one's own opinions
about it. My dual-mode model came in part from reviewing the literature
for the book *Social Cognition* with Shelley Taylor; I noticed that research
groups representing two separate styles of explanation essentially were
not on speaking terms and never cited each other. Again, this was the
data-driven versus theory-driven distinction, which could be integrated
into a more comprehensive model that included both.

Another source of ideas is collaboration. Many people are by nature
collaborative researchers. One of the major things I enjoy about social
psychology is the norm of collaboration. It's fun to work with other people and to brainstorm about a puzzle.

Once you have an idea, I believe you have to learn to play your
strong suit. Some people are better at highly precise, fine-grained analysis that often involves some necessary technology; others are better at
more naturalistic, coarse-grained research that often involves a certain
amount of theater. I am better at the latter, and I can prove it with a lot of
the former kinds of studies collecting dust in the back of file drawers.
One of the most important tasks, early in one's career, is learning what
you're good at and then using your talents.

As for what the future holds, I never know, and that's what's exciting about it. I think I'm taking more risks as I get older, contrary to the common perception, because I feel more confident that something interesting will come out of it. If nothing interesting does come out of it, then it was a nice try. So I think I'm taking a broader perspective on things. I've always pushed social cognition as a field to take a broader perspective, and this is why I kept telling people to pay attention to affect. That was again the still, small voice saying, "Wait, there's something missing here! Affect, emotions, feelings!" And then, more recently, we have been looking at how motivational influences (such as interdependence and power) alter the ways in which people think about other people.

Continuing to make things broader and more accountable to the real world is part of the cycle. In the Supreme Court's decision in the Hopkins case, the justices said:

> The reactions of at least some of the partners were reactions to her as a woman manager. Where an evaluation is based on a subjective assessment of a person's strengths and weaknesses, it is simply not true that each evaluator will focus on, or even mention, the same weaknesses. Thus, even if we knew that Hopkins had "personality problems," this would not tell us that the partners who cast their evaluations of Hopkins in sex-based terms would have criticized her as sharply (or criticized her at all) if she had been a man. It is not our job to review the evidence and decide that negative reactions to Hopkins were based on reality; our perception of Hopkins' character is irrelevant. We sit not to determine whether Ms. Hopkins is nice, but to decide whether the partners reacted negatively to her personality because she is a woman. [*Price Waterhouse v. Hopkins*, 1989, pp. 1794–1795]

> In the specific context of sex stereotyping, an employer who acts on the basis of a belief that a woman cannot be aggressive, or that she must not be, has acted on the basis of gender. . . . We are beyond the day when an employer could evaluate employees by assuming or insisting that they matched the stereotype associated with their group. . . . An employer who objects to aggressiveness in women but whose positions require this trait places women in an intolerable Catch 22: out of a job if they behave aggressively and out of a job if they don't. Title VII lifts women out of this bind. [pp. 1790–1791]

The college student from 1973 couldn't ask for a better hearing than that.

Acknowledgment

Some of the material in this chapter was inspired by an interview, parts of which appear in A. Tesser (producer and editor), P. Frye (director), & W. McIntosh (editor). (1993). *On becoming a social psychologist* (videotape). Athens: University of Georgia.

SUGGESTED READINGS

ERBER, R., & FISKE, S. T. (1984). Outcome dependency and attention to inconsistent information. *Journal of Personality and Social Psychology, 47,* 709–726.

FISKE, S. T., BERSOFF, D. N., BORGIDA, E., DEAUX, K., & HEILMAN, M. E. (1991). Social science research on trial: Use of sex stereotyping research in *Price Waterhouse v. Hopkins. American Psychologist, 46,* 1049–1060.

———— & TAYLOR, S. E. (1991). *Social cognition* (2d ed.). New York: McGraw-Hill.

JONES, E. E., & DAVIS, K. E. (1976). From acts to dispositions: The attribution process in person perception. In L. Berkowitz (Ed.), *Advances in experimental social psychology* (vol. 2, pp. 220–266). New York: Academic Press.

———— & NISBETT, R. E. (1972). The actor and the observer: Divergent perceptions of the causes of behavior. In E. E. Jones, D. E. Kanouse, H. H. Kelley, R. E. Nisbett, S. Vains, & B. Weiner (Eds.), *Attribution: Perceiving the causes of behavior* (pp. 79–94). Morristown, NJ: General Learning Press.

TAYLOR, S. E. (1981). A categorization approach to stereotyping. In D. L. Hamilton (Ed.), *Cognitive processes in stereotyping and intergroup behavior* (pp. 88–114). Hillsdale, NJ: Erlbaum.

ZANNA, M. P., & DARLEY, J. M. (Eds.). (1987). *The compleat academic.* New York: Random House.

M<small>ARK</small> S<small>NYDER</small> *(Ph.D., Stanford University) is Professor and Chair of the Psychology Department at the University of Minnesota, where he has been a faculty member since 1972. His research interests include theoretical and empirical issues associated with the motivational foundations of individual and social behavior and the applications of basic theory and research in personality and social psychology to the practical problems confronting society. His teaching activities include courses on self and identity and personality and social behavior and an interdisciplinary program on ways of knowing. He is the author of the book* Public Appearances/Private Realities: The Psychology of Self-Monitoring.

3

Self-Monitoring: Public Appearances Versus Private Realities

---------- ❖ ----------

The image of myself which I try to create in my own mind in order that I may love myself is very different from the image which I try to create in the minds of others in order that they may love me. [W. H. Auden]

Twenty-some years ago, as a young graduate student in psychology at Stanford University, I happened on this quotation in my then-morning newspaper, the *San Francisco Chronicle*. As it happened, I was at that time searching to define myself both as a person and as a psychologist, struggling to come to grips with matters of self and identity not unlike those described so poignantly by the British writer W. H. Auden. Why, I asked myself, do some people have so much in common with the state of affairs described by Auden? Why do some people seem to be living lives of public illusion, forever striving to create images, always trying to control the impressions they convey? Why do the lives of these people seem to be a kaleidoscope of changing appearances? Why, I also asked, are other people content just to "be themselves" without constantly assessing the social climate around them? Why do these people express what they happen to think and feel, revealing their true selves to other people in their lives? Why, for these people, do the public and the private person seem to mesh so well? And so I began a journey of discovery, of seeking to understand the often tangled web that is woven of the public appearances and private realities of the self.

35

My attempts to answer these questions have grown out of a long-standing fascination with the differences between reality and illusion—the contrast between the way things appear to be and the reality that often lurks beneath the surface—in novels, on the stage and screen, and in people's lives. In time these themes of illusion and reality, of public appearances and private realities, captured my attention as a scholar, leading me to take seriously William Shakespeare's metaphorical assertion in *As You Like It* that "all the world's a stage" and "all the men and women merely players" in a theatrical performance in which "they have their exits and their entrances" and during which they act out many parts (act 2, scene 8). In due course these concerns engaged my dual professional identities as a social psychologist and a personality psychologist. As a social psychologist, I wanted to understand the world of appearances in social relationships: How is it built up? How is it maintained? What are its effects on people and those around them? As a personality psychologist, I sought to answer the question of where the personality resides: Is it in the persona—the public face—or in the underlying private reality?

THE CONCEPT OF SELF-MONITORING

These concerns led me to launch a program of research on the nature of self and identity. Central to my explorations has been the concept of self-monitoring, a concept born and bred of these inquiries. Throughout the course of these ventures self-monitoring has been my theoretical guide for asking questions and my empirical vehicle for answering them, questions not only about the nature of the self but also about the ties that bind personality and social behavior.

Among the lessons I have learned along the way is that even though most people assume that everyone has one and only one true self, this is not always so. Some people act as if they have not one but many selves. Moreover, in spite of the widespread belief that the self is an integral part of one's personal identity, for many people it seems to be largely a product of interactions with other people. These people exhibit striking gaps and contradictions between the public appearances and the private realities of the self. The public appearances of their words and deeds may be a product of deliberate attempts to create images appropriate to particular circumstances, to appear to be the right person in the right place at the right time.

This creating of images in the minds of others, this acting to control the impressions conveyed to others, is no doubt practiced to some extent by just about everyone, but for some people it is almost a way of life. Such people are particularly sensitive to the ways in which they present themselves in social situations—at parties, in job interviews, at professional meetings, in circumstances of all kinds where they may be motivated to create and maintain an appearance. Indeed, such people have the ability to observe their own performances carefully and to adjust those performances skillfully to convey just the right image of themselves. They literally act like different persons in different situations and with different people.

It is as if these people were actors for whom life itself is a drama in which they play a series of roles. It is as if they possessed a repertoire of different selves from which they can choose the one that best fits their current surroundings. I have called people of this type *high self-monitors* because of the great extent to which they are engaged in *monitoring* or controlling the images of the self they project in social interaction.

In sharp contrast, other people—known as *low self-monitors*—think of themselves as consistent beings who value congruence between who they are and what they do. Unlike their high self-monitoring counterparts, low self-monitors are not so concerned with constantly assessing the social climate around them. Instead, they express what they think and feel rather than fashion and tailor their behavior to fit the situation. People of this type can be expected to speak their minds, vent their feelings, and bare their souls even if doing so means sailing against the prevailing winds of the social environment.

When I began my research on self-monitoring, I sought first to find a way to identify two contrasting categories of people: those high and those low in self-monitoring. To do so, I developed the Self-Monitoring Scale, an inventory that includes true-false statements such as "When I am uncertain how to act in social situations, I look to the behavior of others for cues" and "At parties and social gatherings, I do not attempt to do or say things that others will like."

With their responses to this inventory, high self-monitors claim that they regard statements such as the following to be true of themselves:

> I would probably make a good actor.
> In different situations and with different people, I often act like very different persons.
> I'm not always the person I appear to be.

By contrast, low self-monitors claim, in their endorsement of Self-Monitoring Scale items, that

> I have trouble changing my behavior to suit different people and different situations.
> I can only argue for ideas which I already believe.
> I would not change my opinions (or the way I do things) in order to please someone else or win their favor.

Two versions of the Self-Monitoring Scale are available: the original twenty-five-item measure and an eighteen-item revised version (information on how to administer and score these inventories can be found in my book *Public Appearances/Private Realities: The Psychology of Self-Monitoring*). In addition, the Self-Monitoring Scale has been translated into a number of different languages, including Japanese, Arabic, German, Spanish, and Polish.

Although I began my studies of self-monitoring alone, I was soon joined by many other investigators who also were concerned with the self and social life. Collectively, our studies—conducted in a wide variety of research settings and with a wide variety of research methods—have taught us that the propensities identified by the Self-Monitoring Scale are not just idle beliefs that exist in a vacuum. To the contrary, they have widespread effects on people's lives. Self-monitoring meaningfully influences people's views of themselves and the world around them, their behavior in social situations, and the dynamics of their relationships with other people.

THE CONSEQUENCES OF SELF-MONITORING: TWO CHARACTERISTIC INTERPERSONAL ORIENTATIONS

In the beginning, I was most immediately concerned with the striking and undeniable differences in the extent to which people manage their public presentations of the self. Some people do it more often and with greater skill than others. Professional stage and screen actors can do what most of us cannot. It is, of course, very easy to bring to mind examples of highly skilled performers. Some of the more mercurial trial lawyers, the more flamboyant salespeople, and the more persuasive diplomats are but the most readily imaginable of such examples. Needless to say, such highly skilled actors may be the exception rather than the rule.

Nevertheless, within the general population, people differ meaningfully in the extent to which they can and do exercise intentional control over their self-presentations. And it is the high self-monitors who are particularly talented in this regard. In my laboratories I have seen high self-monitors succeed, with little apparent difficulty, in looking and sounding in quick succession first happy and then sad, now fearful and then angry, and so on through a long list of emotions. As studies by Richard Lippa have shown, they often are such polished actors that they can effectively adopt the mannerisms of a reserved, withdrawn, and introverted individual and then do an abrupt about-face and portray just as convincingly a friendly, outgoing, and extroverted person.

Moreover, research on self-monitoring has been revealing about how people resolve a recurring dilemma in social life. In social situations people often must decide how to present themselves to others. Should they march to the beat of their own inner drummers and speak their minds, express their feelings, and reveal their true personalities? Or should they take the pulse of their social surroundings and adopt the public postures that convey just the right image of themselves? As it happens, when confronted with such dilemmas, high and low self-monitors make quite different choices. High self-monitors typically strive for images that are particularly appropriate to the social forces operating in their situations. It is as if they ask, Who does this situation want me to be, and how can I be that person? Low self-monitors, by contrast, characteristically seek words and deeds that faithfully express their attitudes, feelings, and personalities. It is as if they want to know, Who am I, and how can I be me in this situation?

In one demonstration of these contrasting interpersonal orientations, Tom Monson and I tried to bring this dilemma into the laboratory. To do so, we arranged for students at the University of Minnesota to join discussion groups designed to sensitize their members to different reference group norms. In some discussion groups the experimenter led the members to a room furnished with two videotape cameras, a microphone, a videotape monitor, a table, and chairs. Group members then signed release forms to allow their discussions to be videotaped for possible viewing by other students in their undergraduate psychology class. The videotape cameras, the feedback on the monitor, and the explicit consent form all highlighted the *public* nature of the group members' behavior and helped make salient their membership in the larger reference group of undergraduates with its norms favoring *autonomy* in the face of social pressure. In other discussion groups he arranged for the meetings to take place in a room furnished only with a table and chairs. In these groups the most salient norms and cues were provided by the group members themselves. Accordingly, in this relatively *private* situation, *conformity* and consensus within the group (in which members would go along to get along) seemed to be the most situationally appropriate behavior.

Group members who were high self-monitors were acutely sensitive to the differences between the contexts in which the discussions took place. They were conformist in the private discussions, where conformity was the most appropriate interpersonal orientation, and nonconforming in the public discussions, where reference group norms favored autonomy as a reaction to social pressure. Group members who were low self-monitors were virtually unaffected by their social settings. They seem to have largely avoided the impression management activities of the high self-monitors in the group. Presumably, their self-presentations were more accurate reflections of their own personal attitudes and dispositions.

What this and other such demonstrations suggest to me is that high self-monitors literally act like different persons in different situations and with different people. It is as if they possessed a repertoire of selves from which they conveniently choose the one that best fits the current surroundings. These people are the ones for whom Shakespeare's claims that "all the world's a stage, and all the men and women merely players" seem most apt. And these people seem to be precisely the ones about whom William James theorized when he proposed in 1890 that people have as many social selves as there are individuals or groups that recognize and carry images of them in their minds and that people generally show different sides of themselves to each of these different groups. A century later we now have some empirical evidence for James's proposition that people have not one but many selves. Not only do we have some evidence that James's theory is right, we can also see the limits of what he said. He was right only for some people—it is only the high self-monitors who have not one but many selves.

Although high self-monitors are in large measure social chameleons, using their finely tuned self-presentational skills to slip into and out of a wide variety of social roles, one should not automatically assume that they necessarily use those skills for deceptive or manipulative purposes. Indeed, in their relationships with friends and acquaintances, high self-monitors often are eager to put their self-monitoring abilities to use to promote smooth social interactions.

One can find some clues to this motive in the way high self-monitors react to and cope with unfamiliar and unstructured social settings. For example, in one study William Ickes and Richard Barnes arranged for pairs of strangers to spend time together. In these meetings high self-monitors took an active and controlling role in the conversation. They were inclined to talk first and to initiate subsequent conversational sequences. They also felt, and were seen by their partners to have, a greater need to talk. Their partners also viewed them as having been the more directive member of each group.

It was as if high self-monitors were particularly concerned about managing their behavior in order to create, encourage, and maintain a smooth flow of conversation. Perhaps this quality helps explain why high self-monitors often emerge as leaders in groups, organizations, and institutions. Perhaps this quality also may help high self-monitors function well in circumstances that require effective interaction, or function in a "go-between" role with the members of two or more different constituencies (e.g., with management and labor, with producers and consumers, in international diplomacy and negotiations) who may have difficulty interacting directly with each other. And their concern with public appearances may explain why they are drawn to advertising that appeals to the images that one can gain by associating oneself with particular consumer products.

Clearly, the chameleonlike high self-monitoring orientation may give people the flexibility and adaptiveness to cope with diverse social roles. Nevertheless, I should point out that there may be costs associated with this way of life. This orientation may be purchased at the cost of having one's actions communicate very little about one's private beliefs, feelings, and intentions. If high self-monitors habitually choose behaviors to fit the current surroundings, they may create gaps and contradictions between their attitudes and their actions.

By contrast, it is in the domain of correspondence between private attitudes and public behaviors that people low in self-monitoring excel. They are the ones who, when filling out the Self-Monitoring Scale, agree with the statement "My behavior is usually an expression of my true inner feelings, attitudes, and beliefs." They are the ones who claim to value congruence between what they believe and what they do. It follows that consistency between attitudes and behavior should be related to self-monitoring: Low self-monitors should manifest substantially greater consistency between attitudes and behavior than do individuals who are high in self-monitoring.

In one investigation of the links between attitudes and behavior, Bill Swann and I recruited students to serve as jurors in a mock court case involving allegations of sex discrimination in employment. In this simulated court case jurors read summary curricula vitae of two biologists, Ms. C. A. Harrison and Mr. G. C. Sullivan. Both had applied to be an assistant professor of biology at the University of Maine. The university chose Mr. Sullivan for the position. Ms. Harrison subsequently filed suit, alleging that the university's decision reflected a bias against women. All the jurors then considered the arguments advanced in court on behalf of the plaintiff (Ms. Harrison) and on behalf of the defendant (University of Maine). After reaching their verdicts, they communicated them in essays that explained their decisions.

Overall, the relation between general attitudes toward affirmative action and judicial decision-making behavior was at best modest. However, when considered separately for jurors who were low and high in self-monitoring, the relations between attitudes and behavior looked quite different. The verdicts of jurors low in self-monitoring were very closely related to their attitudes. Those who supported affirmative action rendered verdicts favorable to Ms. Harrison; those who opposed affirmative action reached verdicts unsympathetic to Ms. Harrison's complaint. By contrast, the verdicts of jurors high in self-monitoring simply could not be predicted from their attitudes.

Evidently, when it comes to the private realities of attitudes and dispositions versus the public realities of words and deeds, low self-monitors are rather consistent beings for whom the message "To thine own self be true" has particular meaning. They are the people of whom traditional assumptions about the nature of the self speak; they are the people whose unified, consistent sense of self is expressed in consistent fashion from circumstance to circumstance. No doubt, the willingness of low self-monitors to reveal and communicate their inner selves may serve them well in arenas of life (such as close and intimate relationships) where the ability to disclose a "true self" may be the cement that bonds person to person. And their concern with being faithful to their personal standards and principles may account for their preference for consumer products whose advertising stresses the actual functional qualities of the products rather than the images associated with them.

THE SELVES OF SELF-MONITORING: PRAGMATIC AND PRINCIPLED

What accounts for interpersonal styles of self-monitoring? What is it about being high in self-monitoring that leads some people to adjust their behavior to fit their social circumstances? And what is it about being low in self-monitoring that induces other people to act on their attitudes, feelings, and dispositions? As researchers have addressed these questions, they have shed light on the motivations behind self-monitoring orientations. The answers, they have discovered, are to be found in large measure in people's *conceptions of self*.

What, then, are the selves of self-monitoring? It has become increasingly clear that high and low self-monitors have very different ideas about what constitutes a self. It appears that through their responses to the items in the Self-Monitoring Scale people reveal some fundamental truths about their sense of self and identity. They are disclosing their personal "theories" of their nature as individuals and as social beings.

With their responses to the Self-Monitoring Scale, people high in self-monitoring (the ones who claim, "In different situations and with different people, I often act like very different persons") are disclosing that they regard themselves as rather adaptive creatures who shrewdly choose selves to fit the situation. They seem to endorse a rather *pragmatic* conception of self, a theory that construes their identities in terms of specific social situations and the roles they enact in those situations. That is, their sense of self is a rather flexible "me for this situation." For them, the self seems to be whoever they appear to be at a particular moment. As one person put it in describing his "self," "I am me, the me I am right here and right now." Moreover, high self-monitors often sketch their self-portraits in terms of the roles they play. Another person, when asked the question "Who are you?" answered with this recital of roles: "I am a student, I am a post office employee, I am first violin in a chamber music group, I am quarterback of my fraternity's football team."

Some strikingly different ideas about the nature of the self are harbored by people low in self-monitoring. They [the ones who claim, "I would not change my opinions (or the way I do things) in order to please someone or win their favor"] seem to cherish images of themselves as rather principled beings who value congruence between "who they think they are" and "what they try to do." They seem to be endorsing a rather *principled* conception of the self, a theory that construes their identities in terms of inner characteristics and personal attributes. Theirs is a single, unified, coherent identity expressed in consistent fashion from situation to situation, one that must not be compromised for other people and must not bend to the will of circumstance. Their sense of self seems to be an enduring and continuing "me for all times and places," a sense of self they carry with them from role to role and from situation to situation. For example, as one low self-monitor said of her "self," "I am friendly, I am even-tempered, I am reliable, I am a liberal."

These conceptions of self—the pragmatic selves of high self-monitors and the principled selves of low self-monitors—fit well with their characteristic interpersonal orientations. High self-monitors conceive of themselves as rather flexible and pragmatic types, and their social behavior indeed manifests marked situation-to-situation fashioning of the selves they present to others. Low self-monitors conceive of themselves as rather consistent and principled types, and their actions typically are accurate and meaningful expressions of their enduring attitudes, traits, and dispositions. Both types of people seem to be living their lives in accordance with their personal conceptions of the self.

THE SOCIAL WORLDS OF SELF-MONITORING

Just as it has become clear that there are intimate bonds between the characteristic orientations and the self-conceptions of people high and low in self-monitoring, it has become apparent that these ties that bind are not accidental ones. To the contrary, these links seem to be a product of motivated and strategic activities by which people are directly and actively involved in designing and constructing social worlds in which it is easy for them to act in accordance with their self-monitoring propensities. Nowhere are these structuring activities more intriguing, perhaps, than in the social networks of friends, acquaintances, and romantic partners of people high and low in self-monitoring.

Consider the following situation. It's a sunny summer afternoon. You're trying to decide whether to play tennis—one of your favorite pastimes—with your friend Terry or with your friend Val. You know that you like Terry more than you like Val, but you also know that Val is a better tennis player than Terry. What do you do? How you solve this dilemma may reflect your approach to friendship.

If you choose Terry, chances are that you choose your friends on the basis of your feelings of liking for them and that you keep the same friends for most of your social activities. If, in addition to playing tennis, some of your favorite leisure pursuits are discussing politics, listening to music, and going to art museums, you probably prefer the same well-

liked friend as a partner for each of those activities. Overall, you probably strive to spend your time with friends who are highly similar to you
and to each other in their general attitudes, values, and personalities.
And chances are, you are a low self-monitor.

By contrast, if you choose Val, you probably choose your friends on
the basis of their skills in particular areas and are likely to have different
partners for different activities. Not only do you choose to play tennis
with a particularly good tennis player, if they are among your favorite
things to do, you choose to discuss politics with a different friend who is
an expert on politics, listen to music with another friend who happens to
be a music buff, and go to art museums with yet another friend who is
someone who really knows art. In general, you probably tend to fit and
match your friends to the activities for which they will serve well as partners for you. And you are probably a high self-monitor.

Steve Gangestad, Jeff Simpson, and I tested these hypotheses by having college students draw "maps" of their social worlds. To draw these
maps, people made lists of those with whom they regularly spent time
and engaged in social activities. They then nominated the one specific
activity most typical of their social life in each of several categories. For
example, one person specified "going to a fancy French restaurant" for
the category "going out to dinner," "playing tennis" for the category
"competitive recreational activity," and "going to the ballet" for the category "attending live entertainment."

With the matrix defined by the people and activities they had nominated, these people then drew maps of their social worlds. Specifically,
they indicated how likely they would be to choose each of the people in
the matrix as a partner for each activity and how much they would enjoy
each activity with each of those people. Statistical analyses of these maps
revealed considerably more partitioning and segmentation in the social
worlds of high self-monitors and considerably more uniformity and
homogeneity in those of low self-monitors. Typically, high self-monitors
chose specific friends for particular activities, and usually only for those
activities. For these individuals there were clear activity boundaries that
defined and separated their friendships.

The maps of the social worlds of low self-monitors indicated that
they were much more likely to retain the same friends for many, and
sometimes for most, of their activities. Some low self-monitors clearly
had a best friend with whom they engaged in many leisure pursuits.
Others seemed to belong to a group whose members stuck together and
did almost everything as a group. This pattern of segmentation for high
self-monitors and homogeneity for low self-monitors was true of the
social worlds of both women and men.

How do these social worlds come about? How do people actually
structure their social lives? The considerations people invoke when
deciding who they like and when choosing friends as activity partners

help answer these questions. For example, when it comes to choosing between competing leisure-time activities, high self-monitors choose to spend time with people who are "specialists" in the activity at hand, whereas low self-monitors give their time to people they like a lot. One way to watch these choices being made is to present people with choices of the form "playing tennis with ————" (someone who is a particularly good tennis player but only average in general likability) and "going sailing with ————" (someone else who is very high in general likability but only average in sailing ability). In one study, college students made a series of choices of leisure-time activities that directly pitted the partner's specific expertise against his or her general likability. Fully 80 percent of students who were high self-monitors chose friends as activity partners on the basis of their status as specialists in the activity at hand (choosing, for example, to play tennis with the expert tennis player). In contrast, only 33 percent of students who were low self-monitors used this strategy. Within the same set of choices, as many as 67 percent of the low self-monitors chose activity partners on the basis of their global likability (choosing, for example, to go sailing with the well-liked friend) while as few as 20 percent of those high in self-monitoring did so.

Moreover, complementing these findings about friendship choices, researchers have discovered two different and contrasting orientations toward romantic relationships that are clearly linked to self-monitoring. Men and women who are high self-monitors, we have found, tend to adopt an "uncommitted" orientation toward dating relationships. They say they are quite willing to engage in social activities with dating partners other than their current ones. When given the chance to terminate a current relationship and form a new one, they indicate that they are quite willing to do so. Indeed, their recent dating histories reveal the impact of this uncommitted orientation on their romantic lives. These high self-monitors usually have dated steady, exclusive partners for rather short periods of time (on average, barely twelve months), and if not involved in a steady relationship, they have dated a relatively large number of different partners (on average, about six) in the preceding twelve months. When it comes to their sexual behavior, high self-monitors report that they have engaged in sex with a large number of different partners in the preceding year and indicate that they foresee themselves having sex with many different persons over the next five years; they also are more likely to have engaged in sex with partners on one and only one occasion. Finally, their uncommitted orientation is revealed by a relatively slow rate of growth of intimacy in their dating relationships.

Men and women who are low self-monitors, by contrast, tend to adopt a "committed" orientation in their dating relationships. They express little willingness to spend time with people other than their current dating partners even if those people are highly skilled in the social activities under consideration. And when given the opportunity to terminate a current dating relationship for a new one, they overwhelmingly claim to harbor no desire to change dating partners. Furthermore, their recent dating histories reveal just how much this committed orientation is reflected in their romantic lives. They typically have dated steady, exclusive partners for relatively long periods (an average of almost twenty months), and if not involved in an exclusive dating relationship, they have dated a fairly small number of different partners (an average of fewer than four) in the preceding year. When it comes to sexual matters, low self-monitors indicate that they would be rather reluctant to have sex with someone to whom they were not exclusively committed; they also claim that they would be relatively uncomfortable with, and therefore less likely to enjoy, engaging in casual sex with different partners. Finally, their committed orientation is revealed in the growth of intimacy in their dating relationships, which in the long term reach relatively high levels of personal intimacy.

EXPLORATIONS IN APPLIED PSYCHOLOGY

For many of us in the psychological sciences, one measure of the worth of our theories and methods is their ability to speak meaningfully to practical concerns. In keeping with this belief, I and other researchers have devoted much of our attention to the implications of self-monitoring for understanding practical problems. Among our concerns are jobs and careers and advertising and consumer behavior.

Some of the most important and consequential decisions in people's lives concern the jobs they seek and the careers they pursue. What, then, can self-monitoring say about jobs, careers, and professions? Low self-monitors, it seems, select jobs or careers that reflect their personal attitudes and talents. High self-monitors, by contrast, select jobs or careers that allow them to make use of their ability to be different people in different situations. One such type of job is the "boundary-spanning" position. A boundary-spanning position is one in which the employee must act as a go-between for groups that may not be able to communicate with each other effectively face to face. Researchers have found that high self-monitors excel in boundary-spanning positions such as a field representative at a large franchise organization. In addition, researchers have examined the performance of both high and low self-monitors in leadership positions. High self-monitors emerge as leaders in circumstances involving high levels of verbal interaction. Low self-monitors express their leadership potential when they work in relatively homogeneous groups and groups in which their personal inclinations match the needs of the leadership position.

Issues concerning the world of paid work naturally lead to questions about what people do with the fruits of their labors. How do people decide how to spend the money they earn? At least some of these decisions are influenced by the messages of advertising that reach out to us from newspapers and magazines, and from televisions and radios. Two different schools of thought exist within the advertising profession: the soft sell and the hard sell. Advertisers who believe in the soft-sell approach create ads that appeal to images they want the consumer to associate with their products. Those who practice the hard-sell approach create ads that make claims about the quality of the product.

In our studies of the psychology of advertising Ken DeBono and I have found that these two advertising approaches appeal differently to high and low self-monitors. We compared the reactions of high and low self-monitors to these approaches by creating ads with the same picture but different written copy. For example, we paired a picture of a bottle of Canadian Club whiskey sitting on blueprints for a house with the text "You're not just moving in, you're moving up" to create an image-oriented ad and with the text "When it comes to great taste, everyone draws the same conclusion" to produce a quality-oriented ad. We found that high self-monitors preferred the image-oriented ad while low self-monitors preferred the quality-oriented ad.

These preferences for different styles of advertising may translate into actual patterns of consumer purchases. Thus, high self-monitors may purchase a car that looks flashy and sporty rather than a better-handling sports car and may drink an imported premium beer that gives a special status to its drinker rather than a cheaper domestic beer that tastes the same. Likewise, low self-monitors may eat the most nutritious breakfast cereal even though there isn't a star athlete on the box and may purchase the most energy-efficient refrigerator even though it doesn't have a designer-styled finish.

THE ROOTS OF SELF-MONITORING

Why is it that some people are high in self-monitoring and others are low in self-monitoring? Over the years I have been asked this question more often than any other: When it comes to self-monitoring, are people born or made? Or, more formally, what roles do biological-genetic factors and environmental-socialization influences play in the development of self-monitoring? Surprisingly, to me at least, self-monitoring does not seem to vary meaningfully with many of the indicators that are thought to be important in child-raising patterns and practices: social class, economic status, regional origins, geographic movement, and religious affiliation. Perhaps even more surprising is the fact that self-monitoring seems to have genetic roots.

To assess the genetic component of personality, psychologists often compare identical twins, fraternal twins, and randomly selected pairs of individuals. Identical twins share all of their genetic material; thus, if self-monitoring has a genetic basis, they should belong to the same self-monitoring category. Randomly selected pairs of individuals share no genetic material; therefore, any two individuals should have a fifty-fifty chance of having the same self-monitoring propensity. Fraternal twins share half their genetic material and thus should be the same in self-monitoring approximately 75 percent of the time. In fact, Steve Gangestad found that identical twins belonged to the same category of self-monitoring, either both high or both low, 99 percent of the time. Fraternal twins were found to be the same in self-monitoring 74 percent of the time, and randomly selected pairs were the same only 55 percent of the time.

This evidence supports the hypothesis that self-monitoring has a biological-genetic basis. But what does this state of affairs mean? For starters, it does not mean that people are born high or low self-monitors only to rigidly remain that way for the rest of their lives. Rather, it would appear that some people are born with a predisposition to become a high self-monitor and others to become a low self-monitor, predispositions that require an extended course of socialization experiences to translate into reality.

To examine the self-monitoring propensities of children of differing ages, two additional versions of the self-monitoring inventory have been created. One measure is suitable for children between the ages of one and a half and four; another measure has been developed for children between ages six and thirteen. With these versions of the Self-Monitoring Scale, researchers are now working to track the emergence, growth, and development of self-monitoring propensities.

THE MATTER OF VALUE JUDGMENTS

Clearly, high and low self-monitors live their lives in quite different ways. Which is better, I have often asked myself, to be a low self-monitor or to be a high self-monitor? After a few moments' reflection you will no doubt realize why no value judgments should be attached to the interpersonal styles of either self-monitoring category. The more that is known about the many facets of self-monitoring, the more apparent it is that neither orientation is inherently "better" than the other. With a careful choice of words, someone who cared to do so could give either orientation a good name or a bad name. I could, for example, easily describe high self-monitors in rather complimentary terms, pointing to their flexibility and adaptiveness in coping with the diversity of roles required of a person in an increasingly complex society. Or I could just as easily paint a rather unflattering portrait of the same people, depicting them as "silly putty" creatures forever being squeezed and shaped into new and different molds, always posturing and gesturing, forever pretending and occasionally deceiving those around them.

By the same token, I could readily characterize a low self-monitor in glowing terms—an honest, forthright, and direct type, an easy-to-read "open book" in dealings with others, someone with the virtues of being true to his or her values and principles, someone who can be counted on to be the same person at different times, in different places, with different people. Yet I could just as readily turn those virtues into vices. What I had once described as consistency and reliability, I could instead label rigidity and stubbornness. If so inclined, I could make my point with examples such as bosses who are as autocratic and dictatorial with their families as with their employees and teachers who lecture their friends as if they were their students.

Which is better, then—to be high or low in self-monitoring? Clearly, there can be no answer to this question. By choosing words for their shades of meaning, anyone can cast either type in a favorable or unfavorable light. For this reason alone, we should not try to make value judgments; instead, we should recognize that the two self-monitoring orientations represent different approaches to life. We should regard these different approaches as lifestyles each with its own unique assets and liabilities. And until there are clear indications that, on balance and overall, life's pleasures and pains occur disproportionately in the lives of one or the other type, I see no reason to grant more favored status to either lifestyle.

CONCLUSION

At the outset, I characterized my research on self-monitoring as a journey of discovering, a quest to understand the public appearances and the private realities of the self. Clearly, the concept of self-monitoring and the techniques of psychological research have been important in guiding and sustaining this journey. But there is something else: my own personal fascination with the idea of self-monitoring as a basic organizing theme for people's lives and my conviction that it is possible to capture the essence of how people function in important domains of their lives with the methods and procedures of the psychological sciences. And after twenty-some years I am as fascinated as ever.

As I look back over two decades of self-monitoring, I ask myself, Why has the self-monitoring concept been such an appealing one? Why has it led me and other researchers into so many fascinating avenues of exploration? To some extent, I think that the very notion of self-monitoring may capture widespread and shared personal concerns with understanding the human dramas of public appearances versus private realities that are played out in our own lives and in those of other people. Moreover, the fact that self-monitoring seems to touch so many areas of people's lives has meant that I and other researchers have been fortunate enough to work on a wide range of problems not only of concern to us as scientists but of intense personal interest as well. We're not just learning about people in the abstract; we're learning about ourselves, too.

And to some extent I think that the "generativity" of the self-monitoring research program may derive from the fact that it appears to capture one of the fundamental dichotomies of psychology: whether behavior is a product of forces that operate from without (exemplified by the "situational" orientation of high self-monitors) or whether it is governed by influences that guide from within (typified by the "dispositional" orientation of low self-monitors). Perhaps for that reason, self-monitoring has served as a focal point—in theory, research, and application—for issues in assessment, in the role of scale construction in theory building, and in examining fundamental questions about personality and social behavior.

Acknowledgments

Theory and research on self-monitoring, as well as the preparation of this chapter, have been supported by grants from the National Institutes of Mental Health and the National Science Foundation. Portions of this chapter are drawn from my book on self-monitoring, *Public Appearances/Private Realities: The Psychology of Self-Monitoring*, published in 1987 by W H Freeman and Company.

SUGGESTED READINGS

SNYDER, M. (1974). Self-monitoring of expressive behavior. *Journal of Personality and Social Psychology, 30,* 526–537.

———— (1987). *Public appearances/private realities: The psychology of self-monitoring.* New York: Freeman.

———— & DeBono, K. G. (1985). Appeals to image and claims about quality: Understanding the psychology of advertising. *Journal of Personality and Social Psychology, 49,* 586–597.

———— Gangestad, S., & Simpson, J. A. (1983). Choosing friends as activity partners: The role of self-monitoring. *Journal of Personality and Social Psychology, 45,* 1061–1072.

———— & Monson, T. C. (1975). Persons, situations, and the control of social behavior. *Journal of Personality and Social Psychology, 32,* 632–637.

———— & Simpson, J. A. (1984). Self-monitoring and dating relationships. *Journal of Personality and Social Psychology, 47,* 1281–1291.

———— Simpson, J. A., & Gangestad, S. (1986). Personality and sexual relations. *Journal of Personality and Social Psychology, 51,* 181–190.

———— & Swann, W. B. (1976). When actions reflect attitudes: The politics of impression management. *Journal of Personality and Social Psychology, 34,* 1034–1042.

ROBERT **B.** C**IALDINI** (Ph.D., University of North Carolina at Chapel Hill) is Regents' Professor of Psychology at Arizona State University, where he has also been named Graduate College Distinguished Research Professor. His research interests include the study of the processes of social influence, helping, and self-presentation. He attributes a sensitivity to the importance of the social environment to the fact that he grew up in a thoroughly Italian family, in a predominantly Polish neighborhood, in a historically German city (Milwaukee), in an otherwise rural state.

4

A Full-Cycle Approach to Social Psychology

For me, social psychology has always been a serendipitous science, a place for instructive accidents. For as long as I can recall, I have loved the idea (and the art) of turning something entirely fortuitous—an unexpected observation or an unplanned discovery—into a rigorous program of research. Thus I have tried to cultivate an aptitude for drawing psychological implications from the little surprises of ordinary human interaction. And why not? I am a social psychologist, after all, and social psychology is the study of everyday social behavior. As one of its practitioners, I have found no better vantage point than to stand hip-deep in the flow of that behavior, sensitive to the odd or unanticipated ripples at its surface, eager to be intrigued and inspired by them to an understanding of their deeper causes.

But serendipity hasn't shaped only my choice of researchable topics; in a very real sense it shaped my professional identity. Until a day early in the last semester of my senior year in college I had never set foot in a social psychology classroom. What's more, I had no plans to do so. My focus as an undergraduate had been on the experimental study of animal behavior, and I had channeled most of my coursework in that direction. I had worked as a research assistant for a pair of experimental psychologists studying avoidance learning in mice and had even coauthored a paper with my faculty adviser on alarm pheromones in earthworms. In keeping with this kind of background, I had applied the semester before to several universities for admission to graduate programs in animal behavior.

My career direction seemed altogether clear, and I saw no reason to take the time to attend a social psychology class, except for one thing: Marilyn Repinski, on whom I had a powerful crush at the time, was enrolled in an introductory social psychology course that semester. We had begun dating a few weeks earlier and had reached the stage in our relationship of wanting to be together constantly. Fortunately in this regard, I had a free period during Marilyn's social psychology class time and there was an empty desk next to hers. So, when after lunch together she would go off to that class, I would tag along just to be near her.

Two weeks after sitting in on my first social psychology lecture, I knew something important was happening because when Marilyn stayed at the lunch table to study for another course one day, I went to her class anyway. After another week I was so taken with the material that I had approached the instructor, Allan Wicker, asking for advice on good graduate schools in social psychology. He listed a few but suggested that because the time to apply was very nearly gone, I should pick just one or two that best fit my interests and concentrate on them. But I was such a novice to the discipline that I didn't even know what I was most interested in studying. So I went off to the library to look through the journals of social psychology. In the process, I noticed that one of the major journals in the field was the *Journal of Experimental Social Psychology*, which was being edited at that time by the social psychology faculty at the University of North Carolina. *Experimental*, I thought to myself. That's my background. And *social psychology*; that's what I want to study! I'll apply to the North Carolina program. And I did, figuring that if my interest in social psychology faded by the time I had to make a decision, I could always pursue my earlier love and go to graduate school in animal behavior.

By the end of that fateful semester, though, I was more enamored of social psychology than of animal behavior (and, as these things tend to go, of Marilyn). Consequently, when I did receive an admission acceptance from the North Carolina program, I pounced on the opportunity. The instruction I got there was absolutely first-rate; I cannot imagine a better training experience. It turned me from an aspirant into a professional in a field I find as exciting today as I did when I fell in love with it, virtually at first sight, twenty-five years ago.

Still, I can't help but wonder where I would be today if it hadn't been for the fortuitous combination of a hopeless crush, a free period, and an empty desk. My guess is that I would be in a university position but doing something quite different—working as an animal behaviorist of some sort, an ethologist or field biologist, perhaps. Whatever the area of interest, I hope that I would be approaching it the way I like to approach social psychology—as a serendipidist and an opportunist. In the pages that follow I have described some research programs that illustrate the logic and advantages of such an approach.

*T*HE TRAPPER AND THE TRAP

An important event in my professional life occurred one day in Columbus, Ohio. It is quite fitting that it took place not on a traditional workday in the excellent Ohio State University library, in my office, or in the labs of the social psychology doctoral program where I was a visiting professor that year. Instead, it happened on a Saturday afternoon in the stands of Ohio Stadium, where 83,000 people had gathered to delight as a powerful and unbeaten Ohio State team chewed its way through a much weaker opponent. Actually, my day at the stadium had begun considerably earlier. At the time I was there, the social psychology program at Ohio State was located in the football stadium. The stadium is truly immense, and the university was housing some academic units within its bowels. Thus, when I went to my office to do some work that morning, I went to the stadium with the intention of attending the football game later in the day.

My principal purpose in going to the office was to puzzle over some data I had gotten from a laboratory attitude change study. The data were promising enough in that the means were in the predicted direction, but the effect I was looking for was not statistically significant. I was getting about half a point of difference between the two crucial experimental groups on a seven-point scale when I needed a full point of difference to attain conventional levels of significance.

It appeared as though I had probably uncovered an influence on the attitude change process that had not been documented before. The problem was to demonstrate that the influence was a real one. I had been in similar positions before, and so I was familiar with the task that faced me. If the effect was there, my job was to catch it, to snare it. I knew already that it was a phenomenon that tracked lightly. It would be necessary, then, to build an especially sensitive trap.

As I considered how best to proceed, I noticed that it was nearly game time. My office was located so that it was possible to walk through a few empty corridors, pass through a pair of little-used doors, and be out of the deserted academic section and into the richly peopled stands of the stadium. Although I made the physical journey easily, my thoughts remained back below the stands with my data, my nonsignificant statistical test, and my experimental trap. So engaged, I moved toward my seat, mostly oblivious to the behavior around me. Not for long, though, because the Ohio State team had left the dressing room and had begun to run onto the field, *merely* to run onto the field. All at once people began bounding about, waving banners, spilling beer on one another, and yelling encouragement to their favorites below. Arcs of tissue paper crossed overhead. The university fight song was being sung. A large group of fans repeatedly roared "We're number one!" while thrusting index fingers upward. I recall quite clearly looking up from thoughts of that additional half point of movement on a seven-point scale and recognizing the undeniable and intriguing power of the tumult around me. "Cialdini," I said to myself, "I think you're studying the wrong thing."

A short-term result of the above set of events was the initiation of a program of investigation into the psychology of the sports fan. There was, however, a more important consequence for me. I began to think about and understand my basic orientation to research and the basic orientation of experimental social psychology as I knew it. It had definitely been a trapper's approach. We would usually begin with a theory or formulation that would serve as a kind of map. We would use the map to tell us where to look for effects. Reading the map correctly was pretty much an exercise in logical inference. Certain predictions could be derived from the theory and, if followed, would lead us to find certain social phenomena. Once the theory told us the expected location of those phenomena, we could set our traps for them to see if they actually were there and, consequently, determine if the map was correct. Trap construction was a crucial step in the enterprise. It was important to build a sensitive and selective mechanism for snaring the predicted effect. Without a sensitive mechanism, the effect we were seeking could slip through our trap and mislead us about the accuracy of our theory; without a selective mechanism, some other effect could spring the trap (i.e., produce the predicted results) and again provide misinformation about the correctness of the theory. It was desirable, then, to develop experimental conditions that would (1) register even whisper-light effects and (2) allow no phenomenon but the one under direct study to produce the predicted data pattern.

There is a lot to be said for the trapper's approach. It fosters research with methodological rigor, low error variance, and precise measurement. It gives us good information about the validity of our theories. It often directs us to the investigation of intriguing details of behavior that we would not otherwise have thought to study. And, not unimportantly, it is a fascinating pursuit. When done right, it represents a stimulating, absorbing, and personally gratifying use of time. If not for the intellectually challenging character of the work, I am certain that many of its practitioners, myself included, would be doing other things.

But there is a problem with the trapper orientation: the find. Our finely tuned traps allow us to capture phenomena without regard for their importance in the course of naturally occurring human behavior. For instance, I have more than once described a recently obtained finding about which I was both excited and proud to a neighbor or friend, only to be disappointed in the unappreciative reaction I received. In the past I typically attributed the difficulty to a lack of understanding. I still think that was so, but now I am inclined to believe that the lack was mine. I had failed to realize that in a conversational presentation of my finding, I was providing only the end product. And the end product, stripped of the experimental precision and clever design that allowed me to lay claim to a clean and reliable effect, was not especially meaningful by itself. So much of the enjoyment and satisfaction I had derived from my investigation had come from technique. Since I could not communicate the subtleties of sophisticated technique to my listeners (e.g., how my design eliminated this or that potential confounding factor), I should not have been surprised that they failed to understand what I was so pleased about. They were telling me something important by their lack of appreciation. They were telling me that they were unlikely to find much value in my research until I shifted it toward the most powerful features of everyday life. But not until 83,000 of such people jumped up and shouted it in unison did I get their message: "Cialdini, you're studying the wrong thing!"

If we accept the notion that the task of a social psychologist is to study normal human behavior, it is odd that so little of current mainstream social psychology *begins* with the observation of everyday behavior. Much more likely, a research project will have its genesis in a theory or in the prior experimental literature. While both of these starting points allow us to infer the presence of social phenomena that can be investigated, neither tells us whether the phenomena are important in the description of human behavior as it normally occurs. A theory, for example, speaks only to the existence of the effects it predicts; it does not speak to the ecological importance of those effects. Questions about the prevalence or prominence of predicted phenomena in the stream of natural human action are not addressed by theories.

Let us take the example of balance theory, a personal favorite of mine. According to the theory, there is a tendency for people to treat things that are connected to one another, even in trivial ways, as alike. But how strong is this tendency? Is it strong enough to be a genuine influence in a significant portion of people's actions? The theory does not say. It only states that the pressure for cognitive balance is there and, all other things equal, will show itself. To determine if the theory is correct, we would arrange for experimental procedures that at best eliminated or at least held constant all other relevant sources of influence in the situation. But it might well be that these other sources of influence that would interact, interfere, or covary with the action of balance tendencies in our experiment are precisely the ones that are dominant in the natural contexts of the behavior under study. It might well be that by eliminating these external factors, we will have uncovered an influence on human action so inconsequential that it virtually never manifests itself when other factors are allowed to vary.

SCOUTING

So the question remains, If we are interested in more than theory development, how are we to decide what is worth studying? One possibility would be to preface our trapping behavior with a period of scouting activity. Just like the trap setter who scouts an area first to determine what, where, and how plentiful are its big game, we might well begin with systematic observation of the strong and regularly occurring natural effects around us. Perhaps we can reduce the problem of the dubious ecological importance of our derived effects by starting with effects that have already shown themselves to be powerful in the natural social environment. Although this is certainly not a point of initiation that has been previously unknown or unadvocated within social psychology, it does appear to be quite underused. In determining what to research, we seem to have developed a decided tendency to pay less attention to what the people we are supposed to be studying are doing than to what other social psychologists are doing. There are well-known exceptions, of course. The tradition of research on bystander intervention into emergencies is an excellent example. Its impetus came from a powerful social event (a highly publicized murder case) that did not seem to be one of a kind and that people generally cared about. Similarly, Stanley Milgram's work on obedience began with an observation of the chilling strength of authority pressures in producing compliance of the sort seen in the concentration camps of Nazi Germany. I think it is instructive that people outside social psychology know more about these two programs of social psychological investigation than perhaps any other. When I lecture about them to my large undergraduate classes, I am careful to emphasize the incident from which the work sprang. The effect on the students is quite dramatic: I gain their attention almost as totally as if I had mentioned sex. And the academic issues of interest to college students should not be dismissed airily. Students offer a good approximation of what constitutes the "intelligent laypeople," the administrators, attorneys, politicians, and businesspeople who run society. If for no other reason than the public regard for what we do, social psychologists would do well to watch carefully what such people find interesting in our work.

In addition to the fact that they have inherent meaning for individuals who are not social psychologists, there is another reason to study effects that appear to represent important behavioral phenomena. Once the decision about *what* to study has been made on this basis, we can more eagerly set out on the intellectual adventure of determining *why* it works the way it does. With enhanced confidence that we are not dealing with a trivial phenomenon, we can feel justified in expending the time and energy needed to uncover its mediator. With the "what" question out of the way, the sophisticated experimental procedures that are so well suited to answering the "why" question become appropriate. Recall that the problem with these procedures was, paradoxically enough, their precision, which prevented us from knowing whether the things we were studying had a natural impact. But when the task is to explain why an effect that already has been determined to be important exists, we want all the precision we can get. We want to be able to distill the effect to its essence and differentiate among the possible theoretical explanations for its occurrence. Here, when capturing is once again the order of the day, we want our experiments to be elegant, sensitive, and selective.

This, then, is the time for clever designs and operations that will allow us to provide evidence for or against the contending theoretical interpretations for the effect we have observed. Now the fascinating work of testing the applicability of relevant formulations can go on less fettered with worry about its purely academic character. That work is much more than just intellectually engaging, though. It represents the crucial scientific process of theory confirmation/disconfirmation; I trust that the great significance of such a process for the understanding of human behavior need not be argued here. Granted, there are certain advantages to approaching this process in a more deductive fashion than has been suggested in this chapter; the primary benefit appears to lie in the ability to do concentrated theory testing, especially through the prediction of effects that would not otherwise have been expected. Certainly there are times when this sort of approach is appropriate. There are advantages as well, however, to a more inductive orientation that begins with naturally powerful effects and then seeks to determine their theoretical or conceptual underpinnings. In particular, if such a sequence is regularly employed, one result should be a steadily developing sense of which of our formulations account not just for aspects of human behavior but also for aspects of the behaviors that *matter* around us. Earlier in this chapter I suggested that theories can be viewed as being somewhat like maps. To carry the metaphor a bit further, we can see that maps, like theories, may be more accurate in describing certain areas within their boundaries than others. If I set off on a trip, let us say through the land of human behavior, I would want to be assured that the map I used represented correctly the important locations of the journey; it would be cold comfort to know that it accurately depicted the inconsequential ones instead.

SOME EXAMPLES

When Even a Penny Helps

As was suggested by the football fan anecdote at the outset of this chapter, one place to scout for behavioral events worthy of study is in the actions of those around us. An equally suitable place lies in our own actions. Not only are we made aware of the existence of regularly occurring effects in this way, we also may think introspectively about the processes involved and thus obtain hints about their conceptual mediators. Powerful personal experiences are often suggestive of powerful and general psychological influences. One such personal experience led me to the investigation of a highly effective fund-raising tactic and its implications for the way in which compliance decisions are sometimes made.

I answered the door early one evening to find a young woman who was canvassing my neighborhood for the United Way. She identified herself and asked if I would give a monetary donation. It so happened that my university has an active United Way organization and that I had given in-house a few days earlier. It was also the end of the month, and my finances were low. Besides, if I gave to all the solicitors for charity who come to my door, I would quickly require such service for myself. As she spoke, I had already decided against a donation and was preparing my reply to incorporate the above reasons. Then it happened. After asking for a contribution, she added five magic words. I know they were *the* magic words because my negative reply to the donation request literally caught in my throat when I heard them. "Even a penny will help," she said. And with that she demolished my anticipated response. All the excuses I had prepared for failing to comply were based on financial considerations: I could not afford to give to her now or give to her too. But she said, "Even a penny will help," and rendered my argument impotent. How could I claim an inability to help when she claimed that "even a penny" was a legitimate form of aid? I had been neatly finessed into compliance. And there was another interesting feature of our exchange as well. When I stopped coughing (I really had choked on my attempted rejection), I gave her *not* the penny she had mentioned but the amount I usually allot to legitimate charity solicitors. At that, she thanked me, smiled innocently, and moved on.

To try to understand the psychology of what had taken place, I enlisted the efforts of a graduate student of mine, Dave Schroeder. In analyzing the situation, we realized that the request addendum "Even a penny will help" had not functioned as the invitation to contribute; that had come earlier. Rather, it served as a way of making legitimate even the most minimal sort of help. As such, it engaged, we thought, the action of a pair of powerful sources of influence in the social environment—powerful enough, at least, to change me from adamantly noncompliant in expectation to meekly compliant in reality. First, it removed my excuses for not offering aid of some kind. It is very difficult to argue that one does not have the wherewithal to provide as paltry a form of aid as a penny. I needed excuses for my noncompliance. Apparently, it was important that I have reasons to justify my behavior. Without those reasons as anchors, I was easily influenced. Second, by making legitimate a trivial amount of aid, the request had placed some image-maintenance pressures on me. What is the image of someone who will not give even a penny's worth of help to a good cause? It is the image of a decidedly unhelpful person, not the sort of image, public or private, I would like to have associated with myself. To avoid such a characterization, compliance seemed required.

It appeared to us, then, that the real function of the phrase "Even a penny will help" was to legitimize the most paltry contribution and thus allow for the action of the two processes described above. But all this was speculation. We had not yet determined whether the effect was specific to me or substantially more general. The first order of business, then, was to establish that those five magic words did reliably and powerfully increase donations in a naturalistic fund-raising context. So, with the aid of the Phoenix branch of the American Cancer Society, we equipped ourselves with the appropriate identification badges and went soliciting for charity in a nearby middle-income neighborhood.

Our research assistants would go door to door asking for contributions in two ways. The first employed the standard request for funds used by the American Cancer Society's volunteers during its annual area drive: "I'm collecting money for the American Cancer Society. Would you be willing to help by giving a donation?" The other form was identical to the first, except that it included the addendum "Even a penny will help." After contacting forty-two subjects with each type of request, we counted the money. It became immediately clear that I was not the only patsy in Phoenix. The even-a-penny technique that had worked so well on me a few weeks earlier produced nearly twice as much compliance as the standard technique (50 percent versus 28.6 percent). Moreover, just as had occurred in my case, the even-a-penny subjects did not give only a penny: They gave the amount they normally furnished to such a charity organization. Thus, the median and modal contribution for both kinds of requests was $1. The mean contribution among those who gave was also highly alike for the standard and even-a-penny request conditions ($1.54 and $1.44, respectively). It is not surprising, then, that the even-a-penny request provided a significantly higher total yield ($30.34) than did the standard request ($18.55).

At that point we felt comfortable in our belief that we were dealing with an effect worth studying. The first steps in locating the effect and determining its natural impact had been taken. Now it was time to begin the fun of investigating why it worked the way it did. We already had a hypothesis, based on personal introspection, that "Even a penny will help" was effective because it served to legitimize a minuscule form of aid. When the most minimal of monetary contributions is deemed acceptable, excuses for failing to help become inapplicable and the refusal to bestow such aid may jeopardize one's image as a benevolent person. But there was also a competing conceptual explanation. Perhaps the norm of social responsibility that states that people should help those in need accounts for the effect. That is, it is possible that the words "Even a penny will help" cause people to perceive a greater need for aid than they would have if the sentence had not been added to the request. For this reason, they may be more likely to donate funds.

Good. We had plausible alternative interpretations, just what experimental social psychologists love to test and just what our trapper techniques are well suited to doing. The rest consisted of the stimulating process of explanation testing. We would have to design an experiment that assessed the ability of the two alternative explanations to account for the effect. We knew, for example, that the social responsibility explanation proposed an increased perception of need by subjects exposed to the even-a-penny request. If we included a measure of perceived need in our next study and found no such enhanced perception, that would provide evidence against the applicability of the social responsibility formulation to our effect. Thus, when we conducted the study, we incorporated a scale measure of how needful the charity organization (again the American Cancer Society) was of funds, ranging from not at all in need (zero) to extremely in need (six).

We also knew that the legitimization-of-small-favors interpretation implied that any statement with the effect of making a penny seem like a legitimate contribution should result in a greater frequency of compliance. Consequently, we included a condition in our second study that was designed to serve this function without simultaneously implying that the charity agency was badly in need of funds. The solicitor in this condition (social legitimization) legitimized paltry donations by saying, "We've already received some contributions ranging from a penny on up." Here a penny contribution was legitimized via the social comparison–based information that others had given that amount. It was predicted that this condition would produce a compliance level above that of the standard request condition (control) and comparable to the even-a-penny condition.

A final condition was included in the second study to test the derivation from the legitimization hypothesis that it is the legitimization of *minimal* favors that accounts for the effectiveness of the even-a-penny tactic. Subjects in this condition heard the standard request followed by the sentence "Even a dollar will help." Since a person is not as likely to be without excuses for failing to give a dollar and is not as likely to experience image damage in refusing to give a dollar compared to a penny, the legitimization-of-small-favors explanation would predict that subjects in this condition would not show the high degree of compliance of those in the even-a-penny group; instead, their compliance rate might be expected to be intermediate between that of the control group and that of the even-a-penny group.

The findings offered no support for the social responsibility explanation based on perceived need. There was no significant difference between the even-a-penny and the control conditions in the perceived need scores subjects assigned to those requests, yet there was a significant difference between them in obtained compliance (58.1 percent versus 32.2 percent). It seems unlikely, then, that the even-a-penny effect is mediated by the norm of social responsibility. By contrast, there was considerable support for the legitimization hypothesis. First, the social legitimization condition that legitimized a penny contribution through social comparison information produced the highest percentage (64.5 percent) of compliance, a percentage that was comparable with that of the even-a-penny condition. Second, the even-a-dollar request that was designed to weaken the action of the legitimization-of-small-favors process resulted in a percentage of compliance (46.7 percent) that was intermediate between those of the even-a-penny and control requests. The even-a-dollar condition did not produce significantly enhanced compliance compared with the control.

Although the results of our second study supported our thinking about why the even-a-penny effect occurs, a number of additional questions remained unanswered. For example, we suggested that making a paltry favor appear to be an acceptable one increased compliance for reasons of favorable self-presentation—our subjects' desire to look good (or to avoid looking bad) in the eyes of the requester. But the action of this motive was not directly tested in our studies. Other researchers have collected data that support the self-presentational explanation, however. They have shown that the even-a-penny tactic works best when it is made in a face-to-face interaction. It doesn't work as well when the interaction occurs over the phone or, especially, through the mail because the presence of an evaluating requester is reduced in those cases.

To test the self-presentational explanation further, it would be instructive to reduce self-presentational pressures by some other means and see whether the tactic lost effectiveness under those circumstances as well. In a related vein, a researcher could test this explanation by arranging a situation that increased the self-presentational pressures working on subjects and then looking to see if those subjects became even more susceptible to the even-a-penny tactic.

But I am beginning to sound like a trapper again. Exactly. These strike me as interesting conceptual questions requiring sophisticated experimental techniques to answer. The engaging activity of trapping may now be undertaken with increased assurance that the questions being asked refer back to something that is real not just in a statistical sense but in a *real* sense.

In the previous example a research project was begun after an accidental encounter with the effect of interest. The same was true of the series of studies that flowed from the observation I made in the stands of the Ohio State football stadium. There appears to be no good reason, however, for researchers to be so passive about searching for worthwhile effects to study. Certainly it is possible to live our daily lives ready and waiting to be struck by an interesting effect in the behaviors within or around us. But if we have a special topic of interest, it may be advantageous to take a more active, less reactive role. For instance, I am quite interested in the variables that influence compliance decisions. Just what are the factors that affect the likelihood that one person will say yes to another person's request? To begin to find out, I spent nearly three years as an observer, often a participant-observer, in a large number of real-world compliance situations. I wanted to learn which tactics and procedures the practitioners (merchandisers, fund-raisers, con artists, negotiators, advertisers, and so on) thought were effective compliance inducers. Once a sufficiently large sample of such tactics was registered, I could categorize them according to the psychological principles that might explain their effectiveness. With the initial scouting done, I could put on my trapper's shoes again and submit the most intriguing or powerful compliance strategies to experimental analysis in order to test the ability of the likely conceptual principles involved to account for the effects.

Without a doubt, these active scouting opportunities have proved to be among the most edifying experiences I have had. Not only have I become less of a sucker for the techniques that underlie the strategies I have observed, I have also learned a lot of social psychology. That is so because the people I have studied know a lot of social psychology, although they do not know that they do. As far as I can tell, there are six or seven social psychological principles that mediate about 90 percent of the tactics they regularly and expertly employ. High-pressure sales organizations, legitimate charity agencies, waiters and waitresses, Hare Krishna devotees, and Tupperware representatives all use procedures that *work*. If the procedures did not work, they or their practitioners would soon disappear; a process not unlike natural selection assures it. Imagine the little-kid-in-the-candy-store feeling that I had. There I was, a compliance researcher surrounded by compliance tactics of demonstrated impact but indeterminate cause. It was a trapper's dream. I had my effects and my speculations about why they occurred; all that was left was the hunt.

Throwing the Lowball

During one of the times when I was using the technique of participant observation to learn about naturally existing compliance strategies, I came across one that seemed especially intriguing. I had answered an ad for automobile sales trainees and was in the middle of a local auto dealer's program for selecting and training car salespersons. Toward the end of the program, after we had been exposed to a variety of techniques used to get the customer to buy, we were allowed to watch some of the regular salespeople operate. One tactic that enjoyed popularity among the staff is called by a number of names but for our purposes can be referred to as lowballing or throwing a lowball. Although the technique had certain variations, the crucial feature was invariant: The customer was given a price substantially below the amount at which the salesperson intended to sell the car in order to induce the customer to agree initially to the purchase—hence the "lowball" title.

Once the customer had made the decision for a specific car (and had even begun completing the appropriate forms), the price advantage was deftly removed. This could happen in several ways. Sometimes the customer was told that the initially cited price contained a calculation error or did not include an expensive option that the customer had assumed was part of the offer. More frequently the initial price offer was rescinded when the salesperson checked with the sales manager, who voided the arrangement because "we'd be losing money." The most clever variation required the salesperson to propose an inflated trade-in price for the customer's car that was then cut by the used-car assessor upon close examination; in most cases, the customer knew the true worth of the trade-in and thus considered the second evaluation the fair one. No matter which form of the procedure was used, the result was the same: The reason for the customer's favorable purchase decision was removed, and the performance of the desired behavior was made more costly. Further, the increased cost was such that the final price was equivalent to, and often somewhat above, that of the dealer's competitors. However, consistent with car dealership lore, it appeared that more customers remained with the decision to purchase the automobile, even at the adjusted figure, than would have bought it if the final price had been disclosed before a purchase decision had been obtained.

I was amazed at the technique's effectiveness. Why should it work so well? After all, the reason these people had originally decided to buy the car rather than another one was the clear price advantage, and that advantage had been removed by the end of the negotiations. But they still bought! What was going on? I asked the opinions of the old hands at the place. They all said it had to do with getting the customer to make an initial decision to "buy *your* car." After that, their explanations became vague and circular. I should have known. These guys knew what worked; that was their job, and their livelihoods depended on it. But they did not understand why it worked, not in a conceptual sense, at least. That was my job. So, with the invaluable help of three graduate students—John Cacioppo, Rod Bassett, and John Miller—investigation of the lowball technique began.

From what had been already observed, we surmised that the critical feature of the lowball technique was the customer's initial decision to buy. More generally, the essence of the procedure is for a requester to induce another individual to resolve to perform a specified target behavior. Once that determination has been made, it is assumed that the decision will tend to persist even after circumstances have changed to make performance of the target action more costly than it was before. Of course, at this point all we had was my nonsystematic set of observations that this technique is effective. It was even possible, though it struck us as unlikely, that automobile dealers had been deluding themselves about the power of lowballing. The logical first step, as in the prior example, was to establish the effectiveness of the tactic in a natural setting. Since we were not interested in car sales per se, we saw no reason to examine lowballing in the automobile showroom. Indeed, if we could export the technique to a novel context and validate its effectiveness there, we would have valuable evidence for the generality of the effect. It was important, though, to ensure that the context we chose demonstrated that the technique had genuine impact in affecting meaningfully sized compliance decisions. Thus, we wanted to show that the technique could significantly influence people to do something that they did not like to do.

One thing we knew that our undergraduate research subjects did not like to do was to get up early to participate in psychology experiments. At the time, any experimenter who put a sign-up sheet that designated openings before 8 A.M. probably also believed in the Easter bunny. We wondered, though, whether we could get subjects to participate in an early-morning experiment via the lowball procedure.

> *Cialdini:*   Maybe we should see if we could get subjects to get out of bed and come down here for an early psychology experiment. But how early would be early enough?
> *Research Assistant 1:*   Eight o'clock, seven-thirty; how about seven?
> *Cialdini:*   Seven in the *morning*. Are you crazy?
> *Research Assistant 2:*   Yeah, let's try seven. Let's see just what we've got here.
> *Cialdini:*   Okay, seven it is. But don't blame me if this flops.

The study itself implemented the lowball strategy by obtaining a decision from subjects to execute a target behavior (participation in a specific study) and then raising the cost of performing that behavior. The lowball procedure was contrasted with a control procedure in which subjects were informed of the full cost of the target behavior before being requested to perform it. A confederate blind to the experimental hypothesis phoned introductory psychology students and asked them to come to an experiment on thinking processes, for which they would receive an hour of experimentation credit. Before they were asked to participate, subjects in the control condition were informed of the 7 A.M. starting time. They were also allowed to select one of two days for their participation. A subject making such an appointment was considered verbally compliant. Subjects in the lowball condition, however, were asked if they would participate in the thinking processes study before being told about the 7 A.M. feature. Anyone who declined at that point was included in the data analysis as noncompliant. A subject who agreed to participate was *then* informed that the study would begin at 7 A.M. and was asked to choose one of the two possible experiment dates. Again, any subject who made such an appointment was considered verbally compliant. In addition to the measure of verbal compliance, we included a measure of behavioral compliance. We counted the number of subjects in each condition who actually appeared for their early-morning appointments, where we saw to it that they did participate in a thinking processes study.

The results were striking. Of the twenty-nine people called in the control condition, nine agreed to participate and seven of them actually appeared. Thus, only 24 percent of our control condition calls produced behaviorally compliant subjects. The lowball procedure engendered sizably higher success rates, however, as nineteen of the thirty-four subjects who were called complied verbally and eighteen of the thirty-four (53 percent) complied behaviorally with the request. These data offered good evidence that the lowball sequence of obtaining an active decision from a target person to perform an action and only then providing information about the full costs of the action is an effective and powerful way of gaining assent to a request to perform the fully described action.

On the basis of these findings, we felt justified in pursuing the answers to some conceptual questions concerning the phenomenon. One question that suggested itself to us was whether the lowball technique in which a requester secures an active decision to perform a target behavior and then raises the cost of performing that behavior is any different from the foot-in-the-door procedure. A requester uses the foot-in-the-door technique by inducing an individual to perform an initial favor and subsequently asking that individual to comply with a larger second request. While both techniques seek to gain performance of a costly action by first obtaining assent to an apparently less costly request, there is at least one important difference. With the lowball tactic, the behavior requested initially (e.g., buying a certain car) is in fact the target behavior; only the cost of carrying it out changes.

With the foot-in-the-door procedure, the behavior requested initially is not the target, although the two may be related. Whether this difference is just a semantic one or is a genuine one that would manifest itself in the differential ability of the two tactics to produce compliance in given situations is, of course, an empirical question. It was our feeling that the procedural difference between the two techniques would empower the lowball technique as the more effective compliance inducer. That is, an individual who has already decided to perform the target behavior may experience a greater sense of cognitive commitment to the performance of *that* behavior than would someone who has already decided to perform a different, though related action. As a test, we conducted a field study in which three sets of procedures—lowball, foot-in-the-door, and control—were used to induce subjects to perform a charitable action. The decision to employ a charity context was made in order to inquire further into the generality of the lowball tactic. We wanted to know whether the technique could be influential in a charity setting and on benevolent behavior.

Our second lowball study was performed on male graduate students who answered an experimenter's knock at the door of their dormitory rooms. The experimenter uniformly introduced himself as a representative of the United Way who was asking dorm residents to display United Way posters. The target behavior asked of each subject was to display two such posters, one designated for the door and one for a window. Control condition subjects learned from the outset that agreeing to display the posters would require that they procure a "poster packet" containing the necessary materials at the downstairs dorm desk within an hour of the experimental contact. A subject who agreed to do so and to display both posters was considered verbally compliant.

In the lowball condition, the script was similar except that subjects did not learn about the required trip to the downstairs desk until they had agreed to post the materials. Then they were asked if they would perform the fully described target behavior. Subjects in the foot-in-the-door condition were initially asked to display a window poster (all agreed and were given the poster); they were then asked to perform the more costly behavior of going downstairs to obtain a door poster for display.

The data were disappointing to us at first. A high and approximately equal percentage of verbal compliance occurred across all conditions. With ten subjects per group, 80 percent of the subjects in the lowball condition and 70 percent of those in the other two conditions agreed to display the posters after being fully informed of the cost of doing so. It appeared that the very high level of verbal compliance in the control group produced a ceiling effect that prevented any demonstration of the effectiveness of our experimental groups. But the next day, when we measured behavioral compliance with our request by counting the subjects who had actually displayed the posters, we found large differences. As hypothesized, the lowball condition induced significantly greater performance of the target behavior (60 percent) than did the control (20 percent) and foot-in-the-door (10 percent) conditions. Further, the superiority of the lowball treatment maintained itself when only those subjects who verbally complied were considered; that is, 75 percent (six of eight) of verbally compliant lowball subjects complied behaviorally, whereas significantly fewer—28.6 percent (two of seven) and 14.3 percent (one of seven) —did so in the control and foot-in-the-door conditions, respectively.

We learned two things from our second study. First, the lowball procedure appears to be robust across target behaviors and naturalistic situations. Charitable action, a form of behavior quite unlike the target behaviors to which the tactic is typically applied, was strongly affected by this
technique in a setting that was different from both the car sales context
and the subject recruitment context of our first experiment. Second, the
lowball technique does not seem to be a simple variant of the foot-in-the-
door technique. In this regard, it is instructive to examine the relationship
between verbal and behavioral compliance among the three conditions of
the design. The behavioral superiority of the lowball tactic was due primarily to the greater tendency of verbally compliant subjects in that condition to execute the target behavior they had agreed to perform.

One plausible explanation for the form of these data supports our
prior hypothesizing and underscores the need for compliance
researchers to obtain behavioral measures of compliance. It was our feeling that a high percentage of the verbally compliant subjects in the foot-
in-the-door and control conditions never intended to perform the target
behavior; since the full cost of the target action was known to these subjects before they agreed to do it, many may have privately decided not to
perform the costly action but instead to provide only the impression that
they would in order to avoid immediate social disapproval. The comparable subjects of the lowball procedure, however, were induced to decide
to execute the target behavior when it seemed to involve minimal cost;
the resultant cognitive commitment to the performance of the target
action should have existed privately from the outset for them and thus
may have mediated the behavioral superiority of the technique. Whether
or not the above account is the correct one, the form of the results does
indicate that the lowball procedure is not identical in effect to the foot-in-
the-door procedure in that the two techniques produced distinct data
patterns.

At this point we were satisfied that we had located a powerful and
cross-situationally robust influence on the compliance process that was
not a simple variant of an already demonstrated technique. How could
we account for the effect? Additional research indicated that the best
explanation of the lowball effect lies in the commitment formulation presented by Charles Kiesler. Kiesler suggests that a major function of commitment is to impart resistance to change. To the extent that one is committed to a decision, for instance, the decision becomes less changeable.
According to Kiesler's analysis, a person who makes a decision behaviorally and with *free choice* will be cognitively committed to that decision
and disinclined to change it. The applicability of the commitment formulation to the lowball phenomenon is clear: A freely made, active initial
decision to behave positively toward an object (e.g., the United Way)
tends to persist because that kind of decision creates commitment, that is,
a resistance to change that will tend to be impervious to the influence of

subsequent information (e.g., increased costs) concerning the wisdom of the decision. Freely made commitments tend to freeze people in decisional choices.

FULL-CYCLE SOCIAL PSYCHOLOGY

From the outset of this piece I have advocated that social psychological investigators begin work, with much more frequency than at present, from naturally occurring instances of social phenomena. Progressive steps should then be taken to establish the power, generality, and theoretical/conceptual underpinnings of the phenomenon of interest. However, natural observation should not be restricted to the beginnings of the research venture; it also should be used to complete the final arc in the circle. That is, naturally occurring instances should be employed not only to identify effects suitable for experimental study but also to check on the validity of the findings from that experimentation. For example, in the lowball project we ultimately determined that the action of the variable of commitment was limited to a situation involving the perception of free choice. If we look back to the car sales context that originally brought the lowball technique to light for us, we can see that a customer's perception of decisional freedom is represented in that setting. If that had not been the case, we would have doubted the ecological validity of our laboratory findings.

It is noteworthy that in referring to the natural environment to check on this aspect of our results, we can see that not all tactics designed by practitioners to enhance compliance seem to require that free choice be represented. Those which employ the factor of reciprocation, for example, do not. The followers of Krishna who approach airport visitors to pin flowers on them first and then ask for donations try to make use of the cultural rule requiring reciprocation of favors without giving their targets a choice in the matter of the instigating first favor. The same is true of the disabled veterans' organizations that mail unsolicited address labels, greeting cards, or ballpoint pens along with a request for a contribution. Unlike lowball practitioners, these requesters seemingly feel that their tactics (which are among the most cost-effective I have observed) will produce a profitable exchange without the target person's free agreement to the initial stage of the interaction. This sort of comparison between observed compliance procedures cannot help but lead to testable speculation concerning the conditions under which the perception of choice is necessary for the occurrence of compliance. The cycle thus begins again.

The proposal, then, is for a "full-cycle" approach in which initial natural observation gives direction to subsequent controlled experimentation, the outcomes of which can then be given external validation through further natural observation that may stimulate still further experimentation. Systematic recourse to the evidence of the real world both before and after the performance of the experimental work may thus reduce the extent to which current social psychological research can be criticized as artificial and epiphenomenal.

Application

It does not require a careful reading of this chapter to see that there is no suggestion about how to apply the discipline of social psychology to the real world for the sake of society. Instead, it has been suggested that we apply the real world to social psychology for the sake of the discipline. Nonetheless, the two approaches are not independent. If one accepts the idea that it is the social responsibility of the discipline to identify principles that can be applied to areas of societal concern, it is important to have prior confidence in the strength of those principles to affect behavior in natural settings. For example, there is an enormous problem of noncompliance in the area of health behavior. It has been estimated that well over half of physicians' regimens for the remission or prevention of disorders are not complied with by patients. Anyone attempting to design a program to reduce such noncompliance would be wise to look to the techniques that have been determined to be powerful in other natural compliance settings. If the mediating principles that underlie those techniques have also been determined by previous experimentation, the probability of a successful transplant to the health context should be greatly enhanced. Without that vital mediational information, the functional essence of a selected technique is liable to get lost in the translation. Perhaps the most attractive feature of full-cycle social psychology, then, is its ability to foster the performance of solid social science that lends itself easily to social service.

Note, however, that the distinction between science and service remains. Application is *not* the final step in the full-cycle model; it is not even a necessary step. Rather, it is a potential bonus. The model's primary purpose is scientific. It is intended to lead to more realistic information about the factors that influence the preponderance of human behavior. One extremely valuable by-product of such information, however, is a science that is more directly applicable to real problem settings. Clear applicability is such a desirable commodity and yet is in such short supply within much of social psychology that a shift toward a full-cycle approach might be worth a try on that basis alone. After all, even a smidgen more applicability would help.

Acknowledgments

Adapted from the author's chapter "Full-Cycle Social Psychology" in L. Bickman (ed.), *Applied Social Psychology Annual* (vol. 1), pp. 21–47, by permission of Sage Publications, copyright © 1980.

SUGGESTED READINGS

BEM, D. (1967). Self-perception: An alternative interpretation of cognitive dissonance phenomena. *Psychological Review, 74,* 183–200.

BREHM, J. (1956). Postdecision changes in the desirability of alternatives. *Journal of Abnormal and Social Psychology, 52,* 384–389.

BROCKNER, J., GUZZI, B., KANE, J., LEVINE, E., & SHAPLEN, K. (1984). Organizational fundraising: More evidence on the effects of legitimizing small donations. *Journal of Consumer Research, 11,* 611–614.

CIALDINI, R. B. (1993). *Influence: Science and practice* (3d ed.). New York: Harper-Collins.

———— BORDEN, R. J., THORNE, A., WALKER, M. R., FREEMAN, S., & SLOAN, L. R. (1976). Basking in reflected glory: Three (football) field studies. *Journal of Personality and Social Psychology, 34,* 366–375.

———— CACIOPPO, J. T., BASSETT, R., & MILLER, J. A. (1978). Low-ball procedure for producing compliance: Commitment then cost. *Journal of Personality and Social Psychology, 36,* 463–476.

———— & RICHARDSON, K. D. (1980). Two indirect tactics of image management: Basking and blasting. *Journal of Personality and Social Psychology, 39,* 406–415.

———— & SCHROEDER, D. A. (1976). Increasing contributions by legitimizing paltry contributions: When even a penny helps. *Journal of Personality and Social Psychology, 34,* 599–604.

EISENBERG, N., CIALDINI, R. B., McCREATH, H., & SHELL, R. (1987). Consistency-based compliance: When and why children become vulnerable? *Journal of Personality and Social Psychology, 52,* 1174–1181.

FREEDMAN, J. L., & FRASER, S. (1966). Compliance without pressure: The foot-in-the-door technique. *Journal of Personality and Social Psychology, 4,* 195–202.

GOULDNER, A. W. (1960). The norm of reciprocity: A preliminary statement. *American Sociological Review, 25,* 161–178.

HEIDER, F. (1958). *The psychology of interpersonal relations.* New York: Wiley.

JONES, E. E., & HARRIS, V. E. (1967). The attribution of attitude. *Journal of Experimental Social Psychology, 3,* 1–24.

KIESLER, C. A. (1971). *The psychology of commitment.* New York: Academic Press.

REEVES, R. A., MARCOLINI, R. M., & MARTIN, R. C. (1987). Legitimizing paltry contributions: On-the-spot vs. mail-in requests. *Journal of Applied Social Psychology, 17,* 731–738.

R*OY F. BAUMEISTER (Ph.D., Princeton University) is currently the E. B. Smith Professor of Psychology at Case Western Reserve University. He has also worked at the University of California at Berkeley, the University of Texas at Austin, the University of Virginia, and the Max Planck Institute in Munich, Germany. He has over 100 publications, and his recent books include* Meanings of Life *(1991),* Escaping the Self: Alcoholism, Masochism, Spirituality, and Other Flights from the Burden of Selfhood *(1991),* Breaking Hearts: The Two Sides of Unrequited Love *(1992),* Your Own Worst Enemy: The Paradox of Self-Defeat *(1993), and* Self-Esteem: The Puzzle of Low Self-Regard *(1993). He now lives on the shores of the Great Lakes with his beloved wife, his two dogs and three computers, and his well-traveled windsurfer.*

5

The Personal Story of an Interpersonal Psychologist

❖

Social psychology is an extremely popular field in terms of numbers of researchers and exciting ideas. But there is a paradox in the way social psychology is practiced today: It isn't always all that social. Ironically, most social psychologists think of people as largely self-contained units, conceding only that occasionally these units come into contact with each other. Perhaps this is not too surprising. The United States is the nation of rugged individualism, and so American thinkers turn out to be oriented toward individuals.

I grew up with similar notions and conceptions, but somewhere along the way I have become convinced that the individual is not the ultimate or final unit of explanation. In a sense, I have become one of the most social of social psychologists. Although many of my colleagues casually refer to the human being as a "social animal," they mean it in only a limited sense. I have devoted much of my career to analyzing how fundamentally and thoroughly social the human being is. I like to think that a major part of my contribution to the field will be this expanded understanding of the social nature of humanity. Of course, some of my colleagues probably think I'm slightly nuts.

Before examining the personal intellectual odyssey that has led me to these somewhat extreme views, let us pause to examine what it means to say that the human being is a social animal. The simplest meaning is, I suppose, that people like to be together. Unlike species in which individuals flourish in isolation, people are usually found together. A variation on this view might state that there is some sort of "herd instinct" in the human being that motivates people to seek out each other's company and spend time together.

A second meaning may be that people need cooperation from others to achieve any kind of comfortable, stable life. It is extremely difficult to survive entirely on one's own. Long before the beginnings of history, human beings formed groups that did more than enjoy one another's company. They pooled their resources, divided up tasks among themselves so as to maximize productivity and skills, and cooperated in doing things (such as big-game hunting) that were too difficult for lone individuals. These patterns are more true today than ever, a fact that is especially obvious to an intellectual like me. If I had to grow and produce my own food, build my own house, and make my own clothes, I'd be in rather pathetic shape, and even if I somehow managed to avoid freezing or starving to death, I certainly would hardly ever find a chance to work at social psychology.

These aspects of the "social" nature of humanity are rather obvious and are widely accepted. My understanding goes far beyond them, however. Over time I have become convinced that the very nature of selfhood is social in the sense that it is dependent on other people. That is, we would not even have much sense of who we are—of identity and selfhood—apart from other people. I have also come to realize that emotions are not entirely private reactions but are based on interpersonal influences. And recently I have come to think, contrary to what I would like to believe, that people are innately motivated to need certain kinds of relationships with other people.

SOCIAL, ANTISOCIAL, AND INDIVIDUAL

I suppose it is ironic that I ended up with these views, because my background predisposed me toward a heavily individualistic outlook. My parents were an odd pair, an American schoolteacher and a German immigrant businessman, and they always felt somewhat alienated from everyone else, an attitude that they instilled in my sister and me throughout our upbringing. Indeed, they alienated both of their families just by getting married. When my mother left for her trip to Europe after World War II, the last thing her father said to her upon departure was, "Don't bring back any Krauts," so naturally she caused some friction when she decided to marry one. And when my father told his family that he was abandoning his university studies and moving to America, they were outraged. My parents affected a WASPish attitude, complete with a tepid Protestant faith, that was entirely out of step with the heavily Catholic and Slavic suburb where we lived. Neither of them liked to socialize, and they led a rather isolated existence together. Ironically, they were extremely conformist to the patterns that marked highly successful businesspersons, but since those people never really accepted my parents as one of them and my parents looked down on everyone else as inferior, this very conformity contributed to their isolation. Eventually they took early retirement and moved away, spending most of their later years traveling and living in various places, and so they essentially had no stable friends or social network.

Growing up as the child of such parents was not easy, and I soon learned that everybody else seemed to be quite different. I was a relatively lonely kid. My parents thought that rock music and sports and other such pastimes of youth were stupid and wasteful and tried to shield me from the influence of peers. My social isolation was compounded when I skipped a grade and became the youngest and, for many years, the physically smallest member of all my classes. I was generally the smartest kid in the class, but socially I was hopelessly uncool.

Physically I was also at a disadvantage, because in those years of junior high and high school most boys grow quite a bit every year. Athletics were not really available to me, and in gym class I was generally among the poorest performers, with the exception of wrestling. In wrestling, to my and everyone else's surprise, I was unbeatable, because I would be matched against someone who weighed the same as I did; this usually meant that he was scrawny and weak for his age, while I was merely a year younger. Still, in most athletic competitions I was at a serious physical disadvantage for many years. When in my efforts to begin to be a more normal kid I began to join school sports teams, I found I had to make up for my physical deficit by performing to the very maximum of my capabilities just to be competitive. This became a factor in my research in psychology later on. I had to learn the hard way how to get the most out of psychological factors in sports just to keep up with the older, bigger, and stronger boys, and so I gradually developed an understanding of how performance depends on mental responses. Years later I conducted a line of research on why some people perform better than others under pressure and on what causes other people to "choke."

As I said, though, this pattern of social isolation and individualism was gradually replaced by a new outlook that emphasized interpersonal factors in every sphere of human psychology. I can't say for certain what changed me, but there are several apparent factors. Underlying many of them, however, was a basic attitude I adopted during my undergraduate years: not to get too strongly attached to any particular idea. I decided that if I wanted to reach the truth, I had to be willing to abandon any of my views that turned out to be false, and I assumed (stimulated by frequent experience!) that many of my views were false. It was also obvious to me that many people are unable to advance toward a more correct understanding because they cling to views that they like or to views that suit their personal opinions and prejudices rather than abandoning them when necessary. I decided I wouldn't let that happen to me. Over the years it has often been sad or disappointing to me to give up on ideas or opinions that I liked and favored, but I have kept to the faith that to reach correct conclusions it is first necessary to discard many false ones.

My college years, in the early 1970s, corresponded to the "mystical" aftermath of the 1960s. College campuses saw an endless parade of experts and gurus describing new techniques for exploring the mind and expanding consciousness, from psychedelic drugs to meditation practices, and countless lectures expounded new techniques that involved exploring and controlling one's dreams, chanting in unison, doing astral projection, remembering past lives, and more. I was busy rejecting everything my parents had taught me, and I looked eagerly into these putative mind-expanding techniques as a way to shed my false self and discover deep inner truths. Of course, in all those hippie-oriented movements there was a lot of nonsense, but there were some valuable lessons as well. For my part, I developed an escalating realization of how little was really definite and fixed inside me. Even if one takes the cynical attitude that all those consciousness movements were basically nonsense, I still learned something from the exercise of discarding the nonsense I had acquired from my parents and replacing it with alternative nonsense. Contrary to my naive and simple assumptions, I realized that very little of the inner self is nailed down. Almost everything can change. That raised the question of what creates or changes the inner self. The answer, I gradually began to realize, is the interpersonal world. The inner self is a product of human interaction, social influence, and cultural conditioning. When the external social environment changes, the internal person can easily change too.

I had gone to college to major in mathematics. I had been extremely talented at math in high school, and my parents had encouraged that interest as a likely way to make money, on which they placed supreme value. It was also of course an appealing field for a bright young loner because one didn't have to have social skills, emotional maturity, or interpersonal sophistication. Soon, however, I began to realize that advanced mathematics was not the kind of life I wanted to live. The subject matter was so abstract as to be quite dull, and the math majors I knew were the kind of weird eggheads I was striving not to be. Stimulated by the posthippie influence regarding profound questions about the nature of existence and ultimate reality, I decided to study philosophy and comparative religion. I began delving into the writings of the great minds of past centuries.

One set of ideas that affected me deeply was phenomenology, particularly the works of Heidegger. The basic idea of phenomenology is that the primary reality is contact, such as perception or interaction, rather than isolated entities. The human being doesn't exist in isolation from the world, occasionally seeing it or interacting with it. Rather, the idea of an individual human being is deduced from many interactions with the world. The individual inner self is thus the product of interaction, an idea that is still fundamental to the way I think about the social nature of humanity.

Heidegger went on to make the startling point that there is nothing truly private. This idea was at first a shock to me because I believed that the private self is essential and fundamental and I thought I was full of private things. But he pointed out that the so-called private sphere is composed entirely of things taken from the public sphere. At most, one can take or make some public things and keep them secret, but that doesn't change the fact that they are basically derived from the public, social world. If I have a private opinion about, say, government economic policy or Barbara's ugly hairdo, this opinion is a result of my life in society and experiences with the social world, concerns what other people are doing, is amenable to change through discussion and influence by other people, and so forth. Most fundamentally, it is expressed in language, and Heidegger dramatically impressed on me the social nature of language and the extent to which it pervades everything we do, think, and feel. Without language people would not be human, and language is thoroughly and essentially social. After all, it's not a language until two or more people share it.

If language is social, then so is meaning. And meaning pervades everything people do. The meanings of the things people say and do and think and feel are thus dependent on others. If one were to delete everything involving meaning from the human being, there would be hardly anything left, certainly nothing worth talking about. Thus, all the interesting, meaningful, uniquely human aspects of people's experience are social.

SELF-PRESENTATION

Through a series of accidents and coincidences I went into social psychology rather than philosophy. Despite my independent-mindedness, my hippie friends, and my rebellion against establishment values, I still managed to get good grades in college and was accepted into many graduate programs. I chose Duke on the (mistaken) assumptions that the famous professor and researcher Edward E. Jones would be there forever and that my philosophical interests would flourish there. After trying various lines of research with mixed success, I reached the point where I had to choose a topic to focus on for several years. I had become interested in the nature of the self, which was then (even more than now) capturing wide interest among the mainstream public, in the spiritualist/mystical counterculture, and in the intellectual establishment. Of course, the self was too vast a topic to resolve with a master's thesis, and so I had to narrow it down. I decided to explore the interpersonal aspect of the self. At that time the concept of self-presentation was just gaining acceptance in some spheres while being fiercely resisted in others (and ignored in still others). I chose this as my first topic of study.

Up till that point self-presentation had been confined to a rather limited conception. The idea was that people try to make a good impression on others, and so people may change the way they act in order to please others. This view has been called impression management, reflecting the idea that people try to control (manage) the impressions that others form of them. It was suggested that some laboratory results were really the results of impression management: Subjects changed their attitudes or altered their behavior to make a good impression on the experimenter or on other subjects who happened to be present.

My ideas regarding self-presentation were much more radical than this view. I wanted to argue that the self is fundamentally social, that what is inside the individual is very much a product of what happens on the outside. I felt that one's very identity requires validation by others, and so the self cannot have any substantive existence without social recognition. Self-presentation is thus a way of creating one's very self, of claiming a certain identity for oneself.

My thinking on this was shaped by many sources, including George Herbert Mead, Carl Jung, Harry Stack Sullivan, and Martin Heidegger, but probably the oddest of these was Carlos Castaneda. Castaneda had written a series of books on Native American mysticism that were fairly popular in the 1970s. According to the story, he had been a graduate student in anthropology at UCLA, and in the course of doing field research he had come into contact with an old Indian who turned out to be an advanced mystic with a profound understanding of separate realities and with supernatural abilities and powers. This man had supposedly taken Castaneda on as a student and imparted some of his knowledge to him, which Castaneda had then reported in a series of books. The first two books emphasized some drug experiences that Castaneda had had under the old man's guidance and were popular with the drug-oriented mysticism that was rampant on American college campuses at that time. Castaneda's best book, *Journey to Ixtlan,* abandoned the drug approach and emphasized the philosophical lessons these mystical adventures had taught him. This book was accepted as a Ph.D. dissertation by UCLA, although some claimed that Castaneda had made it all up and objected to the idea of granting a Ph.D. for what was essentially a work of fiction, however brilliant it might have been.

One of the points made in this book was that spiritual advancement is hampered by one's "personal history," that is, one's reputation and social network. The idea is that once other people know you, they form beliefs about you and expect you to remain the same. This makes it difficult for you to grow or to change or even to be spontaneous. Much of one's life is thus devoted to responding to the expectations of others.

This idea fit in well with the view of the self I was working to develop. It also, fortunately, fit in with my mentor's work, because it corresponded to the actor-observer bias which Jones (along with Richard Nisbett) had explicated in terms of perceiving other people, but not the self, as having stable traits. Because of this fortunate overlap, I was given the green light to start studying this idea. Thus began what may have been one of the only series of laboratory experiments inspired by the mystical writings of Castaneda!

For my procedures, I began with what was known as the Barnum effect, that is, the willingness of the layperson to accept an expert's evaluation of the layperson's personality as valid and accurate even if in fact it was constructed at random and had no basis in fact. (It is named after P. T. Barnum, the circus entrepreneur whose most famous line was "There's a sucker born every minute.") This was the sort of clever hoax that attracted people to social psychology—the idea that people would fall for such a scam. The usual procedure was to give the subjects a fake personality test and then offer them a chance to see the results of the test, but actually all they got was a standard, randomly assigned personality description that had no relation to what they had written on the personality test and was identical to what other subjects received.

My innovation was to vary whether this false personality feedback was public, in the sense of known to other people, or strictly private and confidential. Most theorizing about the Barnum effect had emphasized that it works by altering the self-concept; that is, it depends on people changing the way they think about themselves in response to an expert evaluation. I thought that if that was all there was to it, it wouldn't make any difference whether other people knew about it. But if the consequences of the Barnum effect involved self-presentation, then people would be affected by it mainly when they thought someone else knew their evaluation. In short, I could give people identical (fake) personality evaluations, but they would be affected by them only if they thought other people had access to them. To measure the effects of these evaluations, all subjects were asked during the lab session to fill out a questionnaire rating themselves on many dimensions. They were told that this questionnaire would be shown to the other subject "to help him (or her) get to know what kind of person you are."

Sure enough, in this experiment the confidential evaluations had little or no effect on the way people rated themselves subsequently, but when the evaluations were allegedly public (i.e., shown to another subject to simulate acquaintanceship), they had strong and significant effects. This encouraged my belief that the self is far more social than we've thought. The same information would have the same effect on the self-concept if private information processing was all that was involved, but if the self was an interpersonal phenomenon, then that information would affect people only if it was publicly known.

In a follow-up I even found that people would conform behaviorally to the bogus feedback about their personalities as long as they thought other people knew their feedback, whereas that same feedback delivered in a confidential fashion failed to alter their behavior. For the behavioral measure, I used the prisoner's dilemma game, in which players must choose between a cooperative response that is moderately good for everyone and a competitive/exploitative response that benefits the self and hurts the other player if the other player responds cooperatively but hurts everyone if both players respond that way. The bogus personality feedback told subjects (by random assignment) either that they were very cooperative by nature or that they were strongly competitive by nature. Only in the public evaluation condition did subjects respond to the prisoner's dilemma game consistently with what we told them about themselves. Thus, again, it is not simply receiving an evaluation and changing how you think about yourself that matters; instead, what is decisive is how you think others perceive you.

These studies formed my dissertation and led to some of my first publications. My adviser helped me adopt a more conventional and seemingly professional approach to presenting them, although I did manage to sneak a citation of Carlos Castaneda into the first article we published on this in a scholarly journal.

A related study was concerned with expectancy effects. The notion of the self-fulfilling prophecy has exerted a powerful influence over social psychology, beginning with the "Pygmalion in the classroom" studies by Rosenthal and colleagues late in the 1960s. These effects also were often understood and conceptualized in terms of private information processing inside the individual mind, but again I thought that the interpersonal dimension might be decisive. I gave people a bogus personality measure and on that basis presented them with supposedly expert information about how they would perform on an upcoming problem-solving test. For this test, we used anagram solving (unscrambling mixed-up letters to spell words), which is a fairly standard test used to study cognitive performance. Our supposedly expert feedback should have been enough to create expectations in the subjects' minds about how well they would perform. Half the subjects received these expectations in private and performed in private, whereas for the other subjects everything was publicly identified. We found that whether the self-fulfilling prophecy effect obtained—or, indeed, whether subjects did the exact opposite of what was expected—depended on the public nature of the situation. Expectancy effects thus seem to have a strong interpersonal aspect too.

As my graduate career came to a close, it was time to find a job, but the times were extremely difficult. Every job opening generated hundreds of applications, and so the odds of getting anything were poor. To complicate matters, my professors thought I was somewhat eccentric (i.e., a nut) and weren't convinced that my seemingly bizarre ideas and philosophical/mystical outlook would really lead anywhere, and I suspect that their hesitation came through in the all-important letters of recommendation they wrote. I applied for jobs for many months with no success. I was lucky enough to land a postdoctoral fellowship, which gave me a year's respite and allowed me to continue applying for jobs, but I still found that prospective employers had little interest in me. It was only as a result of an extraordinary series of accidents that I managed to get interviewed at Case Western Reserve University, where there was no social psychologist on the faculty and the people doing the hiring thus were uncertain about what to look for. In another month or two, my chances would have been up and I would have left the field of academic social psychology, probably ending up as a banker or taxi driver. But through a minor miracle I did get a job and became an assistant professor. Now I could do whatever I wanted within extremely broad limits, subject only to the distant pressure of tenure.

As a new faculty member, I found myself in the position of having to give lectures on a regular basis. I started out going by the course notes and outline I had used as a student, but I soon discovered that my semester schedule was long and I would be giving nearly twice as many lectures per course as my professors had given when I was a student. Like most new professors, I wondered how I could possibly pretend to know enough to lecture for that amount of time. I started spending many hours in the library, reading at random in the journals, looking for interesting topics to cover.

The writing of the lectures for my first social psychology course was a significant turning point in my career. Self-presentation was still a topic that was on my mind, and I had long hoped to write something that would take that topic beyond the narrow and trivial usages to which most of my colleagues seemed to consign it, namely, the view that people sometimes change the way they act in order to make a good impression on others. I felt that the interpersonal dimension of life extends far beyond that, but I was groping for a way to get this message across. I tried writing little theoretical papers to articulate this broader view, but of course they were rejected. I didn't have the intellectual maturity or the professional experience to be making such broad arguments on a theoretical basis.

But when doing the background reading for my lectures, I kept noticing that self-presentation came up in relation to topic after topic. The papers didn't cite each other and no one seemed to have had any inkling that there was a broad pattern, but with each topic somebody had sooner or later come up with the idea of showing that people act differently in public than they act in private. The theories had generally been entirely based on intrapsychic processes, but there was often a data set buried away somewhere showing that the pattern depended on an interpersonal context.

And so the idea of drawing all those scattered findings into a large review paper came to me. It would be a way to make the broad point about self-presentation being more than just a matter of making a good impression, being instead a basic guiding force in human behavior in many spheres. I also thought it might be an easy way to get published and at the time I was acutely conscious of needing to get my publication tally up to keep on schedule for getting tenure. My experiments were still being rejected by the journals, and I was having difficulty getting anywhere. On an obscure shelf in the library I found a journal, the *Psychological Bulletin*, that was apparently devoted to publishing literature reviews. I hadn't heard of this journal; we hadn't paid attention to it in graduate school, where everybody was concerned only with the journals that published experiments. I thought, This must be a relatively unknown journal, and they're probably desperate for manuscripts. I knew that publishing in an obscure journal doesn't really do much for one's career, but I figured it was better than not publishing at all, and so I thought I'd do a review article for *Psych Bull* to help tide me over until my experiments started getting accepted in the important journals. If I had known that *Psychological Bulletin* is actually swamped with manuscripts, has a high rejection rate, and is considered a very prestigious outlet, I never would have bothered trying to write for it, but in the mistaken belief that I had stumbled on an easy outlet to pad my vita, I embarked on what became an important project for me.

I wrote up a first draft, pulling together all these various findings about self-presentational differences in regard to attitude change, helping, aggression, conformity, reactance, emotion, and so forth. I sent it in, and they sent back a very nice, encouraging letter, which seemed to confirm my impression that this would be a relatively easy outlet. The paper was officially rejected, but the editor was very supportive about how I could revise it to get it accepted. I was a bit put out at having to do all that additional work for what I thought was a low-level journal, but the suggestions were quite intelligent and reasonable, and besides, I was desperate to get anything published, and so there was no real choice. I made the changes, including distinguishing between two levels of self-presentational motivations (pleasing the immediate audience versus constructing the self), and sent it back, and it was accepted. The journal was nice enough to put it on the first page of the issue, which again fit into my sense that they were hard up and had made me work harder than ought to have been necessary. When it came out, though, my colleagues soon let me know that this was a prestigious outlet and that the article would be an important step in my career. Indeed, it was the main paper of mine that people knew about for many years and was responsible for most of the citations of my work until the end of my junior faculty phase. I still look back on the episode with a sense of bewildered good luck. When I went up for tenure, that paper was the best thing on my record, and I had written it by mistake! So much for intelligent career strategizing!

Meanwhile, the papers I thought were important were not going anywhere. Part of the reason for this was that I had little sense of the field as a whole. My graduate work had been done in a place with very narrow, specialized interests; this had in fact had tremendous advantages in terms of departmental cohesiveness and collegial interaction but had also had disadvantages in terms of turning out students like me who could not anticipate the field. Coupled with my own relative youth and corresponding lack of intellectual maturity, and followed by my taking a job in a department where I was the only social psychologist and hence had no one to advise me, I was operating on a wealth of false assumptions about the field.

I well recall the paper I thought was going to be the most important one of my early career. It dealt with cognitive dissonance, a topic that had, after all, been the focus of hundreds of articles and had been of great interest to the professors in my graduate program. The latest controversy surrounding dissonance had to do with whether it is a self-presentational phenomenon. The battle lines were drawn, and the conflict was bitter, partly because everyone was still thinking of self-presentation in narrow, trivial terms as just saying something to make a good impression. Dissonance researchers didn't want their phenomenon reduced to such a trivial matter. Indeed, they felt that to admit the role of self-presentation would be to concede that dissonance effects do not represent genuine attitude change but are merely superficial responses of pretending to be consistent.

I saw the matter quite differently, of course. I was working on a view of self-presentation as a basic human motivation and hence as a grand, integrative explanation for all sorts of behavior. To me, self-presentation would most likely produce real attitude change. What I didn't realize was that this position, which I envisioned as a compromise solution to the controversy and one that would make everyone happy, would actually be seen by both warring camps as an unacceptable surrender. Dianne Tice and I conducted several experiments to support our view (e.g., showing that people change their attitudes in public but not private situations and then maintain those changed attitudes in new settings), but reviewers were extremely critical. We kept doing follow-up studies until finally they gave in and let us publish the paper. It too was set to come out on the first page of the journal. I was certain that this paper would launch my career, being the lead article in the top journal and dealing with such an important topic. In reality, most social psychologists had lost interest in dissonance effects years earlier. And although some were starting to accept the idea of self-presentation as a broad, important issue, the idea of showing self-presentational effects on cognitive dissonance was not something they were disposed to care much about. Anticipating a big response, I dug into my meager savings and ordered 200 reprints of the article to send out to all the people who presumably would be requesting copies. I still have most of them. The article was scarcely noticed and rarely cited.

Fortunately, though, self-presentation did catch on in the 1980s, and so I wasn't left completely isolated. The idea that the self is an interpersonal phenomenon has gained increasingly wide acceptance, although of course not everyone believes it. Still, my interest was satisfied: The self is not just something that exists inside the head; rather, it exists in a social context and changes in response to social events.

EMOTION AND OTHER PEOPLE

Having come to regard the self as very much an interpersonal phenomenon, I began to think about emotion along the same lines. Emotion, like the self, is something that one all too readily assumes is entirely contained within the individual psyche. According to standard views, emotions are largely private, personal phenomena, akin to storms or other weather patterns occurring in the inner landscape.

For most of my early life emotions were dangerous forms of vulnerability. My parents' household was permeated with bitter power games and endless petty cruelty, and to show emotion was to open oneself to painful attacks by others. I remember that during my freshman year at college my resident adviser passed along a comment made by one of the other fellows to the effect that I was a very nice guy but never showed any feelings. I analyzed this supposed lack of emotion logically, decided that it was correct, and concluded that it wasn't a desirable way to live, because without emotion life is dull and impoverished. Of course, these logical conclusions didn't show me how to start having emotion! But that was the era of inner exploration, getting in touch with one's feelings, and discovering inner worlds, and I plunged into a pervasive orgy of self-exploration with a clear, logically derived intention of learning to be more emotional. In the process, I discovered that emotions are significantly affected by other people. In fact, often one ended up feeling the emotions that others expected one to feel. Even if you didn't want a particular emotion, in fact, you might end up having it because everyone else expected you to have it.

In my personal life these insights were tied up with my late adolescent efforts to learn to fall in love and maximize the emotional adventures associated with romance, escalating attraction, heartbreak, and the like. Professionally, however, I held on to the hypothesis that emotions can be caused by other people's expectations, and in graduate school I had a chance to test it experimentally. I remember being captivated by reading about an experiment in which embarrassment was measured by having subjects sing a painfully corny song ("Love Is a Many Splendored Thing"), with a cash incentive to sing for a longer time but with a personal or social incentive to finish quickly and put an end to the embarrassing experience. I adapted this procedure by telling subjects that based on something we knew about them, we expected them to be extremely embarrassed and inhibited while singing the song. We recorded their singing, without accompaniment, on the pretext that their voice patterns would be preserved on tape for computer analysis to search for evidence of feelings of inhibition. The running of the experiment presented some problems, mainly because a number of subjects felt no qualms about singing at all and in fact had joined choirs or other singing groups, and so their data had to be discarded because the procedure utterly failed to embarrass them. Still, among subjects who were not habitual singers, we got strong effects that reflected a tendency for them to feel what they believed other people expected them to feel. Specifically, when we told them that we expected them to feel embarrassed and inhibited, they sang faster and quit sooner than did control subjects. This was my first effort in approaching emotion as an interpersonal phenomenon.

The early 1980s was the heyday of social cognition, and emotion was scarcely talked about by the people I knew. Consequently, it was many years before I returned to the topic of emotion. The next step occurred when Robert Hogan asked me to write a chapter for his series *Perspectives on Personality*. He had liked my *Psychological Bulletin* article on self-presentation, and he remarked that the brief discussion of emotion in that work deserved to be elaborated. Accordingly, I spent several months reading about emotion and thinking about how it might relate to self-presentation. In writing it up, Dianne Tice and I tried to develop the view that the natural or inherent function of emotions involves expression and interpersonal communication; that is, emotions are by their very nature interpersonal acts. Although one can learn to keep them secret, to do so is to violate their normal nature and function. I'm still not sure whether this view is entirely correct, but there is a fair amount of evidence that fits it, and I have noticed that other scholars (more knowledgeable than myself) have recently made similar arguments. It is something well worth further study.

More recently, I have begun studying the interpersonal context of specific emotions. The first of these was anger. My path into this research was fairly roundabout; indeed, I was guided as much by the methodology as by any interest in anger itself.

The methodology I used for this work was based on having people tell stories. I have always liked stories, and during my undergraduate years I noticed that many of my favorite parts of psychology books were the clinical case studies in which a person's life and problems were described in detail. Social psychology didn't have much use for stories back then, and when I decided to go into research rather than clinical psychology, one regret I had was that I'd have to miss out on those case studies. Fortunately, that has changed.

The change began quite by accident for me. I was on sabbatical in Texas, researching my most ambitious project: a book on how people find meaning in life. I was still working out the basic framework and looking for interesting marginal phenomena that might give me some new insights, when it occurred to me to examine sexual masochism. I thought that sexual masochism is such an extremely paradoxical, mysterious phenomenon that maybe it would help show me the extent to which people may go to find or alter the meaning of their lives.

One day I went to the library and looked up all the sources I could find on masochism. After several hours of reading, I realized that I wasn't going to learn anything about the meaning of life from those works, but something else struck me. All the phenomena of masochism were blatantly contradictory to social psychology's main assumptions about the nature of the self. Our theories treated the self as geared toward increasing happiness and avoiding pain, maximizing a sense of control over the environment, and raising self-esteem, but masochists sought pain, voluntarily gave up control (as in allowing themselves to be tied up), and desired embarrassing, humiliating experiences. I began to think that masochism represents a fascinating challenge to our theories about the self. I spent several years studying this problem and came to the conclusion that masochism is centrally concerned with helping people escape from themselves, that is, helping them forget who they are and lose their normal self-awareness.

But that is another story. What is relevant here is the methodology I used for my work on masochism. It was obviously impractical to study sexual masochism with my usual methods, namely, doing laboratory experiments with college students. Instead, I collected a sample of first-person accounts of masochistic experiences and fantasies. I found that these stories were extremely helpful in illuminating the subjective experience of masochism and the structure of masochistic desire. I compared letters by masochists with letters by sadists and even a baseline set of letters about ordinary sexual adventures and fantasies. Thus, for example, I found that masochists and their partners were more likely to describe scenes occurring in the context of long-term relationships, compared with ordinary sexual fantasies, which often involve strangers. I searched for evidence of guilt or desire for punishment, but contrary to traditional theories, there was little to be found. Instead, it appeared that masochists liked the experience and wanted to repeat it. Masochists' stories were especially likely to end with wholesale identity change, often involving becoming a full-time sex slave for the new master or mistress, and this pattern confirmed the notion that masochism is centrally concerned with forgetting oneself and escaping one's identity. I also compared male and female masochists to learn how the two sexes interpret the masochistic role differently. The women tended to emphasize being spanked and being displayed nude in front of other people (who were often dressed), whereas the men tended to emphasize stronger forms of pain (such as whipping) and to prefer humiliating experiences that reduced their status, such as being put on a leash like a dog. Female masochists were almost never dressed up as males, but around 40 percent of the male masochists reported being feminized in some way, such as being dressed up in women's lingerie.

Although my research on escape from the self later led me in one direction (into studies of suicide, binge eating, meditation, and alcohol use), my interest in these stories led me to wonder what else I could study with first-person stories. I wanted some standard kind of episode in which there are two roles and in which the two roles might tell systematically different stories about the same event. At that point I came upon the idea of using stories to study the social nature of emotion.

Anger was an excellent choice in this regard. In anger, typically, one person does something that makes someone else mad. The first person (the perpetrator) is likely to tell a very different story than the second person (the victim). To learn about these differences, Arlene Stillwell, Sara Wotman, and I asked a large sample of people to write about one event in which they had made someone angry and another event in which someone had made them angry. The stories were fascinating to read and also showed strong, systematic patterns regarding how perpetrators and victims see things in radically different ways.

To analyze the stories, we first coded them for the presence or absence of many features. For example, we examined each story to determine whether it contained an apology; that is, did the perpetrator apologize to the victim for what he or she had done? We coded for whether the story had a happy ending, for whether it described long-term consequences leading up to the present or even the future, for whether a reason was given for what the perpetrator did, for whether any mitigating or extenuating circumstances were discussed, and many more possibilities. When we finished, we computed the percentage of victim stories and the percentage of perpetrator stories that we had coded as "yes" on each dimension and then used a simple chi-square statistic to test whether there was a significant difference. For example, 22 percent of the perpetrators' stories contained a reference to apologizing, but only 4 percent of the victims' stories said that the perpetrator had apologized. According to the chi-square test, the likelihood of that difference occurring by chance is less than 1 percent, which means that one can be very confident that it is a real difference.

Several of our findings shed light on the discrepancies between perpetrators' and victims' experiences. Perpetrators tend to see things in isolation, whereas victims describe events as being enmeshed in a long-term context that is still relevant to the present. Perpetrators usually describe valid reasons for their actions, but victims often insist strongly that the perpetrator had no valid reason for what he or she did. Perpetrators see single events and think victims have overreacted; victims tend to see multiple, accumulating grievances and see their reactions as thoroughly appropriate and justified. Victims describe perpetrators as inconsistent and immoral and rarely mention an apology, whereas perpetrators often say they apologized and made amends and often state that they could not help what happened.

My students and I were very excited about this research, partly because it was opening new ground, partly because the stories seemed to bring social psychology back to the real experiences of real people rather than the artificial laboratory simulations we usually did, and partly because the paper on anger was published in a very prominent journal that gave our careers a nice boost. In casting about for what to study next, I came upon the idea of trying unrequited love. It often happens that one person feels a strong romantic attraction to someone who does not feel the same way in return, and I had a hunch that the two roles would tell very different stories.

They did. We collected a large set of stories from upper-level college students about their experiences with one-sided romantic attraction. The stories were long, rich, and full of fascinating detail, sometimes very sad and moving, other times very funny. We coded them the same way we had done with the anger stories: using simple yes-or-no decisions about various factors and then computing percentages and using a chi-square test to see whether the percentages were significantly different between the would-be lovers and the rejectors. In this study we actually had quite a long list of dimensions to code, including the following: Was the attraction ever mutual? Did the rejector initially "lead on" the would-be lover? Did the rejector deliver a clear message of rejection? Did the would-be lover keep trying excessively? Did the story contain happy feelings? Did the story contain unpleasant feelings? Is the broken-hearted lover still in love today? Did either person use unscrupulous tactics? Did either person have self-esteem raised or lowered (actually four separate codings)? Did the person change in a negative or undesirable way as a result of this episode? Does the storyteller seem to wish the whole thing had never happened? We found several dozen patterns of difference between the would-be lovers' stories and the rejectors' stories.

As a result, we were able to describe both sides of heartbreak: what it's like to have one's heart broken and what it's like to be in a position of having to break someone else's heart. We realized that although the story of unrequited love is often told in our culture (in thousands of novels, movies, and songs), it is nearly always told from the side of the person who is in love; the rejector's side of the story is almost never told. But rejectors have their own, often powerful and tragic side of the experience. They find themselves abruptly and unwillingly cast in the role of having to hurt someone. They struggle with guilt and wonder whether they are responsible. They find that they don't know what to do and have to scramble to decide how to act and what to say. Often they find that they cannot get rid of the other person and feel pursued and even hounded by this person whom they do not love who refuses to take no for an answer. The stories of the would-be lovers are no less interesting, focusing on themes of encouragement, mixed messages, emotional roller coasters, and often a devastating loss of self-esteem. When our book *Breaking Hearts: The Two Sides of Unrequited Love* came out, I made an appearance on the *Oprah Winfrey* show, which many of my colleagues considered a minor embarrassment but which most of my relatives and neighbors regard as the all-time high point of my career!

Both anger and unrequited love are emotions that arise from a definite interpersonal context and revolve around interpersonal relationships. Our next project—guilt—is one that is often thought of as occurring inside the self. Indeed, many prominent theories about guilt have emphasized that people feel guilty all by themselves by reflecting on their actions and that other people are mostly irrelevant to guilt. I suspected, however, that guilt may well be interpersonal too. For one thing, people often do things that make other people feel guilty. In one study we asked people to describe incidents in which someone made them feel guilty or in which they made someone else feel guilty, and those stories made us see how important interpersonal contexts can be for guilt. We coded each story again with a list of simple yes-or-no questions such as, Did the person who felt guilty change his or her behavior later? Was the relationship (if any) between the two people damaged by the episode? Did one person feel better after making the other one feel guilty?

Slowly I began to realize that guilt is an emotion that basically serves several functions for enhancing interpersonal relationships. Guilt makes people pay attention to their relationship partners (sort of like when you feel guilty because you haven't called or written to your mother or your romantic partner for too long). Guilt equalizes the power in relationships because it allows the person with less power to get his or her way by making the other person feel guilty. Guilt also transfers bad feelings from victims to perpetrators, thus restoring emotional equity.

I was never much afflicted by feelings of guilt myself, and I had always regarded guilt as a wasteful source of suffering that mainly plagues people who are neurotic, or who listen to their parents too much, or who were exposed during childhood to Catholic schools or other guiltmongers. It was very enlightening for me personally to study guilt professionally. I found it a little bit like learning a foreign language: how to say certain things in order to make others feel guilty and how to keep records of who owed guilt to whom ("guilt points," as one of my colleagues put it). The idea that guilt serves positive functions for enhancing relationships was surprising to me and certainly went against anything I was personally inclined to believe, but the data convinced me that it is true. Guilt is strongly correlated with empathy, for example, and empathy is one of the most important and beneficial traits in good relationships. Also, the data showed that most guilt is experienced in the context of close relationships, which again suggests that it serves an important function for them.

Thus, several lines of work led me to understand individual emotions as being rooted in interpersonal contexts and as being fundamentally about human relationships. I haven't put all this together into a grand theory yet, but it is an exciting time to be studying emotion from an interpersonal perspective. As I have started to wonder about the big picture, issues of motivation inevitably arise, because emotion and motivation often revolve around the same issues. Therefore, let me finish this essay with motivation.

MOTIVATION: ANXIETY AND BELONGINGNESS

The history of psychology, in my simple view, can largely be reduced to pendulum swings between the two main poles of motivation and cognition. During some eras (such as Freudian psychoanalysis and the drive theory era of the 1960s) everyone is concerned with motivation, and then in reaction against that extreme (e.g., the "new look" in the late 1940s and the cognitive science revolution of the 1980s) people turn to studying thought patterns and cognitive processes. My sense is that motivation and cognition are the two main roots of psychology. Despite the pendulum swings of theoretical fashionability, both cognition and motivation have to be included in any viable theory of human nature.

I mentioned earlier that psychologists have always recognized some degree of interpersonal motivation. The idea of a herd instinct is a familiar if unenlightening one, and the desire to affiliate with others has long been recognized. So I certainly cannot argue that interpersonal motivations have been ignored. I do think, however, that they have been widely underrated. Over the years, and again contrary to what I wanted to believe, I have come to think that needs for interpersonal attachment and human relatedness are among the most powerful and pervasive motivations that people have.

My first thoughts along these lines were stimulated by a professional conference I attended some years ago. This conference was held on the seashore in North Carolina, at Nags Head, and it was a very pleasant conference because there were only about twenty-five psychologists there, and even though everyone spoke for an hour, there was plenty of time to spend walking on the beach and thinking over the ideas one heard. Several of the researchers (Jeff Greenbert, Tom Pyszczynski, and Sheldon Solomon) were preoccupied with the anthropologist Ernest

Becker's assertion that fear of death is one of the most important human motivations and that anxiety, self-esteem, and culture are all responses to this fear.

Listening to them, I could well recognize that people are afraid of death, but somehow it seemed to me that these researchers were over-stating the case. It just didn't seem plausible that most of what people do every day is driven by fear of death. The theory that anxiety in particular is always fundamentally based on the fear of death seemed dubious. I didn't know much about anxiety, but I wondered if there might be a more plausible and obvious cause.

After returning home, I began to read about anxiety, and it soon struck me that a major cause of anxiety is fear of being excluded by social groups. Anxiety arises over romantic rejection, over being ostracized by others, over losing a job, over not getting into a club or organization or school one wants to join, and so forth. I began to explore the idea that people need interpersonal attachments and feel anxiety over any threat to these attachments and this idea seemed to me to be confirmed over and over. I discovered John Bowlby's work showing how anxiety results from being separated from one's mother, and it seemed likely that other separations could also cause anxiety. Although I didn't deny that people may fear death, it seemed to me that the anxieties people experience from day to day are much more concerned with social exclusion and rejection than with death. The social exclusion idea seemed to keep expanding as more and more phenomena fit it. For example, even the Freudian Oedipus complex seemed to make much more sense when ana-lyzed in terms of exclusion anxiety than when, according to the tradi-tional view, the boy's fear of castration was seen as the driving source of anxiety. Children fear that their parents will reject them or abandon them rather than fearing that their parents will cut off their penises. Also, of course, the exclusion theory of anxiety made the Oedipus complex much more plausible in females than the castration theory.

Dianne Tice and I wrote up our theory about anxiety in a target arti-cle of the *Journal of Social and Clinical Psychology,* where it was followed by a series of commentaries by other scholars. The death group clung dogmatically to its preconceived notions and wrote a hysterical, wildly sarcastic commentary, but everyone else contributed very interesting per-spectives and insights, relating social exclusion to loneliness, evolution-ary selection, blushing, and other phenomena. From reading and think-ing about their comments, I understood that the big picture was even bigger than I had realized. Anxiety was fundamentally concerned with interpersonal relations, but anxiety was only part of the story.

At that time I was also (finally!) putting the finishing touches on my book on how people find meaning in life. One of the chapters in that book dealt with happiness, and to write it I simply read as many empiri-cal studies of happiness as I could find. Some people are clearly happier than others, and various factors predict who will be happy and who won't, although many researchers have been surprised at how weak most of the effects are. (For example, married people are happier than single people and rich people are happier than poor people, but not by much.) One of the few strong effects, however, had to do with interpersonal relationships. To put it simply, isolated or lonely people are hardly ever happy. No particular relationship is essential, whether to parents, friends, lovers, spouse, offspring, or whomever, but it is essential to have some strong and close relationships in order to be happy. This fact suggested to me that we were dealing with one of the basics of human nature. Likewise, my research on suicide showed unmistakably that socially isolated or lonely people are much more likely to kill themselves.

At present, therefore, I am in the process of pulling all these strands together to formulate a general notion of a human "need to belong." The assumption is that belongingness—also known as relatedness or attachment—is one of the two or three most fundamental and powerful motivations people have. It underlies a great deal of what people do, think, and feel. Moreover, it is such a pervasive need that people only rarely go against it. (For example, even if a romantic relationship is unsatisfactory, many people stay in it until they think they can find someone else soon; in fact, people usually try to replace a lost relationship quickly.) When people are forced to be alone, such as in exile or solitary confinement, they become depressed and may start to lose their mental health.

Anxiety is thus only part of the picture. Anxiety results when people experience a threat of losing an interpersonal attachment. But depression and other unpleasant emotions accompany interpersonal isolation. Meanwhile, positive emotions are also tied into belongingness. When people form new relationships or change a relationship in the direction of a more permanent commitment, there is almost always a wave of pleasant, positive emotion. Falling in love, getting a job, joining a new religious group, getting married, having children, and simply making new friends are all happy events, and thus they are familiar examples of the simple principle that social inclusion brings positive emotion, just as social exclusion causes emotional distress.

This new outlook has offered me a new context for understanding the self (which was where I started). I have come to see the self as being, at least to a significant extent, an interpersonal tool. We construct our identities in ways that will attract and keep relationship partners. Self-esteem means thinking that you will be desirable to others: Other people will want to be with you and will like you and include you in their groups. Self-presentation is a means of showing oneself to be the sort of person others want to associate with and form relationships with. Although I have always regarded the self as one of the most compelling psychological structures and its motivations as being among the most basic, they may be derived from the even more basic need to belong. It is

no surprise that the main components of self-esteem and self-concep-
tion—being competent, attractive, likable, and morally good—are precisely the things that make one a desirable relationship partner.

CONCLUSION

If I had clung to my initial beliefs or to the ideas I preferred, I would now
have a radically different outlook. I have approached my professional life
with the attitude that many of my ideas were probably wrong and that I
should always be willing to revise them or even abandon them when the
evidence indicated. I began with a very individualistic way of thinking,
and over time I have come to a strongly interpersonal perspective. People are far more social than most of us are inclined to think. Selfhood,
emotion, and motivation are fundamentally concerned with human relations. No doubt I'll be revising my ideas more in the future, but the cost
of approaching the truth—sort of an admission fee—is relinquishing
many of one's favorite beliefs. For me, that is the only way to derive full
satisfaction from a research career.

SUGGESTED READINGS

BAUMEISTER, R. F. (1982). A self-presentational view of social phenomena. *Psychological Bulletin, 91,* 3–26.

———— (1988a). Masochism as escape from self. *Journal of Sex Research. 25,*
28–59.

———— (1988b). Gender differences in masochistic scripts. *Journal of Sex
Research, 25,* 478–499.

———— (1989). *Masochism and the self.* Hillsdale, NJ: Erlbaum.

———— (1990). Suicide as escape from self. *Psychological Review, 97,* 90–113.

———— (1991a). *Escaping the self: Alcoholism, spirituality, masochism, and other
flights from the burden of selfhood.* New York: Basic Books.

———— (1991b). *Meanings of life.* New York: Guilford Press.

———— & COOPER, J. (1981). Can the public expectation of emotion cause that
emotion? *Journal of Personality, 49,* 49–59.

———— COOPER, J., & SKIB, B. A. (1979). Inferior performance as a selective
response to expectancy: Taking a dive to make a point. *Journal of Personality
and Social Psychology, 37,* 424–432.

———— & JONES, E. E. (1978). When self-presentation is constrained by the target's knowledge: Consistency and compensation. *Journal of Personality and
Social Psychology, 36,* 608–618.

———— STILLWELL, A. M. & HEATHERTON, T. F. (1994). Guilt: An interpersonal
approach. *Psychological Bulletin, 115,* 243–267.

———— STILLWELL, A. M., & WOTMAN, S. R. (1990). Victim and perpetrator
accounts of interpersonal conflict: Autobiographical narratives about
anger. *Journal of Personality and Social Psychology, 59,* 994–1005.

———— & TICE, D. M. (1984). Role of self-presentation and choice in cognitive dissonance under forced compliance: Necessary or sufficient causes? *Journal of Personality and Social Psychology, 46*, 5–13.

———— & TICE, D. M. (1987). Emotion and self-presentation. In R. Hogan & W. H. Jones (Eds.), *Perspectives in personality: Theory, measurement, and interpersonal dynamics* (vol. 2, pp. 181–199). Greenwich, CT: JAI Press.

———— & TICE, D. M. (1990). Anxiety and social exclusion. *Journal of Social and Clinical Psychology, 9*, 165–195.

———— & WOTMAN, S. R. (1992). *Breaking hearts: The two sides of unrequited love.* New York: Guilford Press.

———— WOTMAN, S. R. & STILLWELL, A. M. (1993). Unrequited love: On heartbreak, anger, guilt, scriptlessness, and humiliation. *Journal of Personality and Social Psychology, 64*, 377–394.

BECKER, E. (1973). *The denial of death.* New York: Macmillan.

BOWLBY, J. (1969). *Attachment and loss.* Vol. 1: *Attachment.* New York: Basic Books.

———— (1973). *Attachment and loss.* Vol. 2: *Separation anxiety and anger.* New York: Basic Books.

CASTANEDA, C. (1972). *Journey to Ixtlan.* New York: Simon & Schuster.

GREENBERG, J., PYSZCZYNSKI, T., & SOLOMON, S. (1986). The causes and consequences of self-esteem: A terror management theory. In R. Baumeister (Ed.), *Public and private self* (pp. 189–212). New York: Springer-Verlag.

HEIDEGGER, M. (1927). *Sein und zeit* (Being and time). Tuebingen, Germany: Niemeyer.

*J*OHN F. DOVIDIO *(Ph.D., University of Delaware) is a Professor of Psychology and the former Director of the Division of Natural Sciences and Mathematics at Colgate University. Dr. Dovidio is Editor of* Personality and Social Psychology Bulletin *and serves on the editorial boards of* Journal of Personality and Social Psychology, Journal of Nonverbal Behavior, *and* Review of Personality and Social Psychology. *He has over fifty publications in the areas of helping behavior, prejudice, and nonverbal behavior, including the books* Emergency Intervention *(coauthored with J. A. Piliavin, S. Gaertner, and R. Clark),* The Social Psychology of Helping and Altruism *(coauthored with D. Schroeder, L. Penner, and J. A. Piliavin),* Power, Dominance, and Nonverbal Behavior *(coedited with S. Ellyson), and* Prejudice, Discrimination, and Racism *(coedited with S. Gaertner). He, his wife, and his two children enjoy playing and coaching baseball, soccer, and basketball.*

6

With a Little Help from My Friends

--- ❖ ---

*I*teach introductory psychology, and so I spend quite a bit of time with first-year students. I enjoy first-year students; they come to college eager, interested, and full of optimism. It is a time of excitement, discovery, and maturation. Maturation, however, is often a painful process. Thus, I also sympathize with first-year students. Many become disoriented and confused as their high school identities dissolve and new identities emerge, as they are challenged academically and socially in ways they did not anticipate, and as they struggle to maintain old friendships while exploring new relationships. During the week before Thanksgiving, I often find myself consoling these students as they prepare to visit home for the first time. I tell them what a special period of life it is. I also remind them that they have to be first-year students only once in their lives.

I will never forget my first year in college. It left a lasting imprint on me socially and academically—in surprisingly interrelated ways. Socially, I developed very close friendships that I know will endure throughout my life. Within weeks, I watched a disparate group of students who happened to be assigned to the same first-year dorm evolve into a cohesive group. We studied together, played sports together, and partied together. But most important, we depended on each other, and without ever having to be asked, we helped each other.

Academically, things were changing as well. I intended to major in mathematics or English. I do not recall even registering for a psychology course; I was probably assigned to it because the courses I chose were full and the auditorium in which psychology was taught had plenty of room. Soon I discovered that numbers are not that exciting and that real people are more interesting than fictional or dead people. I was seduced by psychology. Career planning, I believe, is overrated—at least for first-year students.

The match between psychology and me was a good one. I liked it; it liked me. I found that I genuinely enjoyed studying psychology; also, I did well and never felt overwhelmed. That is, until I took an experimental psychology course. The first part of the course covered the basics of research design. It was not especially interesting, but it was not that difficult either. The second part, however, required students, working in groups, to design and conduct an *original* experiment. No one had ever asked me to do something truly original, particularly in a scientifically oriented field. The general topic we were assigned involved helping behavior.

WHY DON'T PEOPLE HELP?

The study of helping behavior had a long but rather limited history in social psychology through the early 1960s. Questions about whether human beings are by nature good or bad, selfless or selfish, altruistic or egoistic have been the subject of debate for centuries; Aristotle and Socrates pondered these issues. Social psychologists seem to have been interested in helping and altruism for as long as social psychology has been recognized as a distinct field. In one of the discipline's first texts, *An Introduction to Social Psychology*, William McDougall in 1908 hypothesized that instincts form the basis for altruistic activity and that these "sympathetic instincts" are stronger in women than in men. Nevertheless, fewer than two dozen empirical studies of helping behavior were published in the social psychological literature before 1962.

In 1964, however, an event occurred that stimulated public interest and greatly accelerated the emerging scholarly interest in the topic. On Friday night, March 13, 1964, in New York City, Kitty Genovese arrived home late from work. She parked her car in the lot outside her apartment. As she stepped out of the car, a man emerged from the shadows, brandishing a knife. Before she could react, he stabbed her. She cried out for help. Lights went on, and faces appeared in the windows of the apartments overlooking the parking lot, but nobody came to help her. The assailant fled from the scene but did not go far. From across the street he watched. When nothing happened, he returned to the parking lot, stalked his victim, and caught her again. He stabbed her, and she cried out again. Again lights went on, faces appeared, and the attacker escaped into the darkness. Still no one came to help. As the wounded woman staggered toward the entrance of her building, the man returned. This time he stabbed her until she died. This event, which actually involved three different incidents over a forty-five-minute period, was witnessed by thirty-eight people from beginning to end. Not one person did anything to stop the attack or help Kitty Genovese.

The Kitty Genovese incident and the controversy surrounding it prompted Bibb Latané and John Darley to begin a program of research, now considered classic in the field, to find out why people may not help another person in distress. Although the behavior of the witnesses to Kitty Genovese's attack seemed cold and uncaring, bystander apathy might not have been the cause. Bystanders could have been concerned but for a variety of reasons decided not to intervene. Latané and Darley's decision model of bystander intervention proposes that whether a person helps depends on the outcomes of a series of decisions. Before a person initiates a helping response, that person must (1) notice that something is wrong, (2) define it as an emergency, (3) decide whether to take personal responsibility, (4) decide what kind of help to give, and (5) implement the decision to intervene. The decision made at any one step has important implications for the bystander's ultimate response: A negative response at any step means that the victim will not be helped.

There we were in 1971, two college sophomores (my roommate, Jim, and I) trying to come up with an original idea and experiment in a "hot" area of social psychology. Like all challenges, the task was exciting and exhilarating at the beginning but frustrating once we got involved. The deadline for handing in our proposal approached, and nothing came to us. We knew the question but not the answer. We were becoming desperate. Fortunately, though, desperation can often lead to inspiration.

*W*HEN DO PEOPLE HELP?

Rather than looking for the answer in books and journals (after all, how original can the answer be if someone has already written about it?), I reflected on my experience. The answer was right in front of me: Jim. Jim and I had lived on the same floor during our first year, and he was part of the group whose members went from total strangers to best friends in a matter of weeks. So the question moved from the abstract to the concrete: What can turn a group of diverse, often egocentric and undisciplined young men into a cohesive and spontaneously helpful group? The answer, perhaps, was that we were bonded together by the stressful experience that we shared—being first-year students.

The pieces fell together. First, we needed to find a way to create stress. One of our friends, the halfback on the football team, had recently participated as a paid volunteer in an experiment in which he had received electric shocks. (Experiments of this type are now rarely conducted.) When he returned to the dorm, he passed the word that the $5 was not worth it. And so we had our stress manipulation: the threat of a painful electric shock.

The design was straightforward. Some participants believed that they would be in the same experiment as another person (a confederate) and that the experiment would involve either an electric shock (high threat) or an easy word association task (low threat). We also included conditions in which the participant and the confederate did not share the same fate. In these conditions, sometimes the participants believed they would be shocked while the confederate worked at a word association task, while the reverse was true for other participants. The dependent measure was whether the subject would spontaneously help the confederate pick up 100 pencils from a container that was "accidentally" knocked over.

The experiment worked! As we expected, subjects were most helpful when they shared a common stressful experience with the confederate. In other words, the subjects were *most* likely to help the other person when they *both* were under the threat of shock. Furthermore, they were *least* helpful when they alone experienced the stress. Two years later, at the encouragement of my adviser, Dr. Bill Morris of Dartmouth College, I replicated that study for my senior honors thesis. He later helped me write it up for publication. I do not have much left from my undergraduate days, but tucked away in storage I have the original copy of my senior thesis.

I believe that if it were not for that study, I would not have gone to graduate school. First, it stimulated my interest in learning. I had believed that the reason for going to college is to get a good job. Learning was a means to an end, not the end itself. This was different, however; this learning was active, it was *my* idea, and it was fun. I wanted more. Nevertheless, I was graduating soon and anticipated being offered a job as a production manager in a meat company. (It paid well.) Then my study had its second impact. In one of our discussions Bill Morris asked me if I had considered graduate school. I explained that I was overextended on college loans and felt that my parents had supported me long enough. He then explained graduate fellowships to me. The idea of someone paying me to go to school was totally alien but appealing. I applied to graduate school.

The next fall I entered graduate school in psychology at the University of Delaware. Ironically, I found that being a first-year graduate student is much like being a first-year undergraduate. There were new pressures and insecurities, but these stresses also facilitated the development of several close and lasting friendships with fellow graduate students. My adviser was Sam Gaertner, and he became my best friend. For the first time my personal relationships, intellectual interests, and potential livelihood all revolved around the same theme: social psychology. But what was I going to do in social psychology? I remember sitting in Sam's office when he said, "I'm interested in racial attitudes, and I'm going to try to get you interested in what I do." And then he added, "I want you to get me interested in what you're interested in." I told him that I was interested in helping behavior. I don't know whether Sam and I were equally persuasive or equally stubborn, but I do know that we eventually conducted a number of studies involving *both* race and helping over the next several years.

My initial problem, though, was that I did not know what specifically interested me in helping behavior. I designed and conducted a follow-up experiment on stress and helping, but it did not work out. My ideas had dried up. The thought that I had peaked as a research psychologist before I was old enough to drink was disconcerting. Around that time Jane Piliavin from the University of Wisconsin presented a colloquium at Delaware on a model of helping behavior that she and her husband, Irving, had been developing. The central point she raised was intriguing. Guided by the Latané and Darley framework, psychologists had been focusing on why people do *not* help others. Emergencies, however, typically involve strangers, and it is frequently dangerous to intervene. It is thus understandable and rational that people often do not help. What may be an equally important issue to examine, Jane and Irving Piliavin suggested, is why people do intervene. By approaching the same subject from a slightly different perspective, the Piliavins stimulated a new line of research.

WHY DO PEOPLE HELP?

The model presented by Jane that day—the arousal: cost-reward model—has two major components. One is emotional; the other is cognitive. The Piliavins suggested that witnessing another person in distress can arouse bystanders. This arousal, when attributed to that event, is unpleasant and therefore motivates people to do something to reduce it. The action that bystanders take in turn is based on a cognitive assessment of the costs and rewards for helping and not helping, as illustrated in Figure 6.1. Costs for helping may include physical danger, effort, and time. Costs for not helping can involve guilt, blame, and the negative feelings associated with knowing that a person is continuing to suffer. The Piliavins proposed that a bystander will choose the response that most rapidly and completely reduces the arousal, incurring as few costs as possible. Thus, the emotional component provides the motivation to do *something*, while the cognitive component determines what the most efficient and effective response will be.

One major appeal of this model, aside from its elaborate and logical rationale, is the elegant way in which it explains an apparently selfless and altruistic action (intervening to help a stranger in an emergency) in relatively egoistic terms. My psychological training was strongly influenced by B. F. Skinner's behavioral approach. The basic principle of this approach, which is fundamentally egoistic, is that organisms are more likely to perform actions that are reinforcing (i.e., associated with positive or negative reinforcers). The Piliavins' model fit well with the gen-

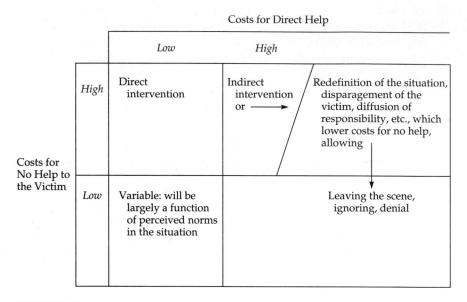

FIGURE 6.1
Predicted responses as a function of costs for direct help and costs for no help to the victim. (Adapted from J. A. Piliavin & I. M. Piliavin. (1972). The effect of blood on reactions to a victim. *Journal of Personality and Social Psychology, 23,* 353–361. Copyright 1972 by the American Psychological Association, reprinted by permission.)

eral assumption of behaviorism. According to this model, I help someone else because it makes me feel better.

I wrestled with the Piliavins' ideas over the next few months. Initially it seemed as if all the good ideas had already been taken. As I immersed myself more in related research, however, I began to realize that there were plenty of interesting questions left. Finally we came up with an experiment to test the model. If it was unpleasant arousal attributed to another person's distress that motivated a bystander's response, changing a person's belief about what caused the arousal should affect that person's intervention.

Several years earlier Richard Nisbett and Stanley Schachter had introduced a "misattribution paradigm." The objective is to lead two groups of subjects who are initially aroused by the same stimulus to believe that the causes of the arousal are different. If what subjects *attribute* their arousal to is critical, the subjects should behave differently. Specifically, Nisbett and Schachter gave subjects placebos, pills that actually have no effects. They led half of the subjects to believe that the pills would soon arouse them (increase their heart rate) and led the other half to believe that the pills would have nonarousing side effects (a slight headache). The experimenters next presented the subjects with a potentially arousing situation: a study of tolerance to pain. Nisbett and Schachter reasoned that subjects in the nonarousing placebo condition, who could attribute their arousal only to fear of shocks, would be more sensitive to the shocks than would subjects who could confuse arousal from the apprehension of pain with arousal from the pill. As predicted, when people could attribute some of their arousal to the placebo, they tolerated substantially higher levels of shock.

We applied this reasoning to a study of helping behavior. The subjects in our study believed that they would be in an ESP study investigating the effects of a pill (actually the placebo) on receptivity to ESP messages. Participants were informed that they would be asked to try to identify which of four answers a person in a nearby cubicle was trying to send telepathically. The ESP "sender" would identify the trials over an intercom system. Following Nisbett and Schachter's procedure, we led our subjects to believe that the pill would have either arousing or nonarousing side effects. Partway through the ESP task, the ESP "sender" (actually a tape-recorded voice) became a victim: She interrupted the ESP task and mentioned over the intercom that she had to straighten out a stack of nearby chairs before they fell. The subject then heard a loud crash of chairs, followed by complete silence.

The results supported the arousal: cost-reward model. Subjects *were* aroused by the accident to the sender, and the way in which they interpreted that arousal was influenced by the description of the pill we gave them. When we had informed participants that the pill had *nonarousing* side effects, they believed that their arousal was due almost exclusively to the other person's problem. Consequently, presumably to relieve this unpleasant arousal, these bystanders helped very often and rapidly. In contrast, subjects who were told that the pill had *arousing* side effects believed that a considerable amount of their arousal was caused by the pill and less of the arousal was related to the other person's situation. They intervened less frequently and less quickly because helping would be seen as less effective at relieving their *own* unpleasant state, since less arousal was perceived to be associated with the emergency and more with the pill. We also asked participants, whether they helped or not, to rate several aspects of the situation on a series of rating scales (for example, "How serious was the other person's situation?" 0 = not at all to 100 = very much; "How upsetting was the situation?" 0 = not at all to 100 = very much). Subjects who received the arousing or nonarousing placebos saw the situation as equally serious and the victim as needing the same amount of assistance. Thus, the difference in intervention was determined more by the consequences of helping for the subjects themselves (that is, differences in their degree of relief from unpleasant arousal) than by the consequences for the person in need (that is, differences in the perceived need of the victim). Helping was egoistically motivated by the desire to relieve one's own unpleasant emotional state.

At around the same time Sam Gaertner received funds from the Office of Naval Research to conduct a study of racial attitudes and helping. Those funds enabled us to purchase biotelemetry equipment and physiographs for measuring a subject's heart rate while an emergency was occurring. Jane Piliavin had earlier tried to use physiological measures of arousal in some of her studies but had encountered practical as well as ethical difficulties. She found that when subjects were wired directly to equipment for measuring galvanic skin response and were left alone to witness an emergency, they often experienced a traumatic dilemma. On the one hand, they were aroused and distressed as a result of the emergency. (Since much of the research at the time characterized bystanders as apathetic, this finding was noteworthy in itself.) On the other hand, because they thought they could be electrocuted, many participants would not disconnect themselves from the apparatus to help.

The biotelemetry equipment that Sam acquired alleviated both the ethical and the practical problems. A small transmitter with two electrodes was attached with tape to the subject's chest. There were no external wires, and participants were shown that they were free to move around. The biotelemetry transmitter sent FM signals to a receiver and a physiograph in a nearby cubicle, where we recorded the subject's heart rate. We also monitored the subject's behavior through a videocamera concealed in a speaker. From the same speaker, as in our other emergency study, subjects heard the confederate perform the ESP task and have an accident. Now, for the first time, we had an opportunity to measure both physiological arousal and bystander response while an emergency occurred.

Contrary to what many people described as bystander apathy, the subjects showed pronounced physiological arousal to another person's accident. In addition, consistent with the Piliavins' model and with the unpublished data they produced with their equipment, bystanders who were more aroused helped more quickly and more often. This study had a strong impact on me. Through the concealed camera I could see the genuine concern and distress of our subjects to the problem of a person they had never met. For some subjects, those high levels of arousal seemed to impel them to action. I frequently had to race them to the door of the cubicle where they believed the confederate had been injured. I could not let them in; there was only a tape recorder inside, and they could become embarrassed or upset. As I tried to reassure the subject that everything was taken care of and begin the debriefing, many subjects still tried to grab the doorknob to enter. We began a brief but subtle tug-of-war that I knew I had to win. From a scientific perspective, the relationship between arousal and intervention represented only correlational data. That is, although we could say that arousal and helping are related, we could not unequivocally determine the cause-and-effect relationship. The arousal: cost-reward model suggests that it was the arousal that caused the helping. It is also possible, however, that helping caused arousal in this study. That is, the subjects who helped could have had higher levels of arousal as a result of mentally and physically preparing themselves to intervene. Nevertheless, the convergence of these data with our other study's results and the impact I had witnessed on bystanders convinced me of the central importance of arousal. The characterization of bystanders as apathetic was far from the truth.

We submitted the results of our studies for presentation at the American Psychological Association convention. In August before my last year of graduate school I gave my first presentation at a professional meeting. I was nervous. I went to the room early to check the layout and familiarize myself with the audiovisual equipment. When I felt that I had things under control, I waited outside the room for some friends. As the time for the session neared, I saw what appeared to be hordes of people coming my way. I escaped back into the room and found a comfortable place at the speaker's table. Actually, our room was only half filled by the time we began the session. (I now attribute my perception of "hordes of people" either to an overactive imagination stimulated by a high level of anxiety or to the fact that there was a session on female sexual fantasies in the room just beyond ours.)

Jane Piliavin was in the audience. She was apparently impressed with the work. A short time after the convention she invited Sam, as the faculty member associated with the work, to coauthor a book on emergency intervention with her and Russ Clark, a professor then at Florida State University. Sam explained my role in the work, and I was also invited to be part of the team. The four of us spent much of the next three years working on the book. It was one of the most exciting and rewarding activities I have ever been involved in. We became very close; I consider them my academic family. We worked hard together, periodically having intensive work sessions in Florida, Wisconsin, Arizona, and New York. Like a family, we had great personal and professional highs. But also like a family, we sometimes disagreed and argued about points. I learned valuable lessons about taking and giving criticism and about how being challenged can expand one's thinking. Being wrong can sometimes be more valuable than initially being right.

I also learned that thinking more deeply may mean thinking more complexly. *Emergency Intervention* was published in 1981 and featured a more elaborated arousal: cost-reward model than the one proposed by Irving and Jane in 1973. In contrast to the original model, the revised model considered a range of new variables (e.g., personality variables, moods and other temporary states), intervening processes (e.g., physiological and attributional processes), and a broader range of interrelationships and outcomes.

As an example of the best and the worst aspects of allowing four psychologists to work together, the revised model is presented in Figure 6.2. Moving from left to right, the model suggests that situational elements (e.g., the clarity of an emergency), bystander characteristics (e.g., moods or individual differences in arousability), and victim characteristics (e.g., a family member) influence the amount of arousal a bystander experiences, the way that arousal is interpreted, and the perceived costs and rewards for various courses of action. These processes in turn determine the bystander's response. For example, consider the influence of victim characteristics. Suppose you witness an emergency involving your best friend (relative to a stranger). You will probably experience a greater sense of "we-ness" (connection to the victim) that will increase your level of arousal, make you feel more guilty if you do not help (i.e., increase costs for not helping), and make the reward for helping greater. As a consequence, the arousal you experience will be more unpleasant. The higher and more negatively interpreted arousal, plus your consideration of the costs and rewards for not helping or for helping, will increase your likelihood of helping the victim. As we begin to appreciate the complexity of human social behavior, it may be necessary to consider more complex models.

For a variety of reasons Jane, Russ, Sam, and I moved away from research in emergency helping behavior soon after the book was published. Part of the reason might have involved the impact of this research

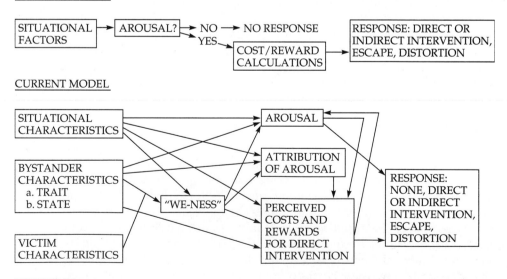

FIGURE 6.2
The original and revised arousal: cost-reward models. (From J. A. Piliavin, J. F. Dovidio, S. L. Gaertner, & R. D. Clark III. (1981). *Emergency intervention*. Reprinted by permission of Academic Press.

on the participants. Once it became clear that we were apparently correct in our hypothesis that emergencies create high levels of bystander distress, the trade-off between the distress of the participants and how much new is learned in each subsequent study tilted increasingly toward minimizing the discomfort of the subjects. The field of social psychology was similarly moving away from such emotionally charged situations. I believe that another element of our decision to move in new directions involved the fact that social psychologists are, as a group, motivated by intellectual curiosity. Once we have found what we believe is the answer to a question, it is time to move on to a new question. We are intellectual nomads. I enjoy the process of coming to know the answer to a problem more than actually knowing it. The directions in which we went after the book were quite diverse, but we all can trace them back to questions unanswered or unaddressed in *Emergency Intervention*. And, like a family, we have reunions. Ten years after the publication of the book we published a chapter updating the model.

Once again I found myself at a crossroad with no signposts. It was not necessarily a question of which road to take but rather a search for a new avenue of research. Opportunity again knocked. Bibb Latané, who had conducted some of the classic research in this area, had acquired a residence on the beach at Nags Head, North Carolina. Because of his dissatisfaction with opportunities for intellectual exchange at large conferences, he was converting the residence to a center for small, focused meetings in which participants lived and worked together for a week. One of his sessions would of course be on helping behavior.

DO PEOPLE HELP TO BENEFIT OTHERS OR THEMSELVES?

The excitement and energy of the conference were invigorating. I met many colleagues who have become research collaborators and good friends. For example, Jane Piliavin and I are currently working with Lou Penner and Dave Schroeder, psychologists we first got to know at the conference, on a new book on helping behavior. In addition, I was pleased that many of the sessions dealt with the general theme that people are motivated to help others to relieve their own distress or, as Bob Cialdini suggested, to improve their moods. Dan Batson proposed an alternative position, however. Although he acknowledged that helping can be egoistically motivated, true altruism, he argued, can also exist. He defined altruistic behavior as helping with the *primary* goal of improving the other person's welfare. This position was in contrast to the prevailing assumption of universal egoism that had dominated American psychology for most of this century. Within the area of helping behavior in particular, Cialdini and his colleagues were demonstrating that helping is a form of *self*-gratification. In addition, despite Jane's concern about the arousal: cost-reward model being egoistic, the closest we could come to acknowledging the potential existence of altruism was noting how another person's need can become coordinated with one's own welfare.

Although I could not uncritically accept Dan Batson's ideas, they were provocative. Indeed, I was provoked. Over the next several years I became involved in a line of research designed to determine whether the altruistic motivation that Batson claimed he had demonstrated could be revealed as disguised egoism. In particular, Batson's empathy-altruism model proposed that under certain conditions (e.g., when there is a bond between the subject and the person in need) exposure to another person's problem creates a special emotional response, empathic concern. Empathic concern is characterized by feelings of warmth, compassion, and tenderheartedness and is distinct from feelings of personal distress and upset. The arousal of empathic concern in turn produces altruistic motivation in which improving the other person's welfare is the main goal. My primary collaborator in this line of research was Dave Schroeder from the University of Arkansas.

This egoism-altruism debate has been a central focus in research on helping behavior over the past ten years. Since motivations are not directly observable, it is difficult to determine somebody's primary motivation. The issue is therefore quite controversial. In a series of studies Dave Schroeder and I identified several testable implications of the empathy-altruism hypothesis. Given my intellectual roots in the arousal: cost-reward model and the fact that as a graduate student Dave had worked with Bob Cialdini, we were confident that we could demonstrate that altruism can be explained in egoistic terms. Although we conducted a number of experiments, I will briefly describe just two to illustrate our strategy.

Our general reasoning was that if empathic concern (compassion for another person in distress) involves an unpleasant emotional experience, then people experiencing high levels of that emotion will be motivated to reduce it. An egoistic interpretation suggests that since helping another person is personally gratifying and improves one's mood, subjects experiencing high levels of empathic concern should be helpful in a wide range of situations. Because the egoistic objective is primarily to make *oneself* feel better, *any kind* of legitimate helping should do. In contrast, an altruistic explanation suggests that empathic concern associated with a specific problem should evoke altruistic motivation only toward that problem. The altruistic goal is to relieve the *other person's* distress.

In one of our experiments we aroused empathic concern, as Batson and his colleagues have done, by asking subjects to imagine how another person feels while that person describes a problem. Tracy Williams, another college student, described the difficulty she was having gathering the data on student activities she needed for her senior thesis before she graduated. She was in desperate need of assistance. In another condition we asked subjects to listen objectively as Tracy described her problem. Then, at the end of the session, some subjects were given an opportunity to help Tracy with the *same* problem she described while other subjects were given an opportunity to help Tracy with a *different* and unrelated problem. The egoistic interpretation predicts that subjects feeling empathic concern (i.e., those who imagined Tracy's feelings) would help her more than would subjects who were not empathically aroused (i.e., those who listened objectively), whether it was the same problem or a different one. Helping Tracy in any way was presumably a good deed and thus would relieve the negative emotion they were experiencing. The altruistic interpretation predicts that empathically aroused subjects would help more only for the same problem that generated the emotion, not for a different problem. Helping Tracy on a different problem might make the helper feel better but would not solve Tracy's main problem. The results, to our surprise, supported Batson's empathy-altruism hypothesis and not our egoistic perspective. Subjects who were empathically (emotionally) aroused by imagining how the other person felt were helpful for the problem that related to their empathy (e.g., providing information for her thesis) but not for an unrelated problem (e.g., providing information for her student committee). We wondered, How could this be? So we attempted another study.

In this other study involving a similar problem we tried to convince empathically aroused subjects that a memory-enhancing substance (actually a placebo) would "freeze" their mood. Using this procedure, Gloria Manucia, Donald Baumann, and Bob Cialdini demonstrated that sadness promotes egoistic helping. Subjects who experienced temporary sadness (by reminiscing about an event) were more helpful to others than were neutral-mood (control) subjects when they believed, as normally is the case, that helping could improve their mood. When subjects believed that their mood was "frozen" by a drug, however, sad subjects were no more likely to help than were neutral mood subjects. Since the motivation to help was based on the desire to make themselves feel better, there was no special reason to help when subjects could not improve their mood. If empathic concern arouses an egoistic motivation, we reasoned that it would show the same result as sadness. If the motivation is altruistic, in contrast, subjects feeling empathic concern should be more helpful *regardless* of whether their moods are manageable or are frozen. After all, the goal of altruistic motivation is to improve the *other person's* situation. Whether or not one's mood will improve should be irrelevant.

The results again supported the empathy-altruism hypothesis. Subjects experiencing empathic concern showed equally elevated levels of helping when they believed that their mood was manageable and when they believed it was not. Batson was right, and we were wrong. Nevertheless, just as I became convinced that another question had been answered, we learned that Bob Cialdini and his colleagues had independently conducted an almost identical mood-freezing study and had obtained the opposite results! Consistent with an egoistic interpretation, empathically aroused subjects who believed that their moods were frozen were less helpful than were those who believed that helping could improve their mood. Who is right? The data are right. The fact that the results *appear* to be inconsistent means that there is still a piece of the puzzle missing. We are back in business and on the trail of the answer. How the story will end is—fortunately for those of us who are easily bored by knowing the answer—still a mystery.

LOOKING BACK, LOOKING AHEAD

As I conclude this chapter, I hope that you see research as a journey through time and ideas. There have been common themes—stress, arousal, and emotion—that have run through my work and have evolved in unplanned ways over the years. When I was younger, I wanted to be an explorer; I wanted to discover new lands. As I grew older, I lamented that there was so little new territory left to explore, and then I gave up—or so I thought. Looking back through this chapter, I realize that I have had an opportunity to be an explorer of human behavior. The analogy seems appropriate. Like Lewis and Clark moving westward, I have been able to move forward a step at a time. There has been no great breakthrough, no immediate upheaval or dramatic change in the lives of people. Often it has been two steps forward and one step back; sometimes it seems like one step forward and two steps back. I can see that there is a path ahead of me, but it is unclear where it leads. Although most researchers may not admit it, it is probably much easier to identify a research program by looking back at the ground already covered than by looking ahead. We think we know where we are going, but there are always surprises and interesting turns. We are never sure exactly where we will end up. However, the process of getting there is the rewarding challenge.

Acknowledgments

I gratefully acknowledge the valuable suggestions and comments offered by Sam Gaertner, Craig Johnson, Jane Allyn Piliavin, and Dave Schroeder on earlier versions of this chapter. I continue to rely on these friends for advice and assistance. I also express my sincere appreciation for the editors' helpful guidance and the suggestions of five anonymous reviewers.

SUGGESTED READINGS

BATSON, C. D. (1991). *The altruism question: Toward a social-psychological answer.* Hillsdale, NJ: Erlbaum.

CIALDINI, R. B., SCHALLER, M., HOULIHAN, D., ARPS, K., FULTZ, J., & BEAMAN, A. L. (1987). Empathy-based helping: Is it selflessly or selfishly motivated? *Journal of Personality and Social Psychology, 52,* 749–758.

CLARK, M. S. (ED.). (1991). *Review of personality and social psychology.* Vol. 12: *Prosocial behavior.* Newbury Park, CA: Sage.

DOVIDIO, J. F., PILIAVIN, J. A., GAERTNER, S. L., SCHROEDER, D. A., & CLARK, R. D. III. The arousal: cost-reward model and the process of intervention: A review of the evidence. In M. S. Clark (Ed.), *Review of personality and social psychology.* Vol. 12: *Prosocial behavior.* (pp. 86–118). Newbury Park, CA: Sage.

GAERTNER, S. L., & DOVIDIO, J. F. (1977). The subtlety of white racism, arousal, and helping. *Journal of Personality and Social Psychology, 35,* 691–707.

LATANÉ, B., & DARLEY, J. M. (1970). *The unresponsive bystander: Why doesn't he help?* New York: Appleton-Century-Crofts.

PILIAVIN, J. A., DOVIDIO, J. F., GAERTNER, S. L., & CLARK, R. D. III. (1981). *Emergency intervention.* New York: Academic Press.

SCHROEDER, D. A., DOVIDIO, J. F., SIBICKY, M. E., MATTHEWS, L. L., & ALLEN, J. L. (1988). Empathy and helping behavior: Egoism or altruism? *Journal of Experimental Social Psychology, 24,* 333–353.

———— PENNER, L. A., PILIAVIN, J. A., & DOVIDIO, J. F. (1994). *The social psychology of helping and altruism.* Boston: McGraw-Hill.

KAREN **K. D**ION (Ph.D., University of Minnesota) is Professor of Psychology at the University of Toronto. Her research interests include stereotyping, close relationships, and, most recently, adult development. Originally from Massachusetts, she was an undergraduate at Wellesley College. Her
interest in the study of attraction and romantic love may have its roots in those
formative college years, when she combined a major in psychology with a minor
in Spanish literature.

KENNETH **L. D**ION (Ph.D., University of Minnesota) is Professor of Psychology at the University of Toronto. In addition to romantic love, his
research interests include intergroup relations, prejudice, small group
processes, gender, language, ethnicity, and stereotyping. Some of his interest in
interpersonal and group processes may stem from his (1) being descended from
two of French Canada's oldest families and raised in a French-Canadian enclave
in New Hampshire and (2) having worked his way through university as lead
guitarist in a rock band that played the college fraternity circuit throughout New
England.

7

On the Love of Beauty and the Beauty of Love: Two Psychologists Study Attraction

❖

When we began to study physical attraction and romantic love more than two decades ago, it came as a surprise to learn that there was little research on either topic in the psychological literature. Since that time we and other social psychologists have been conducting research in both areas, and the literature on these topics has grown extensively. In the first part of this chapter I (Karen) will talk about the relation between physical attractiveness and attraction, and in the second part Ken will discuss our research on romantic love.

WHAT IS BEAUTIFUL IS GOOD

Challenging the assertion that what is beautiful is good are several proverbs such as "You can't judge a book by its cover," "Handsome is as handsome does," and "Beauty is only skin deep." These sayings warn us *not* to evaluate others on the basis of their physical appearance. Reflecting these beliefs, most people would be likely to state that their judgments of others are not affected by characteristics such as beauty. For example, in one study, even when asked what qualities are important in a date, undergraduates ranked "personality" above "looks." However, there is now considerable social psychological research indicating that despite these sentiments, looks do influence liking and evaluations of others.

My research on this topic began in the late 1960s, when I was a graduate student at the University of Minnesota. A number of well-known studies in the social psychology of attraction had been carried out by researchers at Minnesota. One of those studies caught my attention: a "computer dating" study conducted by Elaine Hatfield and her colleagues in which they had examined the impact of physical attractiveness on attraction. Today the term *computer dating* might be assumed to refer to courtship via electronic mail; however, in the 1960s it had quite different connotations. Incoming first-year students purchased tickets to a Friday night "computer dance" where they expected to be paired by computer matching of their questionnaire responses to others of the opposite sex who had expressed similar interests. In fact, the participants in this study were randomly paired (except that a man was never paired with a woman who was taller than he!). Ratings of the assigned date were obtained in an intermission during the course of the dance. Contrary to the researchers' expectations, the date's physical attractiveness was the single most important determinant of liking, regardless of the individual's own physical attractiveness (as assessed by independent judges' ratings). Moreover, whether they themselves were good-looking or not, men preferred the most attractive women, as determined in a follow-up study by whether they tried to go out with their dates after the initial meeting. Contrasting markedly with the importance of good looks, various personality measures and measures of intellectual ability were not good predictors of liking for one's date.

When I read about this research, I was curious about the reasons underlying the relation between attractiveness and liking. I wondered whether attractiveness may influence liking in part because of its possible impact on people's inferences about others. Does physical attractiveness affect one's expectations about other people's personalities and abilities? To examine this question, I designed a study which was conducted in collaboration with Ellen Berscheid, my graduate adviser at the time, and Elaine Hatfield. We presented university students with facial photographs of young adults who differed in physical attractiveness and asked for their first impressions of those individuals on a series of personality traits. In addition, participants were asked to infer how competent they believed those individuals would be in different roles (such as spouse and parent) and their likelihood of achieving success and happiness in their personal lives. We found that physical attractiveness did indeed affect expectations about personal traits. Good-looking individuals were believed to have more socially desirable personalities, and attractive persons were also expected to have greater success in most of the domains of adult life measured in the study. Interestingly, one exception to this pattern was on the dimension of expected competence as a parent; no differences as a function of attractiveness occurred there. The predominant pattern of the results was summarized by the title of the published paper in which our findings were subsequently reported: "What Is Beautiful Is Good."

One issue that subsequently interested me concerned the implications of physical attractiveness for social development. What is the relation between physical appearance and popularity at earlier phases of life? So far the research had focused on young adults, specifically college students. When deciding on an area of specialization, I had debated between social psychology and developmental psychology since I was interested in both areas. Although I had chosen social psychology as my primary area, I also took graduate courses at the Institute of Child Development at the University of Minnesota so that I could strengthen my knowledge of developmental psychology.

While there, I discovered that a sociometric measure of popularity had been administered to preschool children attending the institute's nursery school. The measure involved a picture board technique developed for use with young children. Photographs of classmates were placed on the board, and children were asked whom they liked and disliked in the class. This technique provided the opportunity to begin examining whether attractiveness is related to peer popularity long before adolescence and early adulthood. We found evidence that for the most part good looks are a social asset even among preschoolers.

These findings suggested a promising new direction for research. My interest turned to examining the role played by physical appearance in social development. By this time Ken and I had received Ph.D.s from Minnesota and become faculty members at the University of Toronto. During the next few years the following kinds of questions were the focus of my research: How early does stereotyping based on facial attractiveness appear? Does attractiveness influence behavior toward others?

Among the findings was evidence that the tendency to judge others on the basis of their looks, at least when forming first impressions, begins quite early. In one study I found that preschoolers showed consistent stereotypes based on attractiveness. Using the picture board technique with photographs of children they did not know, preschoolers who were asked to guess, for example, "Who is friendly to other children?" or "Who doesn't like fighting and shouting?" were more likely to point to good-looking children (based on judges' independent ratings of facial attractiveness). When asked "Who scares you?" or "Who might hurt you?" the children were more likely to choose peers who were physically unattractive. At the end of the session each child was asked what it means to be pretty or cute. One preschool girl stated her view of the advantages of good looks quite succinctly: "It's like to be a princess . . . everybody loves you."

During the 1970s and into the 1980s the literature on the social and developmental psychology of physical attractiveness continued to grow. Many studies had provided further evidence that a person's physical attractiveness affects other people's first impressions of him or her. There was, however, little work that addressed *why* people judge others differently depending on their appearance. My interests in recent years have turned to seeking explanations for physical attractiveness stereotyping from several different perspectives.

One of these is a sociocultural perspective. Is stereotyping based on physical attractiveness more likely to occur in particular cultural contexts? Although it was tempting to consider extended travel around the world to examine this issue, there was a more practical alternative. Toronto is a multicultural city, and so it was possible to begin examining this question there. We have now found some evidence that sociocultural factors may be related to the likelihood of stereotyping on the basis of physical attractiveness. Specifically, in one study we found that individuals who reported being very much involved in a community in which group rather than individual concerns traditionally have been important were less likely to show physical attractiveness stereotyping.

We've also found that personality dimensions may be related to the likelihood that attractiveness-based stereotyping occurs. Some years earlier Mel Lerner had proposed the "just world" theory. According to this theory, many people believe that to a certain extent people "get what they deserve" and "deserve what they get." This view of life lets a person see the world as a predictable place. The research of Lerner and his colleagues had largely, if not exclusively, focused on the consequences of believing in a just world for understanding people's reactions to victims. Since good people are not supposed to experience misfortune, people will sometimes go to considerable lengths (such as blaming victims for their fate) to maintain their faith in a just world when confronted with information that contradicts that belief.

Just world theory, however, can also be applied to people's reactions to those advantaged as well as those disadvantaged by fate. Believing in a just world should express itself by being positively biased toward "winners," including individuals who possess favored social attributes such as physical attractiveness. Might the "beauty is good" stereotype itself partly reflect the belief in a just world? Ken and I designed a study to examine that possibility.

We decided to undertake this research at the Ontario Science Centre, where visitors can volunteer to take part in psychology studies. As you'll read in the next section, the Ontario Science Centre has provided us with some unique opportunities for research with a diverse group of individuals coming from a broad range of age groups and representing different occupations and backgrounds. In this study participants came from Canada or the United States. Toronto is a popular city for visitors, and the Ontario Science Centre is one of the top attractions.

People taking part in this study anonymously completed a questionnaire designed to measure the strength of their belief in a just world and also completed a person perception task in which they were asked for their first impressions of a photographed "stimulus person" on a series of items (personality traits, predicted outcomes in areas of adult life such as marriage, occupational success). We found some support for our prediction that believers in a just world are more likely than nonbelievers to favor good-looking people when making personality judgments, but this finding occurred only for first impressions of men's personalities, not for first impressions of women's personalities. By contrast, we found that whether or not they endorsed "just world" beliefs, respondents expected attractive persons of both sexes to have more success and positive outcomes in their lives compared with less physically attractive individuals. However, among believers in a just world (compared with nonbelievers), as predicted, there was a stronger relation between the life outcomes they expected people to have and their view of people's character.

So what do these findings mean? For one thing, they suggest that there may be individual differences in the likelihood that physical attractiveness affects one's first impressions of others. Some people may be more likely to judge other people's character on the basis of their looks. These findings suggest that one (though not the only) explanation of this kind of stereotyping may be linked to personality and other individual differences in people. So as you read about the power of attractiveness to affect first impressions, if you think, but I don't judge people based on how they look, you may be right about yourself. However, are you sure?

*T*HIS THING CALLED LOVE

As it happens, individual differences, including personality variables, are important considerations in a full understanding of another important aspect of interpersonal attraction: people's view of romantic love. When we conducted our first study of romantic love as psychology graduate students in 1968, to our knowledge, no published social psychological research dealing explicitly with romantic love existed to guide us. (Unbeknown to us, Zick Rubin, then a graduate student at the University of Michigan, was independently conducting a study of romantic love at the same time.) We were drawn to the study of romantic love in good part because of the sheer challenge of charting a phenomenon about which, as far as we were aware, little or nothing was known from a scientific, psychological point of view.

We decided on two approaches that have since stood us in good stead. Both strategies stemmed from the issue of finding ways to measure romantic love. There is a time-honored dictum in psychology, attributed to the late intelligence and psychometric theorist Louis Thurstone, that whatever exists, exists in some degree and is therefore measurable. Since we definitely knew that love exists (after all, we had experienced it in relation to each other and continue to do so to this day), it should be measurable. The challenge, of course, was to find ways to measure it. However, in measuring something, one first has to define what the phenomenon of interest actually is, what it consists of.

One strategy was fairly obvious: We would create a questionnaire that asked people about their love lives! Thus was born the "Romantic Love Questionnaire" we have used in one form or another ever since. In the original questionnaire we asked undergraduate students if they had ever been in love and, if so, whether this love was reciprocated, whether they were in love at the time of the study, how long their love experiences had lasted, how intense each had been, and what feelings they had usually experienced while in love. With these questions we attempted to assess some of the different "parameters" of romantic love. We also asked the students to describe their current or most recent experience of romantic love on a series of dimensions. Finally, they also completed some items assessing their attitudes toward love, such as how idealistic or cynical they were toward the idea of romantic love.

Respondents did not seem to mind our questionnaire. As questionnaires go, many respondents found it rather enjoyable. We have hardly been alone in coming up with a questionnaire measure of romantic love. Zick Rubin, for example, had devised a romantic love measure consisting of a thirteen-item attitude scale. Zick conceptualized love as an interpersonal attitude consisting of several interrelated elements (attachment, caring, and intimacy). He defined romantic love as a single underlying dimension on which individuals could be ranked and ordered regarding the strength of their romantic love for a particular partner.

By contrast, we viewed romantic love, even at the outset, quite differently. When we reviewed individuals' descriptions of their romantic love experiences, we were convinced that love was not just a single, uniform experience for everyone; rather, love clearly meant different things to different people. Some people reported experiencing love in the idealized form portrayed in American television and films. They had fallen in love at first sight, were idealistic in their attitude toward love (e.g., by endorsing statements such as "There is only one real love for a person"), and were basically besotted with their partners. By contrast, others described a more rational and emotionally muted experience of love, sometimes with overtones of manipulativeness and attempts at control in the relationship, and in other cases described a relationship that sounded more like good or strong friendship than a passionate or sexual relationship.

Accordingly, in our Romantic Love Questionnaire we deliberately built in a variety of items to measure and reflect these qualitatively different experiences of, and attitudes toward, love. That love means different things to different people can be termed a *multidimensional perspective* on romantic love. Other psychologists and social scientists have since taken a similar approach to defining and measuring love. Indeed, in the 1980s and early 1990s multidimensional perspectives became the dominant approach among psychologists in theorizing about love and measuring it with a variety of questionnaires.

We also believed that the qualitatively different experiences or orientations toward love we and others had observed would relate systematically to key aspects of one's personality. In our view, not only was personality relevant, it was crucial to understanding why people reported qualitatively different experiences of romantic love. Knowing an individual's standing on important personality dimensions, we felt, would enable us to predict who would be prone to experience romantic love and what kind of love experience they would describe.

Our first study focused on the personality dimension of internal-external control—i.e., a tendency to believe that the events and outcomes affecting us are under one's personal control (internals) or under the control of external forces or pressures beyond oneself (externals)—for which well-established personality scales existed. We expected that university undergraduates who were "externals" would differ considerably from those who could be characterized as "internals" in their reported experiences of romantic love. In brief, we expected externals to be more likely than internals to report experiencing romantic love in the traditional way portrayed in the media—as a mysterious, intense, volatile, and idealized experience—because the prevalent stereotype of romantic love in the United States and other western cultures portrays it as an external force.

Fortunately for us, we were right. We found that in a sample of university undergraduates "externals" were more likely than "internals" to report having ever been in love. Among those who had been in love, externals described their experience of love as being more mysterious, more volatile, and less rational and calculated than that of internals. Finally, we (and since then, others too) found that externals were much more idealistic in their attitude toward romantic love than were internals. To summarize, the love experiences of young adults classified as externals were indeed more in keeping with the western cultural stereotype of romantic love than was the case for internals.

Since that first study we've explored other key personality variables (e.g., self-esteem, defensiveness, self-actualization, individualism-collectivism, and gender orientation) and individual difference dimensions (e.g., sex, ethnocultural background) as factors that may be related to the experience of love and attitudes toward romantic love. We carefully selected each personality dimension because its relation to romantic love was controversial. For example, does being an individualist facilitate or inhibit romantic love? Claims have been made for both possibilities. Which is correct? With our studies of personality and love, we were able to test such competing claims. In any case, each of the dimensions mentioned above has turned out to be relevant in helping us understand why some people are more likely to fall in love than others and to have different experiences of romantic love.

This, however, is not the end of the story. Recall that I mentioned *two* strategies for trying to measure romantic love. We felt it was unwise to rely entirely on "self-report" questionnaire measures to assess romantic love, and so we sought other ways to get a glimpse of love as a phenomenon of interest. What situations or paradigms might let us get a glimpse of love, in the same way perhaps that the mist inside a Wilson cloud chamber from a physics laboratory enables one to see traces of electrically charged ions and electrons that could not otherwise be observed?

The department of psychology at the U of T (University of Toronto) is renowned for the study of cognitive processes, especially memory and perception. If we were to persuade our colleagues about the merits of studying love, we would have to show them that the kind of strong, positive feelings and affect reflected by romantic love can influence and distort cognitive processes such as perception and memory, perhaps strongly. Consequently, we began exploring some laboratory paradigms in perceptual and cognitive psychology as candidates for becoming Wilson cloud chambers, as it were, for studying love. Since the American psychologist Herman Witkin had clearly shown that perception and people's responses to perceptual illusions reflect their personality, perhaps these factors could do the same for romantic love. Accordingly, a perception paradigm was our first venture and the paradigm we shall use to illustrate the second strategy. In particular, I had always been intrigued by a Princeton University doctoral thesis in psychology published in 1958 by Warren Wittreich on the "Honi phenomenon," which I'd read as a graduate student at Minnesota. What intrigued me in particular was the charming story behind the Honi phenomenon.

In the 1940s a gentleman with many talents named Adelbert Ames, Jr., devised some intriguing perceptual exhibits and demonstrations which suggested that people do not perceive external reality faithfully in all its details. Instead, people's perceptions are subjective bets about "what is out there" based on their past experience. According to this view, an unfamiliar stimulus array that produces on the retina of the eye the same pattern as a more familiar configuration will be seen by a perceiver as being identical to the familiar one. This principle was perhaps best illustrated by Ames's famous "distorted room," which is large enough for one or two people to walk inside of comfortably.

The distorted room is very unusual indeed. As shown in Figure 7.1, it is trapezoidal rather than square and has several other peculiar fea-

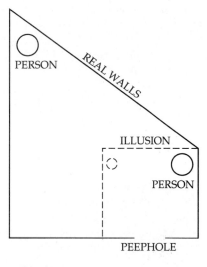

FIGURE 7.1
A two-dimensional representation
of an Ames distorted room.

tures. Inside the room, the floor is not level; it slopes upward to the right of an observer. The wall at the rear recedes farther on the left than on the right. The windows on the rear wall are also trapezoidal and differ in size. This very unusually shaped room, however, has one crucial quality: It has been carefully engineered so that despite its weird shape, when viewed through the "peephole" with one eye by an observer, it produces the same image on the observer's retina as a regular, square room. Though the observer sees the room as square, any persons viewed inside the room are seen as being quite distorted in physical size (see Figure 7.2). An observer watching another person walk along the back wall of an Ames room usually reports that the individual grows or shrinks markedly in physical size, depending on the direction in which the observed person is walking.

The Ames distorted room produces a strong and compelling illusion of perceived distortions in the physical size of persons viewed in it. In 1949, however, a curious exception was serendipitously discovered by a Princeton University psychologist, Hadley Cantril, while he was showing the room to a married couple of his acquaintance: a distinguished lawyer and his wife, whose nickname was Honi. Although Honi reported seeing the usual size distortions in her perceptions of Cantril inside the room, she consistently failed to see her husband as distorted in size. Instead of seeing her husband as distorted in size when she viewed him in the room, Honi saw the room as being distorted. In Cantril's own words in describing the experience, "For her [Honi], unlike any observer

FIGURE 7.2
The Ames distorted room.

until then—the room had become somewhat distorted. In other words, she was using her husband—to whom she was particularly devoted—as her standard." Of hundreds of observers Cantril had tested in the Ames room, all had without exception reported seeing the room as normal and square and people within the room as distorted in physical size, until Honi. Cantril termed this departure from the typical illusion the "Honi phenomenon."

Was this resistance to the typical illusion in the Ames distorted room unique to Honi? For his doctoral dissertation at Princeton in the 1950s, Wittreich set out to see if the Honi phenomenon could be replicated with other people, using young married couples as his subjects. An important feature of Wittreich's research was to devise a quantitative measure of selective perceptual distortion of people viewed in an Ames distorted room.

To an observer, a person walking across the back wall of an Ames room from left to right initially appears to be very small in relation to the room, goes through a stage of being perceived as normal in physical size, and then is seen as becoming progressively larger than normal. The reverse occurs for an individual observed moving from right to left. If the Honi phenomenon is operating, a marital partner should be viewed as comparatively less distorted in physical size standing in either corner and also should not have to move as far along the back wall to appear normal in size. In short, the relative distance traversed by one's partner as opposed to a stranger of the same sex provides a quantitative index of the strength of the Honi phenomenon.

Wittreich found that Cantril's previous observation of the Honi phenomenon was reproducible with *certain* married individuals. Specifically, he suggested that persons married less than a year were less likely to see their marital partners as distorted in size relative to a stranger compared with those who were married longer. I doubted that length of marriage per se was the crucial factor. After all, Cantril's original observation of the Honi phenomenon was based on a deeply and mutually devoted couple who were grandparents and had been married over twenty-five years. To my mind, the Honi phenomenon was a case of romantic love triumphing over the laws of optics, a situation where love for the partner defied an otherwise strong and compelling perceptual illusion. To test this possibility, we would need to administer a measure of romantic love to couples and see if those strongly in love with their partners were better at resisting seeing their partners as distorted in size.

Ames's distorted rooms are not exactly standard issue in university psychology departments these days. Cantril's original Ames room had been dismantled and stored somewhere on the campus of Princeton University, with no one quite sure where. Luckily for us, the Ontario Science Centre in Toronto had a full-size Ames room as one of its most popular exhibits. After a year or two of unrelenting begging and pleading with several of its officials, we were given the use of the exhibit for one weekend to do our research.

This was, we were told in no uncertain terms, our one and only opportunity to use this very popular exhibit. We would get no second chance if something or someone screwed up. Inevitably, the night before the study was scheduled to start and we were finally allowed to set up for our study at the exhibit, disaster loomed as it became abundantly clear that we would need some way for the observer to signal the person walking across the room to stop when she or he was perceived as being of normal size. "Undaunted psychologists" then as now, we solved the problem by applying some high school physics and making a quick trip to the hardware store to pick up a doorbell, some copper wiring, and a 6-volt battery in order to set up a buzzer system for the observer, whose signal now could be clearly heard inside the room by the "target" person(s) being viewed.

The "Honi" study went off without a hitch. We had assembled a crack team consisting of (1) "stimulus persons" of each sex whose task was to be standard "strangers" for all subjects, (2) another person to run up and down the floor of the room, making the physical measurements of distance the observed persons had traversed, and (3) Karen administering Rubin's love scale and other measures after the observations had been made and telling people what the study was about after they had taken part in it. My task was to give instructions to the observer and invite potential participants to volunteer from among the patrons visiting the Ontario Science Centre. As we mentioned earlier, the people visiting the building are wonderfully diverse in age and background. Our sample included a wide representation of couples ranging from grandparents with grandkids bouncing on their knees, to pairs of teenagers I found necking in the corner of the room, to lots of married and unmarried couples between these extremes.

Months later, after scoring the love scale and the related questionnaire measures, transforming the distance measurements in the Ames room to relative position scores for partner and stranger, and analyzing all the information, we finally got some answers. Neither the length of the relationship nor the nature of the relationship (e.g., married versus unmarried) mattered. For the sample as a whole, the strength of romantic love, as suspected, did indeed matter in the way we expected; that is, the stronger the love for one's partner, the less the likelihood of seeing her or him as distorted in size in an Ames room relative to a stranger of the same sex as the partner.

However, there is yet another interesting twist we had not anticipated. When we submitted the paper to a psychology journal for possible publication, a reviewer suggested that we perform separate analyses for men and women. It was a useful suggestion. Men, it turned out, did not show the Honi phenomenon. Rather, only women—to be more precise, only women who were strongly in love with their partners—showed the Honi phenomenon of selective perceptual distortion in the Ames room. Therefore, it does not appear to have been irrelevant or accidental that the phenomenon was first observed in a woman deeply in love with her husband. Nor is this gender difference limited to the Honi phenomenon. In further studies of other cognitive processes (e.g., memory) as reflections of romantic love, we have also found a similar gender difference.

In closing, we leave you with a tongue-in-cheek suggestion. Psychological research on love means that we have advanced beyond pulling the petals off flowers one by one and saying "S/He loves me, s/he loves me not" to find out if your partner *really* loves you. The psychological literature on love provides several ways to gauge a partner's love. A number of "love scales" and questionnaire measures are available in the psychological literature. A problem with such questionnaires, of course, is that it is often fairly obvious what the questionnaire or scale is attempting to assess. However, there is always the possibility of a romantic weekend in Toronto, with a discreet visit to the Ames room in the Ontario Science Centre. But if your partner takes you there, stands inside the Ames room, and asks, "How do I look?" remember to say as you look through the viewing point, "Honey, you certainly look normal to me." Forewarned is forearmed.

SUGGESTED READINGS

DION, K. K. (1986). Stereotyping based on physical attractiveness: Issues and conceptual perspectives. In C. P. Herman, M. Zanna, & E. T. Higgins (Eds.), *Physical appearance, stigma and social behavior: The Ontario symposium on personality and social psychology* (vol. 3, chap. 1, pp. 7–21). Hillsdale, NJ: Erlbaum.

———— & DION, K. L. (1985). Personality, gender, and the phenomenology of romantic love. In P. R. Shaver (Ed.), *Self, situations, and behavior: Review of personality and social psychology* (vol. 6, chap. 9, pp. 209–239). Newbury Park, CA: Sage.

DION, K. L., & DION, K. K. (1988). Romantic love: Individual and cultural perspectives. In R. J. Sternberg & M. L. Barnes (Eds.), *The psychology of love* (chap. 12, pp. 264–293). New Haven, CT: Yale University Press.

*E*LAINE *HATFIELD (Ph.D., Stanford University) is a Professor of Psychology at the University of Hawaii. She has written nine books and over 100 research articles. Two of her books*—A New Look at Love *and* Mirror, Mirror: The Importance of Looks in Everyday Life—*won the American Psychological Foundation's National Media Award, which honors the best books in psychology. She and her husband, Richard L. Rapson, have just completed* Love, Sex, and Intimacy: Their Psychology, Biology, and History. *Dr. Hatfield has won two prestigious awards for her research: the Society for Experimental Social Psychology's Distinguished Scientist Award (in 1993) and the University of Hawaii's Distinguished Senior Scientist Award.*

8

Self-Esteem and Passionate Love Relationships

--- ❖ ---

Serious, rigorous research into the nature of love barely existed when I began my studies. Today one can barely escape it.

THE ENTHUSIASTIC BEGINNINGS

When I arrived at Stanford in 1959, I signed up to work with Douglas Lawrence and Leon Festinger, who were collaborating on a monograph dealing with "cognitive dissonance in rats." At the University of Michigan, where I had just received a B.A., I had worked with Arthur Melton and David Birch, both eminent learning theorists. I spent evenings in their laboratories coaxing rats over hurdles. So it was natural for me to fall in with Stanford's rigorous experimentalists and mathematical modelers. I was also right at home with rats!

There was one problem with this natural alliance, however. I was fascinated by emotions in general and the phenomenon of passionate love in particular. One couldn't help noticing that behavioral theories seemed to lack something when it came to explaining powerful emotional experiences. It was obvious to me that passionate love is a desperately intense motivator. When my friends were besotted with love, they were always a little bit nuts. One male friend could painstakingly articulate why a certain lovely, bright, vivacious but extremely neurotic woman was poison and why he should stay well away from her. Nonetheless, in spite of his piercing logic, one couldn't help but notice that he kept one eye on the laboratory phone, waiting for it to become free so that he could call her to plead for "just one more chance." (Nobody seemed to be desperately in love with the perfectly sensible men and women who loved them and caused no trouble at all.) Clark Hull and reinforcement theory simply did not do a very good job of explaining such weird (and totally human) behavior. Nor could I dismiss passionate love as an unimportant topic. Late in the evening, after our work was done, faculty members and students often confided in one another about their personal problems, all of which seemed to focus on love. For most of us, things were not going well; sometimes they were not going at all! Some of us couldn't find anyone to date. Most were in complicated, confusing relationships. A few of my friends were getting divorces. One night several of my friends complained that they were so discouraged that they sometimes thought about committing suicide.

I began to think about conducting research into passionate love. My fellow graduate students, who were mostly hard scientists interested in constructing mathematical models of rat learning, warned me to avoid such topics. They cautioned that I had to worry about "career management." Passionate love just wasn't a very important phenomenon (!), and there was no hope of finding out much about it in our lifetime. Worst of all, the whole topic just wasn't respectable. And it wasn't "hot." The topic of the moment was mathematical modeling—reinforcement theory and math modeling. One set of interests (reinforcement and math models) during the daytime and another (passionate love and maybe suicide) in the evenings.

I was always stubbornly interested in what *I* cared about rather than in "career management," and so I suggested to Leon Festinger, my adviser, that our Thursday night research group should set aside some time now and then for discussing hazy, half-formed ideas. We could discuss the possibilities of doing research on taboo, neglected, impossible topics such as love, sex, and the emotions. He said that sounded like a great idea. I should go first. I decided to speculate about possible links between self-esteem and one's vulnerability to love. My idea was this: When self-esteem tumbles to an all-time *low*, one should be especially vulnerable to falling in love. I thought that there were two reasons why this might be so.

First, people with high self-esteem are likely to assume that they have a great deal to offer others; they can afford to "demand the very best." Thus, the higher one's self-esteem, the more one might require from a "suitable" date or mate. Second, when self-esteem is low or has been momentarily shattered, one may well have an increased *need* for the affection and regard of others. The lower a person's self-esteem, the more appreciative that person will be when anyone seems to love him or her and the more likely that person may be to reciprocate the affection.

My first step was to check the clinical literature to see if there was any research to support my hypothesis. There wasn't much. In 1949 Theodor Reik had published a wise and witty book entitled *A Psychologist Looks at Love* in which he argued that people are most susceptible to passionate love when their self-esteem has been bruised. Novelists seconded his observations. Mary McCarthy in *The Company She Keeps*, for example, discussed the link between low self-esteem and vulnerability to even deeply flawed love. Her heroine, Margaret Sargent, has been enslaved by love. In therapy, she has made an illuminating discovery:

> Now for the first time she saw her own extremity, saw that it was some failure in self-love that obligated her to snatch blindly at the love of others, hoping to love herself through them, borrowing their feelings, as the moon borrowed light. She herself was a dead planet.[p. 303]

But most clinicians (such as Carl Rogers, Alfred Adler, Karen Horney, and Eric Fromm) said that Reik (and I) had things the wrong way around. It was people with *high* self-esteem who were the most receptive to love. They argued, logically enough, that if people can't love themselves, how can they be expected to love anyone else? The sparse correlational data that existed seemed to support *their* contentions and challenge Reik's (and mine). I suspected that Leon Festinger would probably agree with those theorists as well. Dissonance theory would predict that if we think badly of ourselves, we should experience cognitive dissonance if someone assures us that we are wonderful. One likely way to reduce dissonance would be to assume that these Pollyannas must be stupid or confused or have ulterior motives. Surely, when they got to know us better, they would change their minds.

On Thursday night, as I stood up to present my half-formulated ideas to the research group, I was stunned to discover that Leon, who had arrived late from a merry faculty dinner at a Greek restaurant, had invited some of the celebrants—Al Hastorf, Gordon Bower, Jon Freedman, and Alex Bavelas—back to that night's meeting. I plunged ahead. It is probably unnecessary to mention that my proposal did not knock the socks off the assembled critics. Many of them agreed that the idea just wasn't a very interesting one. One critic noted that in the 1940s theorists had found that rats on partial learning schedules displayed a burst of energy when a reward finally arrived. Presumably, such long-denied rewards were doubly rewarding. The phenomenon even had a name: the Crespi effect. Why bother replicating a well-established finding yet again? People or rats, it didn't matter. An effect was an effect. Others cautioned me that people's perceptions of what is rewarding are elusive. Would we find someone who confirmed our opinions rewarding? What if others agreed that we were miserable human beings? Was even that rewarding? Or did we inevitably prefer those who praised us? Who knew? Why bother? Why not stick to basic research?

So, of course, I proceeded to do just what I wanted to do anyway. I agreed that I would run traditional, sensible dissonance and learning experiments in the daytime. But I would do my own research in the evenings and on weekends.

I set out to test the hypothesis that men and women are most vulnerable to love when their self-esteem has been momentarily shattered. (Well, not exactly shattered. Maybe slightly threatened. I was worried that we might go too far and hurt someone's feelings.) I invited thirty-seven Stanford University and Foothill Junior College women to take a battery of psychological tests: the California Psychological Inventory, a word association test, the Minnesota Multiphasic Personality Inventory, and the Rorschach test. A week later the women reported one at a time for further testing and interviewing. I arranged to have Gerald Davison, a handsome graduate student, waiting for me (the experimenter). Since I was late, the two of them began to chat. The time and conversation stretched out. Eventually Jerry invited the woman to dinner and a movie the next weekend. All the women accepted.

Soon I showed up, breathless, apologizing for being late. I asked Jerry to administer the word association test; I said I could administer the Rorschach test. Jerry read the protocol to the subjects, and I sent him on his way. At the end of the session I asked the women if they were interested in their results. They all were. So I gave bogus feedback designed momentarily to raise or lower their self-esteem or leave it unchanged. If women had been randomly assigned to the low-esteem condition, the analysis stressed their personality problems: immaturity, lack of openness, antisocial motives, limited capacity for successful leadership, and lack of originality and flexibility. If women had been randomly assigned to the high-esteem condition, the report stressed their personality strengths: maturity, warmth and openness, integrity, and so forth. It stated that each of these women presented "one of the most favorable personality structures analyzed by the staff." Women who had been assigned to the control condition were told that their tests had not yet been scored. Thus, they received no feedback.

In later interviews women were asked their first impressions of Jerry and a number of other people, including the experimenter. As predicted, it was the women whose self-esteem had been threatened who were most attracted to him. Women whose self-esteem had been boosted liked him all right, just not so much.

I worried, of course, about the ethics of this deception experiment. In extensive posttesting, I interviewed subjects about their feelings. Did they enjoy the experiment? (Earlier that year Eleanor Maccoby, who was rightly concerned about the ethics of social psychological experimentation, had polled Stanford undergraduates about which experiments they liked and which they disliked, which were ethical and which were not. She had been worried that students would disapprove of social psychology experiments, since they often involved deception. To her surprise, she discovered that undergraduates loved the social psychological experiments and thought they were fun. What they hated were the rote-learning experiments: those long boring lists of paired associates.) Thus, I wanted to be sure students enjoyed participating in my experiment; I thought it probably was a bit unethical to bore subjects to death.

Had the subjects' feelings been hurt? If they had known what they were getting into, would they have agreed to participate? We set aside an hour at the end of the experiment to debrief the subjects. We talked about passionate love in general and the women's concerns in particular. We replayed the experiment and asked if anything about the procedure had bothered them. How could we change it? Because I was concerned about the ethics of deception research, I did a great deal of pretesting and ended up publishing a monograph on the consequences of various debriefing strategies.

THE DISAPPOINTING MIDDLE

Over the next two decades I team-taught a number of social psychology research courses in which faculty members and students speculated about the possible links between self-esteem and passionate and companionate love. A miniteam of economists (Edgar Feige), statisticians (G. William Walster), and computer whizzes (Susan Sprecher) set out to cast these predictions in precise mathematical terms. Finally, Susan Sprecher (a sociologist), Ellen Berscheid (a psychologist), and I decided to investigate the process in a step-by-step fashion. We proposed that self-esteem should affect people's reactions to others in a number of interlocking ways. We conducted five more experiments in an effort to test our hypotheses. The team's theorizing might have been brilliant, but our results were not.

Let us review this ill-fated research.

1. *Measuring self-esteem.* Before embarking on the research, it was critically important to define just what we meant by "self-esteem." Essentially, we were interested in how much self-esteem people had concerning their romantic value, i.e., how much confidence they had that they were lovable, whether they deserved love and were likely to ignite it. Did they possess a basic trust that their relationships were likely to go well?

We were unable to find any existing self-esteem measures that tapped such quiet confidence. One of our students, Edward Wells, set out to review the self-esteem literature so that our team could select the best of the existing measures. He invested so much thought and time in the project that he and Gerald Marwell ended up publishing a monograph on the topic: *Self-Esteem: Its Conceptualization and Measurement.* In four studies, we decided to measure self-esteem, using the measures that seemed closest to the construct in which we were interested:

a. The Berger Measure of Self-Esteem.

b. The Rosenberg Self-Esteem Scale.

c. The California Psychological Inventory. This scale includes measures of poise, ascendancy, and self-assurance, i.e., measures of dominance, capacity for status, sociability, social presence, self-acceptance, and sense of well-being. In addition, in the fifth experiment we followed the procedure we had employed in our original study by manipulating rather than measuring self-esteem. In this experiment, then, we were studying the effect of *momentary* gains or losses in self-esteem on vulnerability to love. In the other four experiments we were exploring the impact of *habitually* high or low self-esteem on vulnerability to love. We thought it should make no difference.

2. *Should we study passionate love, companionate love, or both?* Theoretically, self-esteem should effect vulnerability to both passionate and companionate love. Passionate love (sometimes labeled obsessive love, infatuation, love sickness, or being in love) is an intense emotion. It has been defined as a

> state of intense longing for union with another. Reciprocated love (union with the other) is associated with fulfillment and ecstasy. Unrequited love (separation) is associated with emptiness, anxiety, or despair. Passionate love is a complex functional whole including appraisals or appreciations, subjective feelings, expressions, patterned physiological processes, action tendencies, and instrumental behaviors.[Hatfield & Rapson, 1993, p. 5.]

The Passionate Love Scale was designed to assess the cognitive, physiological, and behavioral indicants of such a longing for union.

Companionate love (sometimes called true love or conjugal love) is a far less intense emotion. It combines feelings of deep attachment, commitment, and intimacy. It has been defined as the

> affection we feel for those with whom our lives are deeply entwined. Companionate love is a complex functional whole including appraisals or appreciations, subjective feelings, expressions, patterned physiological processes, action tendencies, and instrumental behaviors.[Hatfield & Rapson, 1993, p. 106.]

Psychologists have used a variety of scales to measure companionate love. For example, Robert Sternberg assumed that such relationships possess little passion but a great deal of commitment and intimacy; thus, he assessed companionate love by measuring commitment and intimacy. Since we thought threats to self-esteem might have the most profound impact on passionate love and a lesser impact on companionate love, we decided to maximize our chances of discovering how the process worked by focusing on budding romantic relationships.

3. *A step-by-step analysis of the possible effects of self-esteem on romantic attraction.* Finally, Susan Sprecher and I set out to explore the impact of self-esteem on romantic perceptions and feelings in an orderly way.

a. *Self-esteem and perception.* First, we proposed that self-esteem should shape people's perceptions about whether a potential romantic partner is attracted to them. In the early stages of a flirtation it is often difficult for young men and women to assess whether someone is interested in them. We might expect such perceptions to be colored by their own self-evaluations. In one experiment, for example, we studied men and women whose self-esteem had been raised or lowered. We were interested in their reactions to potential dates who were accepting, rejecting, or unclear in their feelings. We had assumed that all the men and women would "correctly" perceive how potential dates felt about them, but we discovered that it was not safe to make such an assumption. Even though we had labored to compose crystal-clear messages of acceptance or rejection, different subjects interpreted those messages in very different ways. For example, after being severely rejected, one man gave a knowing smile and commented, "You can always tell when a girl is interested in you—she plays hard to get." Other subjects had the opposite problem. A few managed to interpret even the most enthusiastic communications as evidencing subtle rejection or pity; if all else failed, they assumed a case of mistaken identity.

Thus, in hypothesis 1 we proposed that young men's and women's self-esteem would affect their perceptions of how much others liked them. Specifically, we proposed the following:

> Low-self-esteem individuals will underestimate how much they are liked by dates while high-self-esteem individuals will overestimate how much they are liked. Such distortions will be especially pronounced when the date's expressions of liking or disliking for the subject are ambiguous.

b. *Self-esteem and liking for others.* People's self-esteem should also affect their liking for others. For the sake of argument, let us assume that all the subjects, regardless of their own self-esteem level, correctly perceived how much they were liked or disliked by others. How might we expect self-esteem to influence their reactions to a potential date's expressions of affection or hostility? As we observed earlier, self-consistency (dissonance) theory and reinforcement theory would make very different predictions. Self-consistency theory assumes that people will most like others who share their opinions, for good or for ill. Reinforcement theorists argue that while everyone prefers praise to blame, people with low self-esteem are more "needy" than their peers and therefore should be especially appreciative of those who provide that rare commodity (affection) and more resentful of those who withhold it. We, and the then existing evidence, favored this latter prediction. Thus, in hypothesis 2 we proposed the following:

> Low-self-esteem people should be especially attracted to those who they perceive like them and especially hostile to those who they perceive do not.

c. *Finally, we attempted to integrate these two predictions.* We predicted the following:

Low-self-esteem individuals will have more volatile relations with others than will high-self-esteem individuals. Low-self-esteem individuals should especially like those who like them and especially dislike those who do not.

Our research team had put so much work into sketching out our predictions and translating them into a complex theoretical mathematical model that we were convinced that we just had to be right.

We then proceeded to conduct five experiments to test our hypotheses. In the first four we began by measuring subjects' stable self-esteem. Men and women completed one of the self-esteem measures we described earlier: the California Psychological Inventory, the Berger Measure of Self-Esteem, or the Rosenberg Self-Esteem Scale. Then the subjects talked to potential romantic partners on the telephone, corresponded with them, or met them for coffee. After the meeting, the subjects and the potential romantic partners were sometimes given a chance to relate their first impressions of each other. Sometimes the answers were scripted, sometimes not. In the cases where they were scripted, the positiveness of the bogus evaluations was systematically varied. In some conditions O's bogus report was totally favorable (for example, the O might say he or she was "really pretty impressed" with the subject). Sometimes O's impression was ambiguously favorable (for example, O might say that it was difficult to tell anything from "just this." Would S be interesting to talk to? "I'd like to talk with him, I think. Why not?"). Sometimes O's impression was ambiguously negative. Sometimes it was totally negative. Then we asked subjects to (1) assess the potential date's real feelings for them, (2) assess how *they* felt about the potential date, or (3) both.

We then conducted extensive statistical tests to determine whether the results matched our mathematical model. The results were disheartening.

First, we had argued that men and women whose habitual self-esteem was either high or low would differ in their perceptions of how much they were liked. This hypothesis was not supported. In general, although there were hints that self-esteem might have a trace of an effect on how messages were perceived, those effects were too weak to worry about. Contrary to our expectations, the biggest determinant of perceptions of how much one was liked was "reality"—how much the individual actually was liked by the other. Scratch hypothesis 1, then.

Second, we predicted that men and women whose self-esteem was habitually high or low would differ in their reactions to expressions of liking or disliking. This hypothesis also was not supported by the data. Subjects' self-esteem seemed to have no impact on how much they liked or disliked accepting or rejecting others. Once again, contrary to our expectations, the biggest determinant of the subjects' liking for the other person seemed to be the other person's actual liking for them. The more the other actually liked them, the more subjects liked the other in return.

Stable self-esteem, then, seemed to have no impact on how subjects perceived other people's intentions or reacted to them.

Interestingly, in one study we had not studied stable self-esteem but, as in the very first experiment we had conducted, had *manipulated* it. There we did find support for our hypotheses. We interviewed college men at the University of Rochester and at Temple University. They were given the Minnesota Multiphasic Personality Inventory, the Strong Vocational Interest Inventory, the Rorschach, and the Thematic Apperception Test. We collected teacher evaluations and high school and college grades. Some men were given favorable psychological reports; others received negative reports. In a telephone conversation the men had a chance to hear a woman's first impression of them. When men's self-esteem had been momentarily raised, they were more likely to interpret a woman's positive or even ambiguous statements of affection as real interest. When men's self-esteem had been lowered, they were unusually skeptical of a woman's expressions of affection. When men's self-esteem had been momentarily lowered, they were unusually volatile. They liked an affectionate woman more and liked one whose feelings were ambiguous or negative less than they normally would. Men whose self-esteem had been raised were more temperate in their reactions. We were perplexed. People whose self-esteem was habitually high or habitually low did not seem to differ in their perceptions of or reactions to potential dates. However, when the same men's and women's self-esteem was momentarily raised or lowered, they reacted as we expected they would. What was going on? We would not be able to answer this question for several years.

The most damaging blow to our research program was yet to come. In 1975 Senator William Proxmire of Wisconsin discovered that the National Science Foundation had granted Dr. Ellen Berscheid, one of my research partners, $84,000 to further her work on passionate and companionate love. He fired off the following press release:

> I object to this not only because no one—not even the National Science Foundation—can argue that falling in love is a science; not only because I'm sure that even if they spend $84 million or $84 billion they wouldn't get an answer that anyone would believe. I'm also against it because I don't want the answer.
>
> I believe that 200 million other Americans want to leave some things in life a mystery, and right on top of the things we don't want to know is why a man falls in love with a woman and vice versa. . . .
>
> So National Science Foundation—get out of the love racket. Leave that to Elizabeth Barrett Browning and Irving Berlin. Here if anywhere Alexander Pope was right when he observed, "If ignorance is bliss, tis folly to be wise."

An attack on my research project soon followed. Senator Proxmire awarded both of us the critical Golden Fleece Award. Subsequently, he gave the same "award" to dozens of other love and sex researchers, supposedly for "fleecing" the government by conducting research that was "junk." Proxmire's joke could have been worth a chuckle, but he was deadly serious. The press, of course, had a field day. My mother's Roman Catholic bishop, the Right Reverend Richard S. Emrich, denounced our work in a Detroit newspaper. He reminded parishioners that Christ had told us all we need to know about love is in the Holy Bible. We should just follow His orders. The *Chicago Daily News* began a daily series on the debate, inviting readers to call in with their votes. Did readers think our love research was worth $334,000 in tax money or not? (That was the amount the National Science Foundation had granted to various love researchers at various times.) The answer of course was a resounding no. To illustrate the relative standing of Proxmire and Hatfield in the informal poll, they showed two cartoon characters' heads—his and mine—pasted on little cartoon bodies and balanced precariously on a teeter-totter. Each day, as irate readers called or wrote in, Hatfield's standing or sitting (and position on the teeter-totter) sank lower and lower. The final standing: Proxmire eight, Hatfield one. Conclusion: Love should remain a mystery.

Senator Barry Goldwater came to my defense. So did columnist James Reston. In his column in *The New York Times*, he wryly agreed that love will always be a mystery, but then stated, "But if the sociologists and psychologists can get even a suggestion of the answer to our pattern of romantic love, marriage, disillusions, divorce—and the children left behind—it would be the best investment of federal money since Jefferson made the Louisiana purchase."

I tried to explain why the study of love is important. In 1978 I wrote a little book *(A New Look at Love)* to explain why the study of love is important and what social psychologists have learned about passionate and companionate love. In 1979 the book won the American Psychological Association and the American Psychological Foundation's National Media Award for the best book in psychology. In 1993 my husband, Richard L. Rapson, and I updated the voluminous findings on this topic in *Love, Sex, and Intimacy: Their Psychology, Biology and History.*

Today many people assume that the great debate is an enjoyable memory for me. They make that assumption because the "taboo topics" I thought were fascinating have been taken up by a generation of young researchers. Today love and emotion are "hot topics." But I remember those "bad old days" with no pleasure. The battle, though it had to be fought and despite the agreeable outcome, was never fun.

THE ENDING: A PARADIGM SHIFT

In the 1980s social psychologists began to look at the relationship between self-esteem and love in a new way, and suddenly our "confusing" findings fell into place. Let me provide the background for this surprising shift.

Developmental psychologists Mary Ainsworth and John Bowlby studied the process of attachment, separation, and loss in children. Infants normally progress through four developmental phases. During the first few months of life infants smile, gurgle, and snuggle into almost anyone. At about three months of age infants begin to notice that their caretaker (usually the mother) is someone special and begin to take a special interest in her. At about six to nine months infants normally become deeply attached to the mother. They smile, jabber, and stretch out their arms to her; if they are separated, they protest. No one else will do. When they are frightened, anxious, tired, or sick, they cling to the mother for security. After about nine to twelve months toddlers slowly begin to take an interest in a wider circle of people.

Parents and infants differ, of course, in personality and skill. Infants differ in the degree to which they have learned to rely on the attachment figure as a source of security. Mary Ainsworth and her colleagues found that children form three kinds of attachments to their caretakers. Most infants are *securely attached*. They are comfortable with affection *and* independence. Others possess an *anxious/ambivalent* attachment. They tend to be anxious and uncertain in their interactions with their mothers and are difficult to comfort after a brief separation. Some infants develop an *avoidant* attachment. They seem to lack whatever it takes to form close relationships with *anyone* and are unemotional and unresponsive.

Philip Shaver and Cindy Hazan pointed out that romantic love is a form of attachment. Children's early patterns of attachment should be mirrored in the passionate attachments they make in adulthood. Men's and women's attachment styles were measured with a single question: Which of the following best describes your feelings?

> *Secure:* I find it relatively easy to get close to others and am comfortable depending on them and having them depend on me. I don't often worry about being abandoned or about someone getting too close to me.
>
> *Anxious/ambivalent:* I find that others are reluctant to get as close as I would like. I often worry that my partner doesn't really love me or won't want to stay with me. I want to merge completely with another person, and this desire sometimes scares people away.
>
> *Avoidant:* I am somewhat uncomfortable being close to others; I find it difficult to trust them completely, difficult to allow myself to depend on them. I am nervous when anyone gets too close, and often love partners want me to be more intimate than I feel comfortable being. [Hazan and Shaver, 1987, p. 515.]

People were asked to endorse one of the three self-descriptions.

Shortly thereafter Kim Bartholomew and Leonard Horowitz tried to extend the previous model. They too proposed that childhood attachments should serve as prototypes for later attachments. They argued, however, that adults' attachment styles should fall into one of four patterns, depending on the lover's self-image (positive or negative) and image of the beloved (positive or negative): (1) Men and women who have positive self-esteem (the self is worthy of love and support) and a positive image of dates and mates (other people are seen as trustworthy and available) should find it easy to become *securely attached* to others. (2) Those with low self-esteem (they are not worthy of love or support) and a positive regard for others should be *anxious/ambivalent* about falling in love; they should be *preoccupied* or *enmeshed* with those they love. (3) Those who have a negative self-image and a negative image of others (other people are unreliable and rejecting) should be *fearful* of becoming close to others. (4) Those who have a positive self-image and a negative image of others should *avoid* getting involved; they should be *dismissing* or *detached* from others.

This framework helps explain previous researchers' confusion about whether self-esteem and love are linked.

A. *Stable self-esteem and love.* It is not global "self-esteem" that is important but the person's own basic quiet confidence that he or she deserves love and that others are likely to provide it. We must know both how subjects view themselves and whether they think they can trust others. When we look at this form of stable self-esteem (attachment), we see that self-esteem does seem to influence romantic behavior. For example, Carl Hindy and his colleagues tested the notion that children who receive inconsistent love and affection will be "at risk" in their later love relationships. They gave men and women a battery of tests designed to determine the stability of their childhoods. How stormy was their parents' marriage? Did they get a divorce? Then the subjects were asked about their own romantic histories. Did they often fall passionately in love? Or did they go out of their way to avoid entanglements? How jealous were they? When their love affairs fell apart, did they sink into a deep depression? They found that young men and women whose parents had been inconsistent in their love and nurturance were more "addicted" to love *or* more afraid of it than was the case with those who came from more secure backgrounds.

Researchers have amassed considerable evidence to support the notion that the lessons people learn as children may well be reflected in the romantic choices they make as adults.

B. *Momentary changes in self-esteem and love.* If passionate love is rooted in the earth of childhood attachments, it would seem that certain types of people, caught up in certain types of situations, should be especially vulnerable to the languors of passionate love. Anything that makes adults feel as helpless and dependent as they were as children, anything that makes them fear separation and loss, should increase their passionate craving to merge with the other. There is some evidence to support these speculations.

1. *Self-esteem.* As we found in the research we detailed earlier, when men and women's self-esteem is shaken, they suddenly become unusually vulnerable to love.

2. *Dependency and insecurity.* A number of theorists have observed that people who are dependent and insecure or who are caught up in

affairs that promote such feelings are especially vulnerable to passionate love. Ellen Berscheid and her associates have argued that passionate love, dependency, and insecurity are tightly linked. When people are passionately in love, they are painfully aware of how dependent they are on those they love; dependency naturally breeds insecurity. In an ingenious study Berscheid and her coworkers found clear evidence to support these contentions. These authors invited college men and women who were not currently involved with anyone but who wished to be to participate in a study of dating relationships. There was one catch, however. To participate, students had to agree to turn their dating lives over to the experimenter for five weeks. They were warned that some of them (those in the high-exclusiveness condition) would be assigned to date one person for the entire five weeks. Others (those in the low-exclusiveness condition) would date that person and a few others. Still others (those in the zero-exclusiveness condition) would be assigned to date a variety of people.

Finally, some of the participants had a chance to get acquainted with one of their dates. (They had a chance to watch him or her take part in a taped discussion of "dating problems on campus.") Sometimes, of course, they knew that the date was the only person they would be dating; sometimes he or she was just one of many. In the control conditions people knew that they would not be dating anyone participating in the videotaped conversation. After viewing the tape, participants were asked their first impressions of the discussants.

Students liked the discussants far more when they expected to date them later than when they did not. Furthermore, the more dependent students were on potential dates (i.e., those in the high-exclusiveness group compared with those in the low- and zero-exclusiveness groups), the more they liked them.

3. *Anxiety.* Numerous theorists, beginning with Sigmund Freud, have proposed that passionate love is fueled by anxiety and fear. This makes sense; passionate love and anxiety are closely related both neuroanatomically and chemically.

Researchers have demonstrated that anxious individuals are especially prone to seek passionate love relationships. In a series of studies my students and I, for example, found that adolescents who were either momentarily or habitually anxious were especially vulnerable to passionate love. In one study forty-one boys and girls from twelve to fourteen years of age, of white, Chinese, Japanese, Korean, and mixed ancestry, were asked to complete the Child Anxiety Scale, which measures how anxious teenagers are generally. Later, the same children completed the Juvenile Love Scale, a child's version of the Passionate Love Scale. Children who were habitually anxious were most likely to have experienced passionate love. In a second study sixty-four adolescent boys and girls ranging in age from thirteen to sixteen were given the State-Trait

Anxiety Inventory for Children, which measures both state anxiety (how anxious children happen to feel at the moment) and trait anxiety (how anxious children generally are). Once again, adolescents who were either momentarily or habitually anxious were especially likely to have fallen passionately in love.

4. *Neediness.* Social psychologists have found that acute deprivation seems to set the stage for passionate love. With two colleagues, we tested this simple hypothesis: When we are sexually aroused, our minds wander, and pretty soon our dazzling fantasies lend sparkle to drab reality.

First, we contacted a number of college men. We identified ourselves as staff members of the Center for Student Life Studies and explained that the center was studying the dating practices of college students. We told each subject that we wanted to know how he felt about a blind date we had picked out for him. Would he participate? Most of the men agreed. While they sat around waiting to give their first impressions of the date-to-be, they whiled away the time by reading articles lying around the office. This material was carefully selected. One group of men was given fairly boring reading material, articles intended to keep them cool and calm. The second group was given *Playboy*-type material designed to make them very "hot."

Finally, the interviewer appeared with the men's files. He showed them a picture of the date (a fairly attractive blond woman) and told them a little about her. (She seemed to be fairly intelligent, easy to get along with, active, and moderately liberal.) What did they think of her? Well, that depended on what the men had been reading.

We proposed that the unaroused men should be fairly objective. Their fantasy life should be in "low gear," and it should be easy for them to assess the woman fairly accurately. The aroused men should have a harder time of it; the luster of their daydreams should keep rubbing off on their dates-to-be. When men were feeling sexy, they should have a greater tendency to see women as sex objects. Hence, they should tend to exaggerate two of their date's traits: her sexual desirability and her sexual receptivity. We found that we were right. As predicted, the more aroused the men were, the more beautiful they thought their date. In addition, the more aroused the men were, the more likely they were to assume that their dates would be sexually receptive. Unaroused men judged their dates-to-be as fairly nice girls. Aroused men suspected that their dates were probably "amorous," "immoral," "promiscuous," "willing," "unwholesome," and "uninhibited."

We see, then, that men and women may be especially susceptible to falling in love when their security has been threatened, especially if they have discovered in childhood that others can be a source of security.

In the childhood of love research we had few "parents" on whom we could fall back, who could grant us security. We were often groping alone in dark thickets, feeling our way uncertainly into new and unexplored territory. We often got lost or were attacked by suspicious folks onto whose terrain we had trespassed. But with a little help from our friends, we have begun to find our way and things have brightened considerably. And as for Senator Proxmire, we invite him into the light and wish him a life filled with love.

SUGGESTED READINGS

BARTHOLOMEW, K., & HOROWITZ, L. M. (1991). Attachment styles among young adults: A test of a four-category model. *Journal of Personality and Social Psychology, 61,* 226–244.

HATFIELD, E. (1965). The effect of self-esteem on romantic liking. *Journal of Experimental Social Psychology, 1,* 184–197.

———— & RAPSON, R. L. (1993). *Love, sex, and intimacy: Their psychology, biology, and history.* New York: HarperCollins.

HAZAN, C., & SHAVER, P. R. (1990). Romantic love conceptualized as an attachment process. *Journal of Personality and Social Psychology, 52,* 511–524.

JACOBS, L., BERSCHEID, E., & HATFIELD, E. (1971). Self-esteem and attraction. *Journal of Personality and Social Psychology, 17,* 84–91.

SPRECHER, S., & HATFIELD, E. (1982). Self-esteem and romantic attraction: Four experiments. *Recherches de Psychologie Sociale, 4,* 61–81.

*L*EONARD **B**ERKOWITZ *(Ph.D., University of Michigan) was the Vilas Research Professor in Psychology at the University of Wisconsin–Madison before his retirement in May 1993. He had been at Wisconsin since 1955, although he also held visiting appointments at Stanford University, Oxford University, the Center for Advanced Study in the Behavioral Sciences, Cambridge University, and the University of Western Australia as well as the University of Mannheim. The founding editor of the series* Advances in Experimental Social Psychology *from 1964 to 1989, he was also one of the first modern social psychologists to study helpfulness experimentally. However, he is best known for his research and writings on aggression since 1957. This work has been recognized with distinguished scientist awards from the American Psychological Association, the American Psychological Society, and the Society for Experimental Social Psychology. Berkowitz fully intends to continue writing about social psychological matters in his postretirement years.*

9

A Career on Aggression

❖

L ooking back over the four decades or so of my professional life, I can now see some continuities that hadn't been altogether apparent to me before. It is true, as I've told a number of people, that chance played a considerable role in shaping my interests and activities. As I think about my career, though, it's clear to me that my research can also be described in terms of several underlying themes. These matters, both circumstances and research themes, reflect to some degree what was happening in contemporary social psychology since the end of World War II and thus may be of some general interest.

CHANCE AND CIRCUMSTANCE

As a start, I should acknowledge the role of luck. A fortunate combination of events, many beyond my control, took me to the University of Wisconsin in 1955. Then too, after my arrival in Madison, external circumstances led to a teaching assignment that brought me to the laboratory study of aggression. My doctoral dissertation at the University of Michigan had been concerned with group leadership, and I considered myself to be more than anything else a specialist in group dynamics. However, the Wisconsin department's senior social psychologist was in charge of the group behavior offerings, and the chairman asked me to take on an advanced undergraduate class dealing generally with social relationships. Since I did not have much of a scholarly background in this particular domain and had no preferences for one topic or

145

another, it was only an accidental encounter with a paper on aggression that led me to the controversy surrounding the frustration-aggression hypothesis and to the relatively few laboratory experiments on this and related topics. I reviewed the extant research literature in this area for my class.

The passage of years has blurred my memory, and I can no longer recall how interested the students were in the psychological arguments we went over in that course. I do know, though, that I was fascinated by the details of the experiments and especially by the theoretical issues. The controversy appeared to be indicating that even some of humankind's most outrageous actions might be explained by a relatively few theoretical principles. Here was the basic idea that had captivated me from the time I was a high school junior and first discovered psychology: There are regularities underlying human behavior, and scientists can identify the laws governing people's conduct. The seemingly inexplicable, including violence and brutality, could be understood if investigators were careful and employed rational scientific procedures.

But to continue, the University of Wisconsin (or at least the Madison campus) has a clear tradition of encouraging and even requiring its faculty to carry out research. This tradition had a strong influence on me from the beginning. It certainly added to my inclination to publish so that, at the end of the semester, I used my class lecture notes as a basis for a *Psychological Bulletin* article summarizing experimental studies of aggression. This review also led to a proposal to the National Institutes of Mental Health for their support of a program of research on aggression. Fortunately, the proposal was successful on the initial try and started me on two decades of federally funded investigations dealing with situational influences on aggression.

I am sure that external circumstances contributed in some way to this continued federal support and probably also contributed to the fairly widespread attention given to aggression research throughout much of psychology. The 1960s was a time of considerable social unrest in the United States, especially in major metropolitan areas. The rate of violent crimes was increasing rapidly, major riots had torn through a good many cities, and President John Kennedy, Senator Robert Kennedy, and the Reverend Martin Luther King had been assassinated. Increasingly troubled by this turmoil and violence, thoughtful Americans tried to understand why these serious disturbances had arisen and what prompted people to assault others around them. Two national commissions were established to inquire into these matters, and books purporting to explain aggression became popular. Psychologists reflected this concern by becoming more interested in research on aggression than before—or since.

RESEARCH THEMES

Even though my research activities undoubtedly benefited from and even responded to these external circumstances, there are some continuities that run through my investigations and writings. The most obvious one has to do with a focus on situational influences, but my work also shows a continued concern with the application of psychological knowledge. I can also see a persistent theme in the nature of the theories that I have found most congenial in accounting for aggression. Each of these has some relevance for contemporary social psychology.

Focus on the Immediate Situation

Many social psychology programs (including the one at the University of Wisconsin–Madison), as well as the leading journal in our field, profess to combine social and personality psychology. In truth, however, most of the research in contemporary social psychology emphasizes the way in which people are affected by particular aspects of the immediate situation confronting them and devotes relatively little attention to the role of persistent individual differences. Lee Ross and Richard Nisbett reflected this focus on situational influences in their 1991 book *The Person and the Situation: Perspectives of Social Psychology*. Although these writers did consider the part played by personal qualities in shaping social behavior, they argued that one of the main core assumptions in social psychology is "the principle of situationism," the notion "that the social context creates potent forces producing or constraining behavior" (p. 9). This fundamental idea can be seen clearly, they maintained, in Kurt Lewin's important pioneering studies in the 1930s and 1940s. Lewin recognized that "behavior is a function of the person and the situation," but as Ross and Nisbett noted, "it was the power of the immediate social situation that was featured in his empirical work and that of his students" (p. 9).

Having grown up in the culture of modern empirical social psychology, I have definitely followed this tradition. My research says nothing about individual differences in the proclivity to be aggressive (although these differences are very clear in our experiments) and is concerned solely with the way certain details in the immediate situation can affect the strength of a person's attack on an available target. My investigations of the "weapons effect" and the aggression-stimulating effects of observed violence are good examples.

These particular studies were prompted more by my theoretically based focus on situational influences on aggression than by a social problem–oriented concern with the impact of violent movies and firearms on

U.S. society. Guided by the stimulus-response/conditioning perspective I was following in those years, these experiments sought to demonstrate that aggression-associated stimuli in the surrounding situation could elicit aggressive reactions from those whose inhibitions against such behavior were relatively weak at the time.

Guns certainly are linked to aggression in many person's minds, and so I asked a graduate student, Anthony LePage, to carry out an experiment for his master's thesis that would test the possible aggression-enhancing effect of the mere sight of weapons. In this study male university students were first either provoked or treated in a neutral manner by the experimenter's accomplice, who was posing as a fellow subject. Each real subject then had an opportunity to give the "other participant" electric shocks, supposedly as a judgment of that individual's work on an assigned task. Since the central question was whether the mere presence of a weapon would increase aggression, some of the men saw a revolver and a shotgun lying on the table near the shock-delivering apparatus, while others saw two badminton racquets and a shuttlecock. (In both cases the experimenter "explained" those objects by saying they must have been left in the room by another researcher.)

The results were very much as I had expected. The provoked men retaliated much more severely when the rifle and revolver were nearby than when no weapons were present. The guns apparently stimulated those men to attack their insulter more strongly than they otherwise would have done.

This finding attracted a fair amount of attention when it was published in 1967, partly because of its obvious social relevance but also because of its demonstration that people's actions toward others are sometimes influenced in a relatively thoughtless and automatic manner by particular details in the immediate situation. Indeed, a number of psychologists objected to this clear implication and rushed to advance other interpretations of the Berkowitz and LePage results. Several reported that they had failed to replicate our original findings, but more generally, critics maintained that the subjects in the experiment had only complied with the researchers' "demands." Seeing the guns lying on the table and disregarding the experimenter's explanation as to why they were there (i.e., that the weapons had inadvertently been left in the room by another investigator), the participants supposedly had realized that the researchers expected them to be aggressive and then had acted to fulfill that expectation.

This is not the place to go into the argument surrounding the weapons effect, but some summary comments are warranted. First of all, even though there have been several reported failures to obtain this effect, there have been quite a few successful replications, and in other countries besides the United States, including Belgium, Canada, Croatia, Italy, and Sweden. Second, some of these investigations (especially a number conducted by a former student of mine, Charles Turner) have shown that the results are not due to the subjects' compliance with the experimenters' demands and arise even when the research participants do not realize they are being studied. Finally, it is also worth noting that the mere presence of weapons sometimes stimulates even nonangered people to increased aggression. If we are ready to be assaultive for one reason or another and are sufficiently unrestrained at the time, there is a good chance that the sight of a gun will make us more aggressive than we otherwise would have been, even though we have not just been provoked.

My experiments on the effects of watching violence and the scores of other studies on this topic carried out by other investigators basically point in the same direction. Again, we have reasonable evidence of the power of the immediate situation. In this case, the depiction of violence on a movie and/or television screen tends to heighten the likelihood that people in the audience will act aggressively. Furthermore, we also now know that this influence is not confined to young children, as many laypersons believe, but can come about in adults as well. Here too, then, the sight of something having a clearly aggressive meaning, whether a weapon or a fight shown on a TV screen, apparently can induce a stronger aggressive reaction than otherwise would have been displayed from persons who are suitably unrestrained at the time.

Although a few social psychologists may question this general conclusion, my guess is that the major argument among those who have looked closely into the available research has to do with the magnitude of the impact. Some reviewers hold that portrayals of violence in the mass media have only a trivial influence. However, Professor Wendy Wood and her associates at Texas A & M University have offered a different view. On the basis of their statistical analysis of twenty-eight different experiments in which subjects were able to assault the available target freely and naturally (instead of through supposedly artificial procedures such as the administration of electric shocks), these investigators concluded that the average effect of exposure to violent scenes on unconstrained aggression is in the "small to moderate range" typical of social psychological predictors.

This question of the size of the movie effect obviously has to do partly with the proportion of audience members who exhibit increased aggression and partly with the variety of situations under which this heightened violence comes about. With my interest in situational influences, I have been more concerned with the latter than with the former, and in a number of studies I have sought to identify some of the conditions that can promote or reduce the probability of aggressive reactions to violent movies. Let me summarize a number of these findings.

A series of studies carried out by Russell Geen and myself proposed that the nature of the target available for aggression affects the likelihood that the violent movie will lead to an open assault. We thought that the aggressive tendencies activated by the violent scene would be intensified if, soon after seeing the movie, the viewers encountered someone who reminded them of the victim in the witnessed aggression. The possible target would be connected with an instance of successful (i.e., rewarded) aggression and, because of this association, might draw a relatively strong attack.

The experiments in this series generally supported this possibility. For example, the male university students in a study Geen and I published in 1966 first were introduced to the experimenter's accomplice, who was posing as a fellow subject, and then were deliberately provoked by that person. Following our standard procedure in this line of research, each subject then saw a brief movie scene of a prizefight or of an equally exciting track race and finally had an opportunity to punish the "other subject" (the accomplice) with electric shocks, supposedly as his judgment of the quality of that person's work on an assigned task.

The important feature of this experiment had to do with the name that had been given to the accomplice at the start of the session. For some of the subjects, he was called Bob Kelly, for others he was introduced as Bob Dunne, and for the remaining people he was said to be Bob Riley. Since the loser in the prizefight scene was named Kelly, while the victor's name was Dunne, the first of these introductions essentially connected the insulting "other student" with the *victim* of the observed aggression, whereas he was associated with the *successful aggressor* in the second condition and had *no name-mediated linkage* with the prizefight scene in the third condition.

Consistent with our expectations, both the nature of the movie and the anger-provoking target's name influenced the amount of punishment given to him. He received more shocks after the prizefight scene than after the nonviolent track race, but most important, he was attacked most severely when he had the same name as the fight loser rather than either of the other names. The tormentor drew the strongest aggression when he was associated with the victim of the observed aggression.

There is another point here that might be of interest. This emphasis on the role of the immediate situation suggests that the aggression-enhancing effect of witnessed aggression may well subside fairly soon as the observers move into other settings. Conversely, even if the violent scene's influence does diminish with time, this influence can be reactivated later if the movie viewers see something that reminds them of the observed aggression. Yet another experiment, conducted outside my laboratory by Dr. Wendy Josephson in Winnipeg, Canada, obtained findings that show just this. When young schoolboys played a game of floor hockey soon after watching a short TV program that was either violent or nonviolent in nature, the boys exhibiting the most aggression in the game were those who (1) had seen the aggressive program and (2) after the movie and immediately before the game had encountered an object (a walkie-talkie radio) that had been featured prominently in the violent scene. Even though this object was neutral in nature, because of its association with the aggressive incident, the sight of it evidently awakened the aggressive inclinations that had been generated by the witnessed aggression.

Other situational influences depend more on viewer's thought processes. As a good example of this, my students and I, along with other investigators, have shown that audience members are more greatly affected by the witnessed aggression when they think they are seeing a real rather than a staged fight. Consider the experiment that Joe Alioto and I reported in 1973. The previously angered subjects in this study had an opportunity to shock their tormentor after they watched a brief World War II movie scene portraying U.S. Marines fighting the Japanese. Half the men had been informed the movie was a documentary filmed during actual combat, whereas the others were told the scene was fictional and had been taken from a Hollywood war movie. When they then punished their antagonist, the men who had seen the supposedly realistic film were more punitive than were their counterparts who had been shown the supposedly fictional reenactment. It could be that the latter people, in thinking that the fighting was only make-believe, had psychologically stepped back from the movie so that they were somewhat less engrossed by it, and consequently it had less of an impact on them.

Another condition that might affect viewers' response to scenes of violence involves their judgment of the propriety of the observed aggression: Is the witnessed attack justified and proper or morally wrong? Audience members conceivably can be "turned off" by any violence they see that they regard as being improper in some way. On the other side, the sight of aggression the viewers believe is justified may color their interpretation of whatever aggressive inclinations they themselves possess at the time. It appears that the observers say to themselves that it is proper for them to attack their tormentor just as it was legitimate for the movie aggressor to punish those who had mistreated him.

Several studies from my Wisconsin laboratory looked into this possibility and obtained very similar results. After the male subjects were first deliberately provoked or treated in a neutral manner by the experimenter's accomplice, they watched a short film showing people fighting. A brief summary of the movie given to the subjects beforehand led half of them to regard the fight loser as a bad person who presumably deserved the beating he received in the film, whereas this movie character was described more favorably in the remaining cases and thus supposedly did not deserve to be beaten. Then, immediately after the movie, when all the subjects had an opportunity to punish the accomplice, the angered men attacked him more severely after seeing the "bad guy" receive his "just deserts" than after watching the presumably unwarranted aggression.

Of course, there can be substantial individual differences in suscepti-bility to these and other situational influences. Some people are espe-cially apt to have aggressive ideas when they encounter emotionally ambiguous stimuli and/or are quick to attribute malevolent intent to another person's ambiguous behavior and/or are relatively deficient in their ability to restrain themselves when they have an opportunity to obtain a desired but socially disapproved goal. Still, the immediate set-ting occasionally has such a powerful impact that it can affect what many people do. Under the right circumstances, seemingly innocuous features of the surrounding situation may even lead quite a few persons to be more aggressive than they otherwise would be.

Application of Psychological Principles

Research into the possible aggression-enhancing effects of weapons and/or scenes of violence certainly is relevant to people's concern about the level of violence in society. Since the findings have policy implica-tions, maybe I should be clear about the lessons I have drawn. In my view, it is best to think of guns and violent TV programs and movies as public health risk factors somewhat akin to cigarettes and alcohol. Not every smoker will develop lung cancer or heart disease, and not all heavy drinkers die from cirrhosis of the liver. These disorders appar-ently do not develop unless other conditions are present that heighten the person's susceptibility to the dangerous substance. All in all, though, we can say that high levels of smoking and/or drinking increase the probability of developing these ailments. Similarly, the sight of guns and/or of other people fighting does not always promote aggression. In the "real world" these stimuli do not lead to open assaults on a target unless other aggression-facilitating conditions are present. But again, if we consider society at large, it is reasonable to suggest that frequent exposure to weapons and/or aggressive movies heightens the chance of violence occurring.

I have made this argument on a number of occasions and have tried to spell out the practical implications of aggression research results in other ways as well. Still, I must confess that I was somewhat surprised several years back when I was given an award as a "distinguished scien-tist in the application of psychology" by the American Psychological Association and then received a similar award from the American Psy-chological Society. I thought of myself only as a social psychologist, not as an applied psychologist. My quick, not well-considered, and stereo-typed conception of applied psychologists was that they dealt primarily with practical matters such as personnel selection, employee productiv-ity, and marketing and did not have much interest in the development of broad, abstract, theoretical analyses of human behavior. By contrast, I saw myself as being concerned more with a general theory of human aggression.

However, it did not take long for me to recognize the appropriateness of the label given to my work. I had truly been interested in applying psychological knowledge to social concerns and practical matters since my undergraduate years. After all, I began my graduate training at the University of Michigan in January 1948 as an aspirant for a career in industrial psychology before switching to social psychology. Furthermore, when I was at Michigan, I was employed as a research assistant on a project investigating decision-making conferences in government, business, and industry. Then, after obtaining a Ph.D. degree in June 1951 (with a thesis on conference leadership), I accepted a job in San Antonio, Texas, with the U.S. Air Force's Human Resources Research Center that was focused on the morale of bomber crews called to fight in the Korean war. What could be more applied than all this?

Yet those experiences were not altogether satisfying. Neither of the two projects came anywhere near fulfilling the hopes and expectations of their directors and sponsors, largely, I have always believed, because they were not guided by theoretical analyses. Both took a raw empirical approach, intending to collect "facts" that supposedly would then dictate whatever theorizing was necessary. But they also floundered around aimlessly, not knowing which "facts" were important. The conference research project and the Crew Research Laboratory both collected lots of data without ever organizing the information in a meaningful manner and as a consequence never developed a good conception of what constituted effective group performance, much less what led to successful group activities.

Both failures, it seems to me, illustrate the wisdom of Kurt Lewin's widely quoted observation that there is nothing as practical as a good theory. Lewin had sought to develop a comprehensive psychological theory throughout much of his highly productive scientific life, but he was also extremely sensitive to social problems and believed that psychology can help overcome them. He was convinced, however, that the "scientific level of understanding" required by government, business, and education can best be achieved through theoretically oriented research. There is little doubt in my mind that the two research projects with which I was associated would have benefited greatly from a guiding theory.

Frustrated by the seeming aimlessness of these two endeavors and probably also influenced to some extent by applied psychology's relatively low status in academic circles, I did not regard myself as having an applied focus after I joined the Wisconsin faculty, even though many of my studies and writings in the 1960s and 1970s actually addressed questions with practical social implications. I also failed to recognize the other side of Lewin's message. It is possible to conduct theoretically meaningful research while investigating problems of everyday life in the world of business, industry, local communities, and larger government. Just as theory can inform practice, applied investigators can contribute significantly to theory development in the behavioral sciences. Perhaps the major difference between, say, academic social psychologists interested in persuasion and attitude change and their psychological counterparts working for market research and advertising firms is not really the subject matter but the greater freedom the former usually have to investigate the conceptual questions raised by their earlier research findings.

At any rate, the research my experimental social psychological colleagues and I have conducted in the area of aggression provides one example of how studies with great social relevance can also contribute to other domains of psychological knowledge. Consider the recent investigations that I and others, especially Craig Anderson at the University of Missouri, have carried out on the aggression-instigating effects of decidedly unpleasant experiences. In my view, the results we have obtained in these studies have important implications for theories of emotions generally and for the appraisal-attributional formulations of emotion in particular.

As is well known, these latter analyses hold that people's interpretations of exciting events determine the feelings they will experience and the emotional reactions they will display in response to those occurrences. And so, according to these conceptions, we presumably will feel angry and exhibit emotional aggression only to the degree that we think some event is personally significant for us and, in addition, attribute the occurrence to someone's deliberate and improper mistreatment of us. Contrary to this line of analysis, however, there is now considerable evidence that anger and emotional aggression can arise without the appraisals and attributions posited by many contemporary emotion theorists. Many persons are apt to become angry, have hostile thoughts, and even assault suitable targets simply as a result of not feeling well for one reason or another.

This is not the place to review all the research supporting this contention. However, some findings obtained in studies of serious social violence are particularly noteworthy. Several social psychologists, including Craig Anderson and Robert Baron, have shown that unusually hot weather had apparently contributed to the urban disorders of the 1960s and that sudden drops in temperature had helped "cool" those riots literally as well as figuratively. Extending these observations even further, Anderson's careful statistical analysis of two years of crime data from Houston, Texas, demonstrated that the frequency of violent—but not nonaggressive—crimes was positively correlated with high temperatures. The numbers of highly violent crimes were greatest on the hottest days. Laboratory experiments have corroborated this temperature-aggression relationship. In studies by Anderson, Baron, and others, many subjects exposed to unpleasantly high temperatures reported angry feelings, revealed hostile ideas, expressed hostile evaluations of others, and even punished fellow students relatively harshly. This occurred, moreover, even when the hostile-aggressive reactions could not possibly lessen the subjects' discomfort. My students and I have obtained comparable findings in experiments in which subjects were asked to immerse a hand in painfully cold water.

It seems to me, as I have argued elsewhere, that any truly comprehensive theory of anger and emotional aggression must account for these observations as well as the more "commonsensical" reports of anger being generated by perceived intentional misdeeds. In neglecting these and other findings obtained in investigations of serious social problems and in more restrained laboratory settings, contemporary appraisal-attribution theories of emotion are at best incomplete in their accounts of why people become angry and assault others in a burst of rage. I'll later summarize my recent theorizing about the effects of unpleasant experiences.

Theoretical Preferences

The last thread running through my research and thinking that I will discuss here involves my theoretical predilections: Partly because I entered psychology at a time when stimulus-response theorizing was dominant but also because of my research interests, I have long been sympathetic to the perspective followed by general behavior theorists such as Kenneth Spence and Neal Miller. I am not a Skinnerian and believe that the cognitive processes through which information is received, transformed, stored, and retrieved play a predominant role in many different aspects of human conduct. Yet I also think that there are important psychological phenomena, particularly in the area of emotions, that are governed mostly by rather primitive associationistic processes.

This general behavior theory–associationistic approach appeals to me partly because of its parsimony. It is scientifically advantageous, I believe, to explain phenomena of interest as simply and with as few theoretical concepts as possible. We would do well not to introduce any more elaborate terms and propositions than are necessary to account for our observations. Thus, in trying to account for, say, a sudden increase in violent crimes during times of considerable social stress, in my view it is preferable to employ as few basic ideas as possible instead of postulating complex motives and thoughts for which no evidence is available. In this vein, I believe it is scientifically undesirable to insist that appraisals and attributions or other such complex cognitions must be involved in all emotional experiences when simpler concepts and propositions can do just as well.

For all the reasons just indicated, I was drawn to the frustration-aggression hypothesis when I first encountered this conception at the time I joined the Wisconsin faculty. It isn't too extreme to say that I found the theorizing aesthetically pleasing (much as, years later, in 1957, I had the same aesthetic sensation when I first read Leon Festinger's monograph introducing his theory of cognitive dissonance). John Dollard, Leonard Doob, Neal Miller, and their associates, all at Yale University, had advanced a line of thought that was for me attractive in both its sweep and its simplicity. In clear and precise terms, they offered a very small number of principles to account for the apparently complex aggressive aftereffects of an unanticipated barrier to goal attainment. I thought they had gone much too far in contending that every aggressive action can ultimately be traced back to a prior frustration. However, it seemed altogether likely to me that people who were unexpectedly blocked from reaching a goal they had been prepared to attain would become instigated to attack a suitable target, especially (but not only) the perceived source of the frustration. I also believed that Neal Miller's 1948 internal conflict model, which extended this reasoning, was a real tour de force. Miller showed that the psychodynamic notion of hostility displacement could be understood relatively simply using the associationistic concept of stimulus generalization and assumptions about the relative slopes of the tendencies to commit aggression and to inhibit that urge. Suppose we have been insulted by John and then, while we're still angry, see a number of other persons. Briefly put, Miller's model holds that in many situations the strength of our inclination to attack any of these others will be a positive function of how closely associated these individuals are with John, the provocateur, in our minds. However, according to the theory, if we are also afraid of being punished by John if we do try to hurt him, this fear will not only dampen our urge to attack John but also will interfere with our inclination to attack any of the others in proportion to their psychological closeness to John. Miller then suggested that the slope of the latter fear-based tendency to avoid attacking (the so-called avoidance tendency) is often—but not always—steeper than the former inclination to carry out the action (the approach tendency). In other words, the avoidance tendency presumably will not generalize as far as the approach tendency. We may be very reluctant to hit Bill, who is closely connected with John in our minds, but will be somewhat more willing to lash out at Joe, who has a much weaker association with John in our thoughts. All in all, according to Miller's analysis, people with a moderate level of connection to the provocateur are apt to draw a stronger open assault than are people with either a greater or a weaker linkage to the perceived tormentor.

It should be apparent from all I've said here that this approach is, for me at least, particularly appropriate in the analysis of many aggressive reactions. I argue, in this chapter and in quite a few of my other writings, that many instances of impulsive aggression are partially affected by situational stimuli that are associated with aggression. All too frequently angered people strike out at someone more or less thoughtlessly, inflicting more injury than they consciously intend, often because they have encountered an external stimulus, such as a gun or even another person, that is linked to aggression in their minds. The association activates emotional reactions, intensifying the aggressive motor acts.

Having expressed all this approval for the general behavior theory–associationistic ideas of years past, I should hasten to add that I also believe that much of the original theorizing advanced by the associationists of the 1930s and 1940s should be altered considerably. Thus, some time ago I offered an important modification of the Yale group's frustration-aggression hypothesis. In recognition of the fact that aggressive reactions do not always arise when people are prevented from reaching their goals, this modification suggests that it is the displeasure generated by the barrier to goal attainment, not the frustration in itself, that creates the instigation to aggression. The factors that affect the strength of the urge to assault someone arising from a frustration—such as the unexpectedness and/or seeming impropriety of the thwarting— have this influence because they determine how unpleasant the experience is.

This revision essentially ties together the evidence for the connection between frustrations and aggression with the evidence cited earlier indicating that decidedly unpleasant conditions can activate angry feelings, hostile thoughts, and aggressive inclinations. The frustration-aggression relationship, I am saying, is only a special case of the more general relationship between strong negative affect and the anger-aggression syndrome.

Most of my research efforts in the past several years have been devoted to the investigation of this relationship. Although many complex factors can intervene to determine whether people who are feeling bad will become angry and aggressive, I can here give you a very brief summary of some of my ideas.

Basically, the model maintains that strong negative affect tends to activate, among other things, both fight and flight response syndromes. This means that persons having very unpleasant feelings are initially disposed to both (1) feel angry and be aggressively inclined *and* (2) be afraid and want to escape or avoid the unpleasant situation. Clearly, it is by no means certain that those experiencing negative affect will be angry and assaultive. In many instances the afflicted people would rather flee than fight, perhaps because of genetic inheritance and/or prior learning about how to cope with aversive conditions, and/or they may think there is a good chance of being punished for aggression. Nonetheless, perhaps because there are "built-in" associative connections linking negative feelings to the various components of the anger-aggression syndrome, displeasure raises the probability that many people will have at least rudimentary anger-aggressive reactions.

This formulation does not exclude the role of cognitive processes. Indeed, along with the traditional emotion theorists mentioned above, I recognize that appraisals and attributions can affect what people do and feel after they are aroused. I propose, however, that these complex thoughts and interpretations are not inevitable and often go into operation only after the initial, primitive associative reactions start. Once this higher-order processing gets under way, though, the afflicted persons may then alter, suppress, or intensify their rudimentary emotional experience, depending on how they appraise the personal significance of the event and what they think is the cause of the occurrence. Cognition can also regulate the intensity of whatever aggressive inclinations arise. Suffering individuals may restrain their aggressive impulses if they are aware of their bad feelings and think that those feelings and/or their aggressive urges are not appropriate under the given circumstances. Still, with all these provisos, I think there is some chance that unpleasant feelings will activate the anger-aggression syndrome often enough that society and psychologists alike should be aware of the possibility.

I find this theorizing fascinating, especially in light of all the evidence that seems consistent with my argument. The search for further support will be intriguing, even exciting, and I believe the endeavor will have considerable practical as well as theoretical significance.

SUGGESTED READINGS

BERKOWITZ, L. (1993a). *Aggression: Its causes, consequences, and control*. New York: McGraw-Hill.

———— (1993b). Toward a general theory of anger and emotional aggression: Implications of the cognitive-neoassociationistic perspective for the analysis of anger and other emotions. In R. S. Wyer, Jr., and T. K. Srull (Eds.), *Advances in social cognition*. Vol. 6: *Perspectives on anger and emotion*. Hillsdale, NJ: Erlbaum.

ROSS, L., & NISBETT, R. E. (1991). *The person and the situation: Perspectives of social psychology*. New York: McGraw-Hill.

PATRICIA G. DEVINE *(Ph.D., Ohio State University) is currently Associate Professor of Psychology at the University of Wisconsin–Madison. She has done research on the factors that affect eyewitnesses' lineup decisions, the processes involved in person impression formation, and the nature of prejudice and intergroup tension. She coedited the book (with David Hamilton and Thomas Ostrom)* Social Cognition: Impact on Social Psychology *and is currently writing a book (with James Jones) on prejudice and intergroup relations. Although too often found in her office, she enjoys a variety of outdoor summer and winter activities and loves music.*

10

Getting Hooked on Research in Social Psychology: Examples from Eyewitness Identification and Prejudice

❖

*I*grew up, intellectually that is, in social psychology. I was one of those students who had the good fortune to get involved in research very early in my academic career. I would like to think that it was good foresight on my part that led me to get involved in research, but I have to confess that my good fortune was largely due to being in the right place at the right time. The right place was a course taught by Roy Malpass at the State University of New York–Plattsburgh. The right time was when I was a somewhat confused, extremely bored, but highly motivated freshman. What I could not have foreseen at that time was how important my decision to get involved in research was. It has affected virtually every aspect of my life.

161

GETTING HOOKED

When I first got involved in research, I had no idea what to expect. What I did know was that despite the fact that I was doing well in my classes, I was bored. I already knew how to "do school." That is, I knew how to read and study my text and class notes to prepare for exams, and I knew how to write papers for classes. This isn't to say that my classes weren't good or challenging, but simply that I wanted something more. When Roy Malpass first asked me if I wanted to get involved in research, I was hesitant. However, I figured that I might as well give it a try and see what it was all about.

The first research project I worked on was designed to determine which factors affect an eyewitness's decision either to identify someone from a lineup as the guilty party or to decide that the person who committed the crime is absent from the lineup. The problem was clearly important. We were interested in how the instructions given to eyewitnesses affect whether they will identify someone in the lineup as the criminal. We looked at two different types of instructions. The first we labeled "biased instructions" because the way they were phrased presumed that the guilty person was actually in the lineup. These instructions told the eyewitness to look over the lineup and choose the person who committed the crime. Think about real lineup situations. Is it the case that the guilty person is always present in lineups? Surely not. The lineup procedure is part of the investigation to *determine* if the person the police *suspect* is guilty is indeed the criminal. If the police already knew that the person they suspected was guilty, there would be no need for a lineup. How would such biased lineup instructions, which we found were used in many real police lineup procedures, affect a witness's willingness to make an identification?

To find out, we compared biased instructions with "unbiased instructions." The unbiased instructions allowed for the possibility that the guilty person was not in the lineup. Specifically, they told the eyewitness to look over the lineup and decide whether the person who committed the crime was there. If he was in the lineup, the eyewitness was to identify him; if he was not, the eyewitness was instructed not to identify anyone. Would the unbiased instructions be fairer? How could one know?

We decided that it was extremely important to see how the instructions affected eyewitnesses' decisions under two different conditions: when the criminal was present in the lineup and when he was absent from the lineup. At the time we did this study (the late 1970s), most of the research had examined only situations in which the criminal was present in the lineup. This type of situation did not enable the researchers to see what would happen in perhaps the most important situation: when the criminal was absent from the lineup. The last thing the criminal justice system wants to do is prosecute and convict innocent people. Thus, it is crucial to examine how eyewitnesses respond to lineups in which the criminal is absent.

Therefore, we set up an experimental situation that provided an opportunity to examine how eyewitnesses behave in all possible combinations of the two variables of interest: instruction type (biased versus unbiased) and lineup type (criminal present versus criminal absent). While deciding that these were the variables we wanted to examine, we had designed an experiment. I thought that this was a really interesting way to go about learning the answers to the questions we had. We could set up the conditions of interest and then see how eyewitnesses behaved in those conditions. This was only part of the story, however. We needed a crime. We wanted a crime that many people could witness simultaneously and one that would appear realistic to our prospective eyewitnesses. This was a really exciting part of the research.

We decided on a vandalism that would occur in the course of a large lecture demonstration. To pull this off, we needed the cooperation of many people: Henry Morlock of SUNY–Plattsburgh, who gave the lecture demonstration; a young man, Tim Varano, who was our vandal; a young woman who would jump up and volunteer to call the police; police officers who would come to take statements at the scene of the crime; several young men to be lineup participants; and several other student volunteers who helped coordinate the activities during the lecture demonstration and vandalism. Having cast the principals in our drama, we needed a compelling script—the crime had to be believable. The vandal would destroy some expensive electronic equipment after an argument with the professor. We had to have a realistic escape route for the vandal after the crime, lest he be detained by an energetic eyewitness. We had to anticipate every way that things could go wrong and try to plan options for each possibility. Lines had to be learned. Places had to be marked on the stage. We had to rehearse and rehearse and rehearse. Every detail had to be planned, timed, and executed perfectly or the whole experiment would be ruined and we would not be able to find the answers to our questions.

Scene 1: The Crime

The script went as follows. About 350 students filed into a large lecture hall for a demonstration on biofeedback techniques that was to begin at 7 P.M. When the lecture started, the professor asked for some volunteers who would agree to be hooked up to biofeedback apparatus and participate in the demonstration. Three students volunteered. All were accomplices of the experimenters, called confederates. One of the confederates was the vandal. During the demonstration, a young woman was hooked up to the biofeedback apparatus and a television monitor displayed her image so that students sitting in the back of the room could see where electrodes were placed and follow the demonstration. The other confederates waited for their turn to be hooked up to the apparatus. While the professor explained the principles of biofeedback, the television image became fuzzy. Before the professor noticed and could attempt to bring the image back, the vandal began to play with dials on the monitor. When the professor noticed, he quickly admonished the young man and began to work on the monitor. After successfully regaining the television image, the professor sternly reprimanded the young man and asked him to refrain from touching the expensive, well-calibrated equipment. The vandal retorted that he was just trying to help, and that elicited another stern reproach from the professor. Their discussion escalated into a rather heated argument, obscenities were yelled, and the vandal pulled the rack with the television monitor and electronic apparatus to the floor, shattering the monitor and damaging the apparatus. The vandal quickly ran out a front door of the lecture room (and back to the safety of our research lab). An audible gasp was heard from the audience, followed by a moment of shocked silence and then a buzz of discussion: "I can't believe that happened." "Who was that guy?" "Did you get a good look?" "What a jerk!" "I'll call the police."

Scene 2: The Aftermath

It worked! The crime and the escape were a success. The students believed that the crime was real. But the drama was not over yet. The professor looked visibly upset and justifiably concerned over his destroyed equipment. Some fifteen to twenty minutes later the police arrived and distributed forms that asked for descriptions of the person who destroyed the equipment. After the police collected the information sheets, the researchers entered stage left. At this point the students were told that the crime had been staged for the purpose of doing research. They were told why we had staged the crime and were invited to come to our research lab and view a lineup during one of the following three nights. Many were shocked because it had seemed so real. How weird, others thought. Why would someone go to all the trouble to stage a crime and set up lineups? When the curtain closed on scene 2, we were exhausted. We had invested so much hard work and so much emotional energy. I had never worked so hard in my entire life. And still we did not have answers to our questions about the effects of instruction type and lineup type on how eyewitnesses respond. Now the crime was over, and the data collection would begin the following evening.

Scene 3: The Lineups

During the next three nights between 7 and 10 P.M., students who had witnessed the criminal event showed up at our research lab to view a lineup. As with the crime and the aftermath, every detail had to be planned perfectly. It was very important that every eyewitness be treated exactly the same way. The only thing that differed for the eyewitnesses was whether they received biased versus unbiased instructions and whether they viewed a vandal-present versus a vandal-absent lineup. Everything else was identical (the way the eyewitness was greeted, the demeanor of the experimenter, the lighting condition for the lineup, the behavior of the lineup participants). To the extent that anything except our key variables differed across the eyewitnesses, we would not be able to determine the effect of these variables (instruction type and lineup type). The goal of an experiment is to isolate and vary only the key variables of interest. If this part of the experiment was not executed with the same precision as the early phases of the research, the whole experiment could be ruined. Thus, our script for the lineup was executed over and over as the eyewitnesses showed up to view the lineup.

After randomly assigning each eyewitness to one of the four experimental conditions, the experimenter followed a carefully planned script in which he gave the eyewitnesses the appropriate instruction and escorted them to a one-way glass through which they could observe the appropriate lineup. For each eyewitness, we recorded whether he or she made an identification (chose one of the lineup participants as the vandal) and whether his or her decision was correct or incorrect.

Epilogue: The Results

When all was said and done, 100 student-eyewitnesses had come to the lab to view the lineup. Now we could get down to finding the answers to our questions. Did the type of instruction given to eyewitnesses affect the rate of making an identification? Did the presence or absence of the offender make any difference? The answer to both questions is yes. But perhaps most important, we can see the most dramatic effects of these variables when they are considered together. When the vandal was present in the lineup, the type of instruction given to eyewitnesses didn't make much of a difference in choosing rates (100 percent for the biased and 83 percent for the unbiased). Keep in mind at this point, however, that we also have to consider the types of mistakes people make. I'll return to this when we examine the error data. Let's look at what happened when the vandal was absent from the lineup. When the instructions were biased, 78 percent of the eyewitnesses selected someone as the vandal; when the instructions were unbiased, only 33 percent of the eyewitnesses made an identification.

This is a huge difference, particularly when we consider that any choice made when the vandal is absent is an *incorrect* identification of an innocent person. Eyewitnesses are much less likely to incriminate an innocent person in vandal-absent lineups when the instructions are unbiased compared to when they are biased and imply that a guilty person is present. When the vandal was present in the lineup, people were pretty good at identifying him, but eyewitnesses in this experiment made different types of identification errors depending on which instructions they were given. The biased-instruction, vandal-present condition had a 25 percent error rate—all misidentifications of an innocent person. In contrast, the 17 percent errors in the unbiased-instructions, vandal-present condition were all failures to identify anybody (i.e., the 83 percent who made an identification chose the guilty person). We believe that the latter error (missing the guilty person when he is present in the lineup), although a serious error, is less serious than wrongfully incriminating an innocent person.

Thus, we had answers to our questions about the effects of instruction type and lineup type on choosing and error rates among eyewitnesses. Unbiased lineup instructions may reduce the overall number of errors that are made and may lead to less serious errors compared with biased lineup instructions. We were very excited by these data and thought that they might be useful in the criminal justice system. We were eager to communicate our findings to those who could put them to the best use. However, it occurred to us, as I'm sure it has occurred to you, that as nice as this experiment was, there was one important limitation: The eyewitnesses knew they were participating in an experiment. Maybe laboratory subject eyewitnesses behave differently from *real* eyewitnesses to a criminal event. After all, there's more at stake for real eyewitnesses. Their decisions matter and can affect the course of a criminal investigation and the fate of another person. Also, identifying a suspect commits eyewitnesses to possibly testifying at a trial. These are only some of the possible consequences that can affect the decision of a real eyewitness. The important point is that the first experiment provided us with some useful information, but perhaps more important, it encouraged us to ask new questions which we would explore in subsequent studies.

Participating in that first study was a significant event. I was hooked. We had labored to create an experimental situation that would enable us to test our ideas, and once we had followed it through, we found that all the effort had been worthwhile. We had not only answers but also new questions. This research had everything. It dealt with important issues, was interesting, required creative problem solving, and had the potential for application. Most interesting and somewhat surprising to me, it was fun. In fact, I've been asking questions and designing experiments ever since. Getting involved in research helped solidify my decision to major in psychology and helped me decide that I wanted to pursue a Ph.D. in social psychology and continue to do research throughout my career. I had no idea when I was an undergraduate that I would end up doing research on prejudice and intergroup tension. Although one obviously needs to work on the problems he or she finds most fascinating, it was not a topic area that drew me to research but rather the *process* of doing research.

*T*HE PROCESS OF DOING RESEARCH

Throughout my undergraduate and graduate school days I had the good fortune to study with a number of outstanding social psychologists, including Roy Malpass, Tom Ostrom, Tony Greenwald, and Gifford Weary. Each of these people contributed greatly to the way I think about doing research. When I was a graduate student at Ohio State University, Tony Greenwald shared with us a general framework for thinking about research. Over the years I have found this framework invaluable, and I would like to share it with you. Tony suggested that one could think about research in terms of the "three worlds of science" and the "four phases of scientific activity." The three worlds are the *real world* (the everyday world people live in), the *theory world* (the world of ideas and hypotheses), and the *research world* (the world where researchers conduct research). As can be seen in Figure 10.1, the four phases of scientific activity bridge the three worlds of science. I will take you through the three worlds of science and four phases of scientific activity in terms of the research on eyewitness identification discussed earlier in this chapter, but the ideas are relevant to any research area. This framework simply provides a broad overview of what's involved in doing research, but in my opinion, it is the process of going through these phases that is exciting, rewarding, and fun.

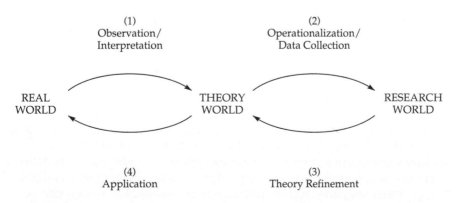

FIGURE 10.1
A framework for the process of doing research (cf. Anthony Greenwald). The three worlds of science and the four phases of scientific activity.

Phase 1: Moving from General Questions to Specific Hypotheses

Many research ideas come from observations people make of things that happen in the real world. For example, our concern over the nature of lineup instructions given to eyewitnesses and our studies of the effect of varying the presence of the criminal in a lineup came from looking at how lineups are conducted in the real world. We didn't stop with our observations and interpretations of the real-world events, however. We also looked to see what the research literature had to contribute to our thinking about these issues. This is phase 1 of scientific activity. The activities of phase 1 serve to connect the real world with the theory world. In the theory world, we formulate our best guesses or hypotheses about the relationships between variables. In our specific example, we were interested in the relationship between the variables we could control (instruction type and lineup type) and the outcome or consequence variables (choosing rates and error rates). We hypothesized, for example, that biased lineup instructions would lead to high choosing rates whether the vandal was present in or absent from the lineup. Moreover, we hypothesized that unbiased instructions would lead to more caution in identifying anyone, especially when the vandal was absent from the lineup. Thus, in the theory world one lays out one's hypotheses and the logic underlying them as completely as possible. Doing this prepares a researcher to move into the activities of phase 2, in which abstract theoretical ideas are translated into the concrete manipulations and measures that make up the experiment.

Phase 2: Designing Experiments and Collecting Data

It's in phase 2 activities that the actual experiment takes shape. We decide exactly how we will manipulate and measure the key variables. In our experiment, in operationalizing instruction type, we had to determine precisely how the biased and unbiased instructions would be phrased. Lineup type was easy to operationalize (finding six possible lineup participants who were similar in appearance proved to be rather difficult). In vandal-present lineups, the vandal was among the lineup participants; in vandal-absent lineups, the vandal's place in the lineup was taken by an alternate. We also had to operationalize our key outcome variables in terms of concrete measures. Choosing rate was defined as whether eyewitnesses made an identification. Error rate was defined as whether they made an incorrect decision (chose the wrong person or failed to identify the vandal when he was present). Part of the phase 2 activities also included setting up the procedure for the experiment, detailing what would happen at every point. For us, this was the script for the crime and the script for the lineups. After operationalizing our variables and preparing our script, we were ready to collect the data. Specifically, we had the eyewitnesses look at our lineups and make their identification decisions.

Scripting the drama. In describing the eyewitness identification study, I characterized our script in terms of a drama or play, referring to the major parts of the study in terms of scenes. This is one of the aspects of doing research that I enjoy most. In much of my work I have had to create dramas in which the subjects are the only naive actors. Everyone else's lines are scripted, and the timing of behaviors is carefully planned and well rehearsed. In essence, each subject determines the end of the play or drama by virtue of how he or she responds to the situation. This aspect of the research provides some of the greatest opportunities for excitement, creativity, and fun. The researcher takes on the role of scriptwriter, stage manager, set and costume designer, and director. Some of the fun in research lies in scripting the drama, for it is here that one sees one's theoretical ideas take shape in the form of manipulations (independent variables), measures (dependent variables), and procedures. In addition, curiosity about how each drama will end (i.e., how subjects will respond in the situation) is part of what contributes to the excitement of doing a study.

Some studies require more elaborate types of scripts, while others require less elaborate scripts. However, in every study the script has to be very well planned and carefully executed. The goal is to create experimental situations that have what Eliot Aronson refers to in his book *The Social Animal* as "experimental realism": The experimental situation should have an impact on the subjects so that they are involved in the situation and take it seriously. This is very much different from what Aronson has termed "mundane realism," which refers to how similar the laboratory experiment is to events that frequently happen to people in the outside world. It is important to recognize that an experiment does not have to be high in mundane realism to be good. All experiments, however, should be high in experimental realism. If subjects do not take their tasks seriously and are not involved in the tasks, the results are not likely to be valid or reliable.

Phase 3: Evaluating Results against Hypotheses

Once the data have been collected, they have to be analyzed and the researcher has to determine if the findings support or challenge the hypotheses. These are the activities of phase 3. This is one of the most nerve-racking aspects of doing research, as you wait anxiously to find out whether your ideas are supported. When the findings support the hypotheses, the researcher has at least two choices. First, the researcher can determine the next important question and cycle back to the theory world and to phase 2. With a new hypothesis to test, the researcher designs a new study and collects new data. Back to phase 3. This is exactly what we did when we decided that we needed to create a lineup situation in which the subjects believed that the crime was real and that their decisions would have real consequences. In fact, we cycled between phases 2 and 3 often as we developed a full program of research on factors that affect eyewitnesses's lineup decisions. Second, if the researcher has real confidence about the findings, he or she can move on to phase 4 activities and apply the findings from the research to the real world (see below).

When the results of a study are inconsistent with the researcher's hypotheses, the researcher is placed in somewhat of a quandary and must take on a new role—that of a detective. The researcher looks for clues concerning what went wrong in the study and decides what steps to take to remedy those problems. The detective has to consider carefully a number of possibilities. First, it is possible that the hypothesis is incorrect. Alternatively, it is possible that the hypothesis is correct but that the variables investigated in the study were not operationalized effectively (the manipulations and measures need to be fine-tuned) and the procedure needs to be revised (the drama was not well scripted). To avoid this problem, researchers often go through painstaking pretesting to ensure that before they conduct their studies, they have developed good manipulations, measures, and procedures. Whichever possibility is determined to be the source of the difficulty, the detective/researcher returns to the theory world and phase 2 activities in his or her quest to understand the phenomenon of interest. Concluding that one's hypothesis is incorrect can be disappointing as well as threatening, but it can also lead to new discoveries.

Just when you thought you failed . . . surprising results, important discoveries. To provide you with a feel for the situation of confronting findings that fail to support your hypotheses, I want to leave the eyewitness research for a bit and tell you about my experiences with my dissertation research. First, some background information is in order. I was very much interested in studying the relationship between stereotypes and prejudice. My dissertation research concerned prejudice toward blacks. It seemed to me that a primary difference between low- and high-prejudice people is that whereas high-prejudice people believe in the stereotype (that blacks are lazy and criminals), low-prejudice people believe that the stereotype is wrong.

Thus, it seemed reasonable to me that low-prejudice people would be less likely to use the stereotype in making judgments about blacks. At the time when I was developing my hypotheses and designing my studies, priming techniques were becoming very popular as a way to activate cognitive structures and examine the effects of such activation on social judgments. Priming simply means presenting people with information that brings a whole set of ideas and memories to mind before having them work on related tasks. It occurred to me that this would be an effective way to show the differences between low- and high-prejudice people. I could present stereotype-related words (e.g., primes such as *lazy*, *Afro*, *musical*, and *poor*) to low- and high-prejudice people and then give them a social judgment task, a judgment task that should be affected by the stereotype. The idea was that priming stereotype-related information should lead to stereotype-congruent judgments for high-prejudice people but not for low-prejudice people. Because low-prejudice people do not believe in the stereotype, they should not make stereotype-congruent social judgments.

Whenever one does research on prejudice, social desirability concerns have to be considered. In scripting one's procedures, it is important to set up the situation so that it is unlikely that subjects will try to please the experimenter by giving "socially desirable" responses. Cognitive psychologists have developed priming techniques that have enabled researchers to present primes below the level of conscious awareness. This is achieved by presenting the priming words extremely rapidly (e.g., for just 80 milliseconds) and outside the central field of vision. Thus, although the stimuli can be detected (i.e., the subject sees the images), they cannot be recognized. I thought that this would be a perfect strategy for avoiding social desirability concerns. I could present very few stereotype-related primes (low stereotype priming) or a large number of stereotype-related primes (high stereotype priming) to both low- and high-prejudice subjects. These were my key manipulations. My central dependent measure was designed so that if the stereotype was affecting subjects' judgments, the subjects would make extreme ratings on an impression scale. It is well known that hostility is part of the stereotype of blacks. Therefore, after the priming task, subjects read a paragraph about a stimulus person named Donald who engaged in a number of ambiguously hostile behaviors. These behaviors (e.g., refusing to pay rent until his apartment was repainted) were likely to be interpreted as hostile only if the concept of hostility had previously been primed. Because hostility is part of the stereotype, when the stereotype is primed, these behaviors should be interpreted as higher in hostility than is the case when the stereotype is not primed.

I predicted that in the low-stereotype-priming condition, ratings on the impression scale would not be extreme and there would not be a difference in the ratings of low- and high-prejudice subjects. However, in the high-stereotype-priming condition, I thought that there would be a difference between the impression ratings of the low- and high-prejudice subjects. Specifically, I predicted that high-prejudice subjects would be strongly affected by the priming and that their impression ratings would be extreme (they would rate Donald as very hostile). In contrast, because low-prejudice people don't believe in the stereotype, I thought that they would not be affected by the priming and that their ratings would not be extreme (Donald would not be rated as hostile).

In this study I measured prejudice in a very straightforward fashion. A few weeks before participating, prospective subjects filled out a standard attitude questionnaire called the Modern Racism Scale that measured their attitudes toward blacks. This scale, which was developed by John McConahay, is designed to detect even subtle prejudice toward blacks and has been demonstrated to be both valid and reliable. Using this scale, we were able to identify high-prejudice (scored in the upper quartile of the scale) and low-prejudice (scored in the lower quartile of the scale) people. Once identified, these people were invited to participate in the study and were randomly assigned to the low- and high-stereotype-priming conditions. After collecting my data and analyzing the results, I was dumbfounded. I was wrong! Both low- and high-prejudice people were similarly affected by the stereotype priming. High levels of stereotype priming led to extreme ratings on the impression scale for *both* high- and low-prejudice people.

At first I was incredibly disappointed. I felt stupid. I felt threatened. This was my first truly independent research project. I had had some wonderfully successful experiences working with others, but now, on my own, I had failed. I briefly entertained thoughts that I was not good at research and couldn't design a good study. But I realized that I had enough experience with research to know that things don't always work out the way one wants them to and that this is part of science and the process of discovery. So I got into the detective mode. What had gone wrong? I spent a great deal of time staring at the graph of the actual results. I puzzled over them. I checked my data coding to see if I had made an error there. I hadn't. I thought about the procedure and whether it was appropriate for testing the hypothesis. I decided that it was. I thought about the measures and whether they were good. I decided that they were. So I was left with these data, and I had decided that they were valid. Therefore, it was these data that needed to be explained. This was a frustrating process. It took a while, but finally I had an "Aha!" experience and the data made sense to me. The explanation I developed seemed so sensible in retrospect that I could not believe that I hadn't seen it earlier. Moreover, making sense of these data provided me with the theoretical analysis that has served as the cornerstone set of assumptions that has guided all my subsequent work.

Here's how I made sense of the findings. First, I did not change my assumption that whereas high-prejudice people believe the stereotype, low-prejudice people do not (to make sure, I did a study to test this assumption). Indeed, low-prejudice people renounce stereotypic thinking and have developed egalitarian personal beliefs. Thus, low- and high-prejudice people have different personal beliefs about blacks. However, having been socialized into the same culture, both low- and high-prejudice people are equally knowledgeable about the cultural stereotype of blacks (I did a study to test this assumption explicitly). Indeed, this is a very frequently activated knowledge structure for all people in our culture. As a result, whether one believes that the stereotype is valid or not, it is very easily activated. The priming task activated the stereotype. And because the priming was done below the level of conscious awareness, it could not be monitored and inhibited by subjects who believed that they should not make stereotype-congruent judgments (i.e., low-prejudice people). When they are aware that the stereotype can affect their judgments, low-prejudice people make a conscious decision to refrain from making stereotypic judgments. What is really important about this analysis is that people are not always aware of when the stereotype affects their judgments. It is so easily activated that one has to be extremely vigilant in detecting instances when judgments of others may be clouded by the stereotype. Indeed, it appears that the stereotype (rather than one's personal belief) is what gets activated by default. It takes conscious attention, energy, and effort to inhibit the stereotype and instead activate one's personal beliefs.

This theorizing led me to develop an analysis of the challenges associated with reducing prejudice. Conscious decisions to renounce prejudice do not immediately eliminate prejudiced responses. That is, overcoming prejudice requires overcoming a lifetime of socialization experiences. I have likened the process of reducing prejudice to that of breaking a bad habit in that people must make a decision to eliminate the habit and then *learn* to inhibit the habitual responses. It does not occur all at once. It is a long process that requires a great deal of hard work and effort. As with breaking any habit, people are likely to meet with mixed success.

I also began to think about new questions. What are the consequences of violating one's nonprejudiced beliefs and standards? What processes are involved in overcoming prejudice? What are the implications of this analysis for intergroup tension and our prospects for improving intergroup relations? Indeed, what was exciting to me about this analysis was that it provided me with a whole new set of questions to explore. I had a research agenda that would extend well into the future. Moreover, I wasn't stupid and I hadn't failed!

Phase 4: Coming Full Circle: Applying Science to the Real World

The final phase of scientific activity involves coming full circle and applying research findings to the real world. When a substantial body of literature has been accumulated, it sometimes becomes possible to use the knowledge in applied settings. The really difficult issue here is deciding how much knowledge is sufficient for applications to be successful and productive. For example, the research we did on lineup instructions and the presence or absence of the criminal from the lineup could help people who regularly conduct lineups generate fair and effective lineup procedures. I have had the opportunity to see the application of the scientific findings on the factors that affect eyewitness identification decisions to a very important real-world situation in an up-close and personal way. Because of my expertise in the eyewitness literature, I have been a consultant to defense attorneys in trials involving eyewitness testimony and have been invited on occasion to testify in court on the reliability of eyewitness testimony. It is not the job of an expert to offer an opinion about whether a given eyewitness was accurate but rather to educate jurors about the current state of knowledge concerning factors that can affect the accuracy of eyewitness identifications in general.

Testifying in court proved to be interesting, exciting, and stressful. It is a huge responsibility. I found it interesting to see the adversarial system up close, and it was exciting to play a role in criminal trials (one was a robbery, and another was a rape case). It was stressful because, as you might imagine, in an adversarial system both the defense and prosecuting attorneys want to win their cases. Thus, they have different goals in questioning the expert. The defense attorney, who is trying to discredit the validity of eyewitness testimony, structures his or her questioning to highlight the factors that may adversely affect a witness's ability to make an accurate identification. The prosecuting attorney has another goal in mind: to do everything he or she can to undermine the credibility of the expert or, alternatively, to highlight inconsistencies in the research literature that can shake jurors' confidence in the expert's testimony. Testifying in court is also stressful because you are playing a role in something that can dramatically affect people's lives (i.e., the defendant and the victim). That is, an expert's testimony may affect whether jurors return a not-guilty or a guilty verdict. This type of interplay between science and the real world highlights for me the reasons why the application of scientific findings must be approached cautiously. It is important that the applications derive from well-established, well-replicated findings.

RESEARCH AS A JIGSAW PUZZLE

In many ways, doing research is like putting together a jigsaw puzzle. Some of the pieces can be found by reading through the literature and seeing what other researchers have done on the topic you wish to study. The goal of every study you design is to provide a new piece. However, unlike puzzles that come in a box, research puzzles have no picture that illustrates what the full puzzle will look like. In addition, there are no clear border pieces that provide the outline shape of the puzzle. Although this can often be a source of frustration, it is one of the main reasons why research is so stimulating and challenging: Research is a process of discovery that it is intellectually and personally satisfying.

Every experiment is designed with the goal of adding a new piece to the puzzle. Choosing the independent variables that will be manipulated and the dependent variables that will be measured determines the shape of the piece to be added. The results from the study, then, should neatly fit into the puzzle. However, the results don't always cooperate. Sometimes the results produce a piece that does not fit neatly into the puzzle. Its shape is different from the one expected, and so the researcher is required to see the puzzle differently. I believe that very often these unexpected findings (or oddly shaped puzzle pieces) lead to the most important discoveries. Unexpected findings cause researchers to think in novel and creative ways as it becomes clear that the current way of thinking about the phenomenon is not adequate to explain the new findings. As I indicated in the discussion of my dissertation research, this process can be frustrating. However, when one successfully works through the issues, it is fabulously rewarding.

Another interesting and rather seductive aspect to this notion of research as an amorphous puzzle is that you never really have the feeling that you are done. The puzzle is never complete. That is, the findings of the study you just completed provide answers to part of the puzzle but also lead to new questions. Before you have an opportunity to complete the project in terms of writing a research article for publication, you move on to the next step: designing the next study to provide the next piece to the puzzle. As a result, the research enterprise is always new. It creates new challenges, frustrations, and exciting opportunities.

The Importance of Programmatic Research

In thinking about research as a puzzle, it is important to realize that the puzzle is not completely without shape or direction. That is, one of the most important things I have learned about the process of doing research is how new questions build on the work one has done previously. Each new puzzle piece must build on and add to the existing pieces. Nowhere has this been more evident to me than in my ongoing program of research on prejudice and intergroup relations. You can think of this process of adding to the puzzle as tantamount to asking the following questions: If this finding is valid, then what question follows? What hypothesis should be tested next? To illustrate the process, let me take you through some of the key developments in my research program on prejudice and intergroup relations.

The cornerstone piece. My early work addressed an important paradox in the literature on prejudice: the persistence of prejudiced tendencies among those who claim to be nonprejudiced. The dissertation research I described earlier was designed to address this issue. The coexistence of these contradictory reactions has often been regarded with suspicion in the literature. Several theorists have resolved this conflict by assuming that verbal reports are not trustworthy indicators of attitudes and beliefs. In fact, the theme of most contemporary theories of prejudice is that individual prejudice has not been reduced but rather that the *expression* of prejudice has been modified (i.e., become more subtle) in response to legislative changes such as civil rights laws. These theories are somewhat discouraging because they offer little guidance or encouragement with regard to reducing prejudice. It was my belief that these conclusions are too simplistic. The question that my research addressed was, Can people who renounce prejudice have prejudiced tendencies? The answer is yes.

My dissertation research showed that there are automatic components to racial stereotypes and that those components are present even among people who report low-prejudice attitudes. It is only with effort and the exertion of controlled processes that low-prejudice people are able to overcome their stereotypical ideas. By exploring the structural representation of stereotypes and personal beliefs held by prejudiced and nonprejudiced individuals, I was in a unique position to address the question of whether in contemporary society people are less prejudiced (as suggested by many survey researchers) or whether their prejudices are simply more subtle and better disguised. This was incredibly exciting. My model suggests that conscious decisions to renounce prejudice do not immediately eliminate prejudiced responses. A strength of this model is that it explains the role of both conscious (mostly intentional) and nonconscious (unintentional) processes in one's responses to members of stereotyped groups. The change from being prejudiced to being nonprejudiced is viewed not as an all-or-nothing event but as a process during which the low-prejudice person is especially vulnerable to conflict between his or her enduring negative responses and endorsed nonprejudiced beliefs. For those who renounce prejudice, overcoming the "prejudice habit" presents a formidable task that is likely to entail a great deal of internal conflict over a protracted period.

Adding to the puzzle. The next step in my program of research was to examine the consequences of this type of internal conflict. My students and I have been interested in examining the challenges faced by individuals who have internalized nonprejudiced personal standards and are trying to control their prejudiced responses but who sometimes fail. Specifically, we examine the emotional and motivational consequences of the fact that negative emotions and stereotypes may be automatically activated even in nonprejudiced individuals. How do you think they should respond to such failures? How would you feel? And why would you have such reactions?

Our empirical strategy for exploring these questions is quite straight-forward. We simply ask subjects to report how they should respond to members of stigmatized groups (e.g., blacks, homosexuals, women) and then ask them to report how they actually respond. Although people who score low on traditional measures of prejudice indicate that they should not respond with prejudice, many of them also report that very often they do. That is, many low-prejudice people respond with more prejudice than they personally find acceptable. When their actual reactions violate their personal standards, low-prejudice people experience guilt or "prejudice with compunction," but prejudiced individuals do not. For low-prejudice people the coexistence of such conflicting reactions threatens their nonprejudiced self-concepts.

Putting it all together. Seeing the developments in the research program over the years has truly been rewarding and stimulating. By putting the pieces of the puzzle together, we really had something to say about the processes involved in overcoming prejudice. In contrast to the rather pessimistic view that little progress is being made toward the alleviation of prejudice, our analysis suggests that many people are embroiled in the arduous task of breaking the prejudice habit. The first step in the model is the establishment and internalization of nonprejudiced standards. However, the establishment and internalization of non-prejudiced personal standards does not imply that change is complete.

During the early phases of the prejudice reduction process, we can expect that contact with members of a stereotyped group will lead to the automatic activation of the stereotype and its associated affect. Moreover, during these early phases of the prejudice reduction process, low-prejudice people should be particularly likely to experience discrepancies between their nonprejudiced standards and their actual responses. If low-prejudice people do not evaluate their actual responses in light of their personal standards, they will exit the process and will not experience a negative affect. If, however, they do evaluate their actual responses and recognize them as being more prejudiced than their personal standards permit, they will experience a threat to their nonprejudiced self-identity and guilt.

We have also found that failures to live up to well-internalized standards, along with the guilt such failures engender, can actually help people more effectively live up to their nonprejudiced standards in the future. The guilt associated with such failures serves as a psychological signal that something has gone wrong and needs attention. The signal causes low-prejudice people to slow down their responses, attempt to understand why the failure occurred, and try to figure out how to avoid failures in the future (and thus avoid future guilt feelings). These reactions to failure experiences help low-prejudice people learn to inhibit unacceptable (prejudiced) responses and replace them with responses based on their nonprejudiced beliefs in later phases of the prejudice reduction process. The encouraging aspect of this model is that it suggests that people can benefit from their failure experiences and make progress in learning to respond consistently with their nonprejudiced standards. Although the process is not easy and clearly requires effort, time, and practice, prejudice appears to be a habit that can be broken.

But we are not done yet . . . Although this prejudice reduction model has encouraging implications concerning the progress being made toward the alleviation of prejudice, the puzzle is far from complete. The model needs additional testing and further development, and we are working on those issues. In addition, we are exploring new directions for our research program. For example, I think an important limitation of our previous work is that we have focused almost exclusively on the nature of the *internal* conflict (i.e., the conflict between personal standards and actual responses) experienced by low-prejudice people. This may limit the applicability of our analysis in addressing the everyday types of interpersonal situations in which prejudice is problematic. Indeed, I believe a limitation of most models of prejudice in addressing pressing social issues is that they have focused primarily on intrapersonal processes (i.e., change within the person). Few theorists have explored the implications of their models in the interpersonal arena in which people have to manage or negotiate interactions with others (i.e., majority group members with similar and dissimilar values and minority group members who have been the target of prejudice historically).

To address these issues, we are currently expanding our research program in two major directions. The new lines of research hold great promise for adding important new pieces to the puzzle of intergroup prejudice. The first line of research focuses on the consequences for low- and high-prejudice majority group members when there is conflict between their standards and social pressure from other majority group members. The second line of research explores the interpersonal dynamics of intergroup contact.

Majority group members often encounter situations in which there is pressure from other people to respond in ways that conflict with their own personal standards. It is important to consider how people negotiate situations in which their personal standards are at odds with situational social pressures. Social pressures that conflict with personal standards can be especially powerful when the "others" have the power to allocate rewards or punishments (material or social). For example, an employee with a low-prejudice personal standard may feel compelled to laugh at her boss's derogatory jokes about homosexuals because she doesn't want to hurt her chances of getting a raise. In situations like these, it appears that the individual is pulled in two directions by competing motivations. That is, he or she must either (1) risk social disapproval and/or sanctions from others or (2) risk self-disapproval or self-criticism for violating his or her personal standards. Such competing motivations are likely to create conflict and momentary decision uncertainty for the individual. How is the uncertainty resolved? Which motivation wins out? And how do people feel about their behavior in these situations?

In a sense, we are asking how people deal with interpersonal situations when their standards are put on the line. Nowhere are people's standards more on the line than when they interact with members of minority groups. We are exploring the relevance of our work on the nature of personal standards to understanding the nature of intergroup tension. The tension that results when members of different groups come into contact is presumed to underlie the conflict and the interpersonal difficulties faced by both majority group and minority group members as they try to negotiate or manage their intergroup encounters. The goal of this most recent aspect of our research program is to provide an analysis of the psychological experiences and challenges that may underlie the tension felt by both majority group and minority group interactants. I believe that the nature of intergroup tensions in interpersonal relations must be understood before intervention strategies to alleviate such tensions can be developed.

To explore these issues, we are up to our old trick of scripting elaborate dramas for subjects and allowing them to determine the end of the drama by virtue of how they respond to the scenarios we have created. For example, to address the social pressure issue, we scripted a simulation of the employee-boss scenario discussed above. Our cover story was quite elaborate and required a fair amount of acting on the part of the experimenter and the confederates. In this study, the experimenter and the two confederates have specific roles to play. The experimenter explains that the goal of the study is to examine the relations between employers and employees in a simulated job scenario. The situation is set up so that the subject and one of the confederates are told that they are to play the role of two new employees in a television network programming team. The other confederate is assigned the role of program director and thus has power over the two employees. The program director will, based on the performance of the employees on preliminary tasks, assign the employees to subsequent tasks, one of which is highly desirable (it involves selecting comedians for the network comedy special) and the other is clearly less desirable (it involves verifying entrant numbers for those competing for the special). One of the initial tasks involves rating jokes told by a comedian. We arranged for the subject and the program director to watch the initial set of jokes together. Here was where the key manipulation of social pressure was introduced.

Two of the comedian's jokes were made at the expense of homosexuals, the target group of interest in this study. The social pressure conditions were created by the nature of the program director's response to these key jokes. In the low-prejudice social pressure condition the programmer indicated displeasure at the jokes by shaking his head and sighing. In the high-prejudice social pressure condition he indicated approval of the jokes by chuckling and nodding. In an ambiguous condition the program director showed no obvious reaction to the jokes. Because we had low-, moderate-, and high-prejudice subjects in this study, we could examine how subjects at each level of prejudice responded to social pressure that was consistent with or at odds with the subjects' personal standards. One of the key dependent variables is subjects' rating of the jokes about homosexuals. We know from pretesting that low-prejudice subjects believe that they should not rate these jokes as funny. High-prejudice subjects believe that rating the jokes as funny is acceptable. Thus, if low-prejudice subjects rate the jokes as funny, they will violate their personal standards, which our previous research suggests, should make them feel guilty.

As with the eyewitness identification research, our scripts have to be believable and each phase of the study must be executed with precision. Creating situations in which the subject can legitimately behave in a prejudiced fashion and not flag to the subjects that we are studying prejudice is quite challenging indeed. We appear to have been successful. High- and low-prejudice subjects alike appear to be highly responsive to social pressure. Although high-prejudice subjects generally rated the jokes as more funny than did low-prejudice subjects, low-prejudice subjects rated the jokes as more funny in the high-prejudice social pressure condition compared with either the ambiguous or the low-prejudice social pressure condition. Similarly, high-prejudice subjects rated the jokes as less funny when there was social pressure to behave without prejudice compared with the other conditions. We are currently in the process of exploring the consequences of responding to social pressure in ways that violate people's personal standards (e.g., Do low-prejudice people feel guilty when they violate their standards?).

This type of research brings with it a whole new set of challenges. We have to know subjects' prejudice levels before they participate in the study. Thus, we have to obtain a measure of prejudice in a setting that appears to be unrelated to the research setting. To accomplish this, we typically collect a measure of prejudice when subjects fill out a large number of questionnaires in the classroom setting early in the academic semester. We then have to invite subjects of varying levels of prejudice into the lab to participate in our studies. It is important that neither the experimenter running the study nor the confederates be privy to the subjects' prejudice levels. If they were to know this information, it might affect their behavior and contaminate the research findings. We go to great lengths to ensure that experimenters and confederates are blind to the subjects' prejudice levels; for example, the person who calls the subjects and thus knows the subjects' prejudice levels is never the person who runs the experimental session.

I've very much enjoyed adding to the puzzle of intergroup prejudice. My work in this area, as was true of my work with Roy Malpass on eyewitness identification, illustrates the process of doing research. Many of the questions I have asked derived from real-world observations. In working on these issues, we took our questions into the research world, where we could design studies to test our hypotheses. Over the years we have cycled often between the theory world and the research world. Our ultimate goal is to add sufficiently to the puzzle so that we can move on to the application phase and use our knowledge to help people learn to overcome their prejudices and contribute to the reduction of intergroup hostilities. The good news is that we have, I believe, made substantial progress in addressing these issues. The other good news is that our previous work has provided the foundation for us to move forward so that we can add new pieces to the puzzle of intergroup prejudice. The key to this success is that our work is programmatic. Each study builds on the last. Thus, our work is cumulative. It is through the process of doing such programmatic research that the puzzle takes shape.

WHO DOES RESEARCH?

When I first read textbooks and saw studies discussed with citations indicating the authors of an article, somehow these people didn't seem real to me and the process of doing research was not at all apparent from the brief descriptions of the studies. In textbooks, you read only about the conclusions of research studies. It all seems so abstract, so neat and tidy. You don't get a real feeling for what goes into a single study, let alone a whole program of research. So when you think about who does research, most often images of faceless people working at universities and research institutes come to mind. Rarely do you get the feeling that people like yourself do research, nor do you get the image that research is fun. However, if you take a look around any university, you will find many scholars actively involved in research, and in many instances you will find people like yourself playing key roles in the research enterprise. In addition, if you were to chat with these people, you would probably come away with the image that research is a dynamic and enjoyable enterprise.

Over the years I have had the good fortune to have a great number of outstanding graduate and undergraduate students collaborate with me on research. Indeed, without them, it would be virtually impossible to do the type of research we do and it would not be as much fun. We have a very active and dynamic lab. Every semester between fifteen and twenty undergraduates participate. These students participate in all aspects of the research. They contribute to hypothesis generation and the operationalization of our independent and dependent variables as well as contributing to the scripting of the dramas and the data collection. They are centrally involved in the data-coding phase of the research and in interpreting the findings from our studies. Every week we have a two-hour meeting in which we discuss the various projects we are working on that semester. Oddly enough our preferred meeting time is Friday afternoon from 2 to 4 P.M. We find that this is an enjoyable and relaxing way to cap off the week. During these meetings some of our discussions are theoretical. Others are problem-solving meetings (i.e., how to effectively operationalize a variable, how to develop a compelling script that will involve the subjects, how to get around social desirability concerns). Our discussions are typically lively and spirited. What makes them so enjoyable is that we all feel that we are working on important issues and developing high-quality research projects.

After they have been involved in the research for awhile, most of the students tell me that they didn't really know what to expect. If anything, they saw it as a necessary evil (i.e., it would be a rather stuffy, dry, and tedious enterprise) if they wanted to get into graduate school (i.e., it would look good on a résumé). However, in the process of working in our lab, students come to learn that their preconceptions were wrong and also come to learn a lot about themselves and how smart they are. They figure out that they can think creatively about research and have good ideas. Many of the students who have worked in my lab have done independent research projects (some of which have been published), and a very large number of them have gone on to graduate school. Our research team is a very closely knit group. After students graduate, they regularly send me letters and postcards to let me know how they are and what they are doing. When they visit Madison, they stop by to participate in our Friday afternoon meetings. They are interested in seeing what progress we've made and what our latest findings indicate. I find this quite remarkable.

For me, one of the most rewarding aspects of research is working with students. I enjoy watching students get excited about ideas and "get hooked" by the process of doing research. The students who participate in my lab work incredibly hard and have contributed greatly to the research. Thus, when Gary and Matt (the editors) asked me to submit a picture of myself to appear in this book, the idea of sending a picture of "just myself" didn't feel right. Instead, I submitted a picture of all the people currently working in my lab (unfortunately a few people were out of town that day, so only their names appear).

CONCLUSION

Getting involved in research was clearly a career-shaping event for me. I am happy to report that my passion for research has grown over the years and that I cannot imagine myself in a different career. This is not to say that research is for everyone, but an important thing to take away from this chapter is the idea that you should seek out opportunities to get involved in your area of interest. Whether your interest is in psychology, sociology, political science, economics, biology, chemistry, physics, mathematics, astronomy, geology, women's studies, or music, at most universities you will find people actively engaged in research. Not everyone will be so fortunate as I was, to be asked by a faculty member to join his or her research group. But wonderful opportunities are there for the person who is willing to go after them. Seek them out and enjoy!

Acknowledgments

I would like to thank all the students who have participated in my research program over the years. Pictured in the photograph with me are the students (a wonderfully fabulous group) who worked with me during the spring semester of 1993. These students and those who preceded them are part of what has made my research career so rewarding. Their tireless efforts have been invaluable and are deeply appreciated. I'm the person in the front and center of the photograph. Surrounding me on the steps in front of our psychology building are Sophie Evett, Ivan Amodt, Dave Froning, Julie Zuwerink, Terri Conley, Kathy Lepage, Paige Levin, Dan Pilloff, Craig Meyer, Jennifer Zerbst, Renee Fry, Sam Shapiro, Jana Price, Sara Andrews, Michele Marvich, Kevin Thompson, Sharon Jenik, Tracy Sweeney, Kelli Duehning, Kathy Zeitz, and Tracy Holz. A couple of our lab members were not able to be at the picture session: Sarah Pressley and Ireliz Martinez.

SUGGESTED READINGS

ARONSON, E. (1992). *The social animal* (6th ed.) New York: Freeman.

———— ELLSWORTH, P., CARLSMITH, M., & GONZALES, M. (1990). *Methods of research in social psychology* (2d ed.). New York: McGraw-Hill.

DEVINE, P. G. (1989). Stereotypes and prejudice: Their automatic and controlled components. *Journal of Personality and Social Psychology, 56*, 5–18.

———— & MONTEITH, M. J. (1992). The role of discrepancy associated affect in prejudice reduction. In D. M. Mackie & D. L. Hamilton (Eds.), *Affect, cognition, and stereotyping: Interactive processes in intergroup perception* (pp. 317–344). New York: Academic Press.

———— MONTEITH, M., ZUWERINK, J. R., & ELLIOT, A. J. (1991). Prejudice with and without compunction. *Journal of Personality and Social Psychology, 60,* 817–830.

———— & ZUWERINK, J. R. (1994). Prejudice and guilt: The internal struggle to control prejudice. In W. J. Lonner & R. S. Malpass (Eds.), *Readings in psychology and culture* (pp. 203–207). Boston: Allyn & Bacon.

MALPASS, R. S., & DEVINE, P. G. (1980). Realism and eyewitness identification research. *Law and Human Behavior, 4,* 347–358.

———— & DEVINE, P. G. (1981). Eyewitness identification: Lineup instructions and absence of the offender. *Journal of Applied Psychology, 66,* 482–489.

*M*ICHAEL *HARRIS BOND* (*Ph.D., Stanford University*) *was born in Toronto, Canada, where he received a transplanted public school education from teachers with British accents. His cultural confusion was reinforced by trips to Quebec, where he heard a euphonic language and saw people drinking wine at lunch. His fate was sealed when he was enchanted by another foreigner, Edwin Hollander, whose television programs on social psychology were beamed across the border from Buffalo. Subsequent travels took him to exotic cultures such as California. His appetite for the extraordinary thus whetted, he continued going west as a young man until he arrived in the far east, where he has now reached middle age teaching psychology at the Chinese University in Hong Kong. His most recent act of cultural hubris was writing* Beyond the Chinese Face *in 1991.*

11

$\mathcal{D}$oing $\mathcal{S}$ocial $\mathcal{P}$sychology $\mathcal{C}$ross-$\mathcal{C}$ulturally: $\mathcal{I}$nto $\mathcal{A}$nother $\mathcal{H}$eart of $\mathcal{D}$arkness

—————— ❖ ——————

If I succeed, you shall find there according to your deserts: encouragement, consolation, fear, charm—all you demand—and, perhaps, also that glimpse of truth for which you have forgotten to ask. [Joseph Conrad, preface to The Nigger of the Narcissus]

Time for the truth, at least as I experience it. Of course, the elephant of truth portrayed in the Sufi story has many parts. To one man searching in the pitch-black chamber, that elephant appears as a massive tree trunk; to another, as a pulsating fire hose; to yet another, as a fibrous shaving brush, and so it goes. Each person grasps part of the whole, but by traveling around the darkened room one may learn that there are many takes on the truth.

Cross-cultural psychology is done by many searching men and women from varied cultures, of different personalities, for different reasons. I am a male

Anglo-Canadian of rebellious and open disposition trying to carve out a career as a psychologist while living in Hong Kong. Other cross-cultural types have their own backgrounds which they take to their tasks, as I do to mine. These resources and orientations become especially important in the cross-cultural enterprise, I think, because these researchers become our guides through the "alien corn" of other cultures. It is important to know how prepared they are to lead us into "the heart of darkness," for there are many pitfalls along the way. Let me introduce you to my compass, escort you around a few of the traps I have explored, and then show you the vision I have discovered through my travels around this darkened room we call the earth.

ONE POINT OF DEPARTURE

Chance favors the prepared mind. [Louis Pasteur]

I often tell my students that I am totally unprepared for the life I am leading. In some senses that statement is true, and it certainly gets their attention, for I typically drop this bombshell on Chinese undergraduates taking cross-cultural psychology from someone they perhaps believe, and certainly hope, is an expert, an authority on whose judgment and goodwill they can rely. Indeed, in Chinese culture one is especially vulnerable and exposed if those in authority cannot be trusted.

But, let's examine the facts. How can I claim to be doing cross-cultural psychology with Chinese people when I speak and read no Chinese; studied no Chinese history, philosophy, sociology, or anthropology; and had never read a cross-cultural study during my undergraduate and graduate schooling? Is cross-cultural psychology a refuge for amateurs, an outpost for the ill prepared?

Qualifications

The answer to that question depends on one's assessment of preparedness. I certainly lacked much useful information about the concept of "culture" both in general and in specific cases, such as that of the Japanese whom I first encountered on my odyssey. Of course, this knowledge business is a daunting one. A trip to the journal room of any library is enough to depress me for a day. How little I know! How impossible it seems to accumulate even the basic information needed to pose a useful question. Where to begin? How to proceed?

Well, I have good news and bad news. The good news is that you can do it—you can master the cultural knowledge you need to learn if you are hungry. As Peter Medawar claims in *Advice to a Young Scientist,*

> The great incentive to learning a new skill or supporting discipline is an urgent need to use it. For this reason very many scientists (I certainly among them) do not learn new skills or master new disciplines until the pressure is upon them to do so. [p. 16]

Having arrived ignorant on the shores of Japan and later Hong Kong, I had pressure aplenty to become culturally literate. Four thousand years of recorded history requires a lot of "catch-up ball," but I'm slowly moving forward. And as the Chinese say, "It takes ten years to grow a tree but a hundred years to make a scholar." There is time for you as there is for me, and the process never ends.

The bad news is that cultural retooling does take time and that a good cross-cultural study probably takes two to three times the effort, resources, and patience required for a good monocultural study.

Incentives

So why do cross-cultural research? In my case I was blissfully ignorant of the dangers, and at age twenty-seven the world was my oyster anyway. If things didn't work out in Japan, I could always retreat to a received career in my home country.

More to the point, I was then and am still fascinated by difference: How could so much behavioral variety exist and still be called human? Surely this was an intellectual puzzle worth unraveling.

Buttressing this curiosity was a kind of democratic prejudice, an insistent belief in people's sameness beneath the external trappings. Its spirit is captured in these lines from Kipling's "We and They":

> All good people agree,
> And all good people say
> All nice people, like us, are We
> And everyone else is They.
> But if you cross over the sea
> Instead of over the way
> You may end by (think of it) looking on We
> As only a sort of They

In my boyhood simplicity the Sunday school distinction between the damned and the saved never rang true; surely my Muslim, Buddhist, Hindu, Zoroastrian, Baha'i, and Jewish (whom have I forgotten?) brothers and sisters were struggling with the same divisive wisdom from their elders, wisdom which left me, likewise, beyond the pale. It didn't seem fair or fair-minded then, and it still doesn't. Although I didn't know it then, I had already sided with Confucius, who asserted, "All men are the same; only their habits differ." I was fascinated by these differences and unwilling to condemn others because of them.

I mention this "democratic prejudice" because I now consider it essential equipment for a cross-cultural psychologist: When we are striving to understand people of another culture, ethnocentrism, however innocent, has no place. It leads to intemperate, superficial conclusions about our subject matter and pulls us out of the race before we have finished the course. Instead, we need the willingness to explore any behavior long and hard enough to answer the question, Under what set of social premises does that behavior make good sense? I believe that persuasive answers to this basic question require enough generosity of mind and openness of heart to keep a person in intimate contact with the cultures he or she wishes to study.

All my colleagues in cross-cultural psychology who do good science seem to possess these qualities of mind and heart. It takes so long to learn the necessary skills of the trade that one would abandon the struggle prematurely without them. So, fair warning: You will need more than technical skills on this voyage. By the same token, take courage. If you already like Thai food, or Chinese philosophy, or Indian music, or Sufi poetry, or Nigerian proverbs, or Brazilian novels, or Persian carpets, or Indonesian batiks, or Russian dances, or Navajo jewelry, or Japanese painting, you probably have the basics already.

LOST AT SEA

> Kynna kept a cheerful countenance, but felt her spirits flag. The alien speech of the passersby, the inscrutable monuments, the unknown landscape, the vanishing of all she had pictured in advance, were draining her of certainty . . . she had known that the world was vast, but at home in her native hills it had had no meaning. Now, on the threshold of the illimitable East, she felt like a desolate in its indifferent strangeness. [Mary Renault, *Funeral Games*]

It is one thing to study a culture at a distance and quite another thing to live in one, however well insulated. For a social psychologist of culture, this direct contact is a working necessity, and I know of no competent culturalist who lacks it. This contact gives one the immersion necessary to appreciate the fullness of the culture and experience the daily stuff from which hypotheses are generated. Let me give some examples:

Case 1: I love swimming, and in Hong Kong our university pool is open eight months a year. The problem I have experienced since I arrived is collisions—head-on, broadside, rear-endings, you name it—from people doing the backstroke in a crowded pool, freestyle with their eyes closed, the breaststroke with bone-crushing kicks. After such collisions, Chinese people typically pull up surprised and wave an apology as they continue on their (to me) careless ways.

Hypothesis: Life in an environment with heavy academic and family demands is exhausting and leads to civic indifference. The result is more physical contact with strangers in public. Automatic apologies reduce everybody's irritation. Life in Canada is less focused on school success and family obligations, people are socialized to associate and work smoothly with strangers, and civic rules are used and enforced to maintain smooth exchanges.

Case 2: A prospective Chinese candidate for a job opening in our department introduces his seminar presentation to the faculty members by apologizing for his lack of preparation and incompetence in the topic compared with some of the listeners present. He then proceeds to give a perfectly adequate presentation about a subject on which he is obviously an expert.

Hypothesis: In a hierarchical society emphasizing smooth interpersonal relationships, it is prudent to show deferential, humble form. Your content may deserve such abasement, of course, but even if it is outstanding, those who may work with you afterward want to be sure that you play the courtesy game. In Canada one is socialized to have "proper self-regard" and not to show "false modesty." Self-presentations are tailored accordingly. Individualistic social logic requires that people negotiate their interpersonal relationships on the basis of truth, openness, and their real selves to achieve a proper social order.

Case 3: I am shopping in Kowloon with a Chinese friend. In front of us at the checkout, a demure Chinese woman is shouting furiously at the cashier in Cantonese. Suddenly she throws down her purchase and curses him loudly in English with "Oh, shit, screw you!"

My Chinese friend laughs. My ears are ringing; I have never heard a Chinese lady swear in English. I ask my companion if she had also been cursing in Cantonese, but he says no. Why had this porcelain lady, I wondered, switched language codes for the purpose of abusing the salesclerk? As I ponder this puzzle, I ask my friend how to translate those choice English expletives into Chinese. He blushes. I persist until he provides some possibilities. I roll them across my tongue but notice no physiological rush.

Hypothesis: Could it be, I mused, that the use of a second language for emotionally charged exchanges has the effect of defusing the impact on the speaker of what is said? Because one has learned the forbidden words from a book or movie, they may lack the emotional impact with which they are conditioned in a first language. One can then abuse another person in a second language without risking as much social censure or becoming aroused oneself. A sort of having your cake and eating it too. This line of reasoning suggests an experiment. . . .

The Context of Discovery

This term, which was coined, I believe, by Hans Reichenbach, refers to the medium out of which hypotheses are generated and experiments are run. If you peruse a scientific journal, these hypotheses roll out of introductions like cars freshly minted roll off a conveyor belt. Where do they come from, I always wondered, these elegant jewels of scientific reasoning? I knew how to test a hypothesis once I had one; courses in scientific methodology equip a student with an armamentarium of techniques for what Reichenbach called "the context of evaluation." These courses, however, are usually silent about the voice of inspiration, the source of hypotheses.

Arthur Koestler has tackled this juggernaut in his book about creativity, *The Act of Creation*. Anthologies of writings on creating have been compiled (e.g., Brewster Ghiselin's *The Creative Process*, 1952), and psychologists such as Frank Barron have studied creative persons. We scientific practitioners, however, are still left to our own devices in generating good ideas that are worth testing.

Enter the Delights of Living Overseas, of Being a "Stranger in a Strange Land"

As Edward Hall put it, "Most cross-cultural exploration begins with the annoyance of being lost." The unending procession of irritations, surprises, and puzzles afforded by daily contact across cultural lines is a mother lode of hypotheses waiting to be decoded. Life becomes one's guide, silent but endlessly inventive. One must simply survive the process with body and soul intact, itself no mean feat, to have a cornucopia of creative stimulation.

So what is my preparation for receiving this cornucopia? In short, it is twenty-one years of socialization as a Canadian. Blundering around Chinese culture with these unconscious expectations and values on display results in effortless friction and some light. André Malraux identified this looking glass of a foreign culture when he said, "A people is a mirror in which each traveler contemplates his own image." If one enjoys such contemplation, then each day spent in a foreign culture can provide a rich harvest.

Thereafter, Medawar's assurance that one will pick up the necessary skills and information takes over. Trips to the library, chats with colleagues, feedback from reviewers, and attendance at seminars all conspire to focus my thoughts and connect them to previous scholarly work. The wind has filled my sails, and I am moving forward as a scientist, hypothesis before me.

AN EARLY LANDFALL?

As they gain experience, scientists reach a stage when they look back upon their own beginnings in research and wonder how they had the temerity to embark upon it, considering how ignorant and ill equipped they were. [Peter Medawar, *Advice to a Young Scientist*]

Some time ago I was asked to select my "six best papers" for a promotion committee to consider. This selection took me back over twenty years of cross-cultural research and left me cringing in amazement at some of my early folly. Well, "nothing succeeds like failure," as Bob Dylan allowed, so I thought I might illustrate the perils of cross-cultural research by selecting a classic "failure."

I put the word *failure* in quotation marks because the study was published in the *Journal of Cross-Cultural Psychology*, has occasionally been cited by others, and may well have produced accurate results. But it surely left no scientific purists singing its praises, and it highlights some basic problems in cross-cultural research. Let me elaborate.

THE FOREIGNNESS IN CROSS-CULTURAL RESEARCH

In his reflections on twenty years of cross-cultural study, George Guthrie put the challenge in a nutshell:

Surely the methods of research one may use in cross-cultural studies are, at a very basic level, the same as those used in one's home setting. Taking those methods to an alien culture, however, is hazardous because the materials, the tasks, and the relationship between subject and experimenter may be very different. Coping with those differences as well as extensive understanding or good advice about the new setting is the heart of the matter; that is the problem of cross-cultural research. [pp. 349–350]

We have already discussed the dynamics involved in developing "extensive understanding or good advice about the new setting," but what about coping with the different understandings of materials, tasks, and relationships?

How Not to Do It

In 1973 an old and dear friend wrote to me about a study he had run on "Barnum personality descriptions." These are character analyses presented to respondents who have completed a battery of personality inventories. The descriptions, however, are pitched at a general level and supply content that could apply to anybody. Indeed, respondents receive the identical description of their character regardless of their actual responses to the personality questionnaires: "Despite receiving an interpretation filled with personality clichés, Ss tended to congratulate the examiner for his penetrating insights."

At least that was the case for Caucasian Americans and Japanese-Americans. They, however, had been socialized into a heavily psychologized culture where the armamentarium of personality surveys, sophisticated tests, and clinical pundits is common currency. What would happen if the same "materials, tasks, and relationships" were imported into Japan, a very different culture in all these respects? If Japanese gave the same high endorsement to the Barnum personality description, the acceptability of such general analyses would be applicable across cultures. American astrologists could then be syndicated in Tokyo!

The procedure appeared to be straightforward: All I had to do was have the instructor of the psychology class administer cards II and X of the Rorschach inkblot test, give the subjects the (translated) Barnum description, and have them rate its accuracy in assessing their character, using a translated version of the American scale.

That, in short, is what we did. The findings? To quote, "These results indicate that native Japanese students and both Japanese-American and Caucasian American students are equally likely to endorse highly general personality impressions as being true of themselves" (p. 232). By way of explanation we asserted, "The absence of cultural differences may be attributed to these students' sharing a larger metaculture characterized by the changing values of the 1970's" (p. 233). Well, maybe. Before being hasty, however, let us look at possible sources of inequivalence arising from "materials, tasks, and the relationship between subject and experimenter."

First, the materials. In this experiment they were the Rorschach cards, the personality description, and the rating scale. The American subjects were undoubtedly more familiar with the inkblots than were the Japanese, both through general media presentation and because the Americans responded to the cards as part of a lecture on personality tests about which they had already read; the Japanese had not yet reached the personality part of their course.

As for the description itself, one problem was the method of translation. Back-translation to Japanese and then to English using independent translators was not employed. Instead, a "consultative" translation was produced by a native Japanese speaker (then) moderately skilled in English working with me, a (then) beginner at Japanese. In time we both became much better speakers of each other's language, but who knows what kind of translation we produced without the strict requirement of back-translation.

This translation problem became acute with the key rating measure. A single question was asked, using a five-point rating scale with steps labeled "excellent," "good," "average," "poor," and "very poor." These labels were, as usual, converted to numerical scores from five to one, implying, indeed requiring, psychologically equidistant steps from one label to the next.

Was this requirement met in Japanese? Who knows? A back-translation procedure was not followed. Even if it had been and the labels had been translated similarly, one would have legitimate concerns about whether they were equidistant in Japanese (let alone in English!). Recall that this scale constituted the only dependent variable for the cross-cultural comparison. The slightest inequivalence thus could become pivotal in changing the results.

Second, the tasks. The subjects had two jobs in this experiment: responding to the cards and then assessing the personality profile. With respect to responding, the Americans were undoubtedly more familiar with taking a personality test. This difference is of little moment here, however, because any response they made would be assessed by omniscient clinical psychologists. Different amounts of responding would have no bearing, then, on the key dependent variable of accuracy.

The way in which the subjects assessed the profile, however, would directly affect their assessment of the description's accuracy. Do clinical psychologists carry the same authority in Japanese culture as in America? Do Japanese students practice introspection and receive as much personality-relevant information as American students do? Will the expected contents of a personality description in Japan focus on the same issues as those in America? A no answer to any of these questions, or to any others one may generate, means that the evaluation task is different for the subject populations involved. As the rated accuracy of the personality description emerges from this evaluation task, any inequivalence at this point renders a comparison questionable.

Third, the relationship between the subjects and the experimenter. The American data were collected by the first author of the paper as part of a course he had been teaching; the Japanese data were collected by a female graduate student who came into the class only twice, once to administer the cards and once to deliver the personality descriptions. Would this greater contact experienced by the American students with their experimenter lead them to (1) trust him more, (2) pay more attention to the personality description, (3) assume greater competence in the clinical psychologists assessing their Rorschach protocols? Who knows? But again, any inequivalence here bears directly on the dependent variable of description accuracy.

Of course there was an additional "relationship" involved in the experiment: that between the subject and the clinical psychologist who purportedly made the Rorschach assessment. This relationship was impersonal, since the assessment is delivered on paper rather than face to face. Are Japanese more respectful of printed communications than Americans or do they show more deference to authorities who are physically present? Again we cannot be sure, and the answer has implications for the key measure in the study.

Fourth, the subjects. Guthrie did not mention subject differences as a potential trip wire, perhaps because we know that they must be different in cross-cultural research—different by virtue of their cultural background only, however. In all other respects the subjects should be similar with respect to age, sex, social status, and so forth.

In this experiment all subjects were students of psychology courses at the university. The verbal equivalence here may, however, mask substantial differences. A larger portion of the population attends university in America than in any other country. Hence, American undergraduates are less highly selected and more representative of their culture. Furthermore psychology courses are extremely popular in America, much more so than elsewhere. In Japan, such courses are less in demand and those who take them are more atypical of their peers.

The way in which these types of subject inequivalences may affect the results is unknown, but one may speculate. Japanese students may be brighter and hence more critical of the personality assessment, or those who choose psychology may be more drawn to psychology and hence more accepting of assessments by clinical psychologists. These subject differences might have made a difference in their assessment of the Barnum description. Again, who knows?

The Impossible Dream?

What I have been demonstrating is the ability to generate "plausible rival hypotheses"—possible alternative explanations for a result other than one based on cultural differences. Each of these possibilities has a varying likelihood of being true, but taken as a whole, they cast a considerable cloud of doubt over our 1974 explanation.

Of course, I'm smarter now. I know much more about Japan than I did in those early days. Such knowledge would have enabled me to alter many aspects of our study. In addition, ten years of experience in evaluating the cross-cultural research of others and planning my own has alerted me to a host of hazards.

Another constraint in improving our 1974 study, however, was the fact that it was "safari research," an opportunistic imposition of ideas, procedures, and instrumentation developed in one culture upon another. Because the study has been designed before being considered for export, no changes are possible. The result, then, is a study which produces very "iffy" results that are open to a legion of plausible rival hypotheses.

How can this situation be improved? The first step is to formulate your research as cross-cultural from the beginning. Then read all you can about how to do it better (*Cross-Cultural Research Methods* was my first research Bible). Thereafter talk to people who are knowledgeable about the cultures you are going to compare in an effort to discover how the research is likely to be understood by the subjects you are using. Indeed, you may want to ask these cultural informants for their opinions about the subjects you ought to select, given the purposes of your research.

Even then it will be a challenge to produce a cross-cultural study that cannot be faulted by someone creative enough to generate an intelligent "yes, but." I once heard an editor of the *Journal of Cross-Cultural Psychology* assert that he had never published a study whose outcome he could not subject to a plausible rival hypothesis. Culture is a megalopolis of variables, all energetically interacting to yield the endless variety of human behavior. How can we ever exercise sufficient care to produce a sound piece of cross-cultural research?

*T*HE TRUE SPICE ISLANDS?

> What kind of truth is this that is bounded by a chain of mountains and is falsehood to the people living on the other side? [Montaigne]

Under supportive circumstances folly yields to a measure of wisdom. Ten years after my joint study of Barnum personality descriptions I published another cross-cultural study with Kwok Leung, a Chinese psychologist from Hong Kong. It avoided many of the obvious pitfalls that compromised my earlier work and embraced some of the more subtle virtues that are recommended for comparative research. It still has problems, of course, but we are all continuing to learn, and as the Chinese say, it takes 100 years to make a scholar.

The Platonic Ideal

This particular study may be assessed against an ideal for such studies. As I now conceive it, a study embodying this ideal begins with behavior which has universal status; that is, it can be found anywhere. This behavior is embedded within a theory which orchestrates the various situational factors which influence that behavior. One of these factors would concern the culture of the actors and the culture of the setting for the behavior. Both factors must then be linked to the behavior in generating predictions. So, for example, the values of the actors may reflect their culture, as do the situational norms in the behavior setting. Both norms and values have to be measured before or during the study to prevent after-the-fact "explanations" from being created to justify the outcome. Perhaps the following example will clarify this idea.

Resource Allocation

The goods of this world are limited; human claims on those resources are loud and insistent. All societies therefore must confront the problem of allocating resources in the face of competing demands. Procedures for resource distribution are developed and legitimized in each society so as to minimize disruptive struggles among its members.

This universal conundrum is resolved differently by resource allocators depending on their relationship to the recipient. A parent may divide allowances among children on the basis of their perceived input to production. This equity solution may be dropped in favor of an equal distribution when that employer is giving meal vouchers to members of the Little League team he or she coaches after work.

These approaches to distributing resources affect people differently. The equity solution, for example, is perceived by people as being fair and as promoting productivity. The equality solution is perceived as being nondiscriminating and as promoting harmony. As one might anticipate, these two solutions will be differentially preferred in cultures which emphasize either fairness or harmony.

The Impact of Collectivism

My American friends who visit Hong Kong express great difficulty with an apparent paradox: Chinese persons are rude and careless with strangers in public but attentive and courteous at home with guests. At least that is how Chinese appear to western minds socialized in a democratic ethic. To quote from the Declaration of Independence, "We hold these truths to be self evident, that all men are created equal." To realize this state of nature, we raise children to treat all people by the same set of rules and to apply those rules universally—to all persons regardless of race, creed, or color.

Could one not, however, imagine a cultural world where there are two sets of persons: strangers and those with whom one has an ongoing relationship? Strangers are given the necessary respect their size, speed, and passing presence require but nothing more. Acquaintances, however, are treated like family, people whose welfare matters and whose good opinion we strive to achieve and maintain, often at considerable cost. Such was the distinction that Kwok Leung and I came to advance as an explanation for the puzzlement of our American visitors.

This outsider-insider distinction is fundamental to the concept of cultural collectivism, and in our intellectual bull sessions Dr. Leung and I found that it applied easily to the problem of resource distribution: Outsiders should be treated in strict accordance with the equity or fairness criterion by Chinese in order to avoid disputes; insiders should be treated in accordance with the quality or harmony criterion in order to foster a sustaining relationship. In other words, Chinese allocators draw the sharp collectivist distinction between strangers and friends whereas Americans do not, or at least do so less sharply.

To our knowledge, nobody had yet tested this speculation about the concept of collectivism in an area of social psychology such as resource allocation. However, the idea seemed well grounded to us, since we both had lived in each other's culture. Furthermore, the hypothesis was theory-driven. As such, its confirmation promised to have some impact on mainstream psychologists who were jaded by a history of opportunistic cross-cultural studies run on available subjects and having no theoretical significance. Hofstede's earlier research had established that the Hong Kong Chinese were collectivist and that the Americans were individualistic, and so the stage was set to test our ideas.

Tasks, Materials, Relationships (and Subjects!)

As Guthrie has warned us, the

> major problem that faces us in cross-cultural research is that of determining whether differences found among samples from different societies are real or merely the artifacts of data-collection procedures that mean different things to people from different cultural backgrounds. [p. 350]

This equivalence problem faces journal editors when they evaluate a cross-cultural manuscript and, as a result, must be considered in detail by researchers who are planning to run such a study. This Kwok Leung and I did in the sweltering summer of 1982, sitting in my office at the Chinese University when he was on vacation from graduate studies at the University of Illinois. Here are the considerations we made.

Task. The task we gave subjects was to copy words from a known language and an unknown language correctly for a total of forty minutes. They were paired with another subject whom they had never met (i.e., a stranger) and who supposedly was working in an adjacent room. We told subjects that to heighten motivation and make the work more lifelike, they and their partners would be rewarded for their joint output in the copying task. We manipulated feedback about the relative outputs so that the subjects believed they had done either twice as much or half as much as their partners. They then had to divide a fixed amount of money between themselves and their partners.

Here was our attempt to examine resource allocation with a stranger in collectivist and individualistic cultures. We knew that both Chinese and American subjects have experience working in groups and being rewarded as a group (e.g., on academic projects in class), and so there would be no inequivalence in task familiarity. Furthermore, the mathematics involved was easily within the grasp of university students, and so no group would choose an equality solution simply because the calculations for an equity division were too difficult. Finally, the performance feedback was equally plausible for both groups, as subjects had no knowledge of the partner's performance or the accuracy of their own. As all subjects were taking introductory psychology, we might of course expect them to be somewhat, although equally, distrustful of any feedback from the experimenter. Again, no inequivalence.

Materials. The familiar language to be copied was English for the Americans but Chinese for the Chinese; the unfamiliar language was French for the Americans but Japanese for the Chinese. Although these languages are different for each of the cultural groups, they are conceptually similar with respect to the familiarity variable. Straightforward operational similarity is obviously inappropriate when one is running subjects from different cultures.

So too in the case of money. To equate the importance of the allocation task, the same value of total reward must be divided by the allocators, but the value of a given sum depends on the relative income of each cultural group. In the early 1980s Hong Kong Chinese students were relatively less affluent than American students. How, then, could we equate the value of the total reward? Our solution was to make the total for each cultural group about twice the cost of a lunch at the student canteen. Operationally, then, the exact amounts of the total reward differed for Americans and Chinese. Conceptually, however, their value was equivalent.

Relationships. The subjects and the experimenters must have the same quality of relationship in each cultural group studied: the same levels of acquaintanceship, formality, and status. Inequivalences here could affect the subject's motivation to concentrate on the task at hand, trust the experimenter's feedback, or impress the experimenter with one allocation strategy or another. Acquaintanceship was equated by using local experimenters who did not know the subjects; formality was equated by focusing the exchanges exclusively on the experiment; status was made equivalent by using graduate student experimenters in the United States but senior undergraduates in Hong Kong. The greater hierarchy in Chinese culture means that one can achieve the same status effect with smaller distinctions of rank. Again, a strict operational sameness is rejected in the effort to achieve conceptual equivalence in the relationship between subject and experimenter.

Subjects. To choose university students as subjects does not guarantee that they are the same sorts of persons from culture to culture. This is especially true for women, whose access to higher education is restricted in certain countries. Generally speaking, the poorer the country, the more demanding the criteria for university admission and the smaller the proportion of the population in universities. In the United States, for example, more than one-third of the age cohort receives a university education; in Hong Kong, only about 2 percent.

Fortunately, academic achievement is the litmus test for university admission in both cultural groups. To equate roughly for achievement, however, one must choose subjects from an American university that has admission standards as high as those in Hong Kong. We believed that the University of Illinois was equivalent to the Chinese University in this respect.

A further difficulty arises, however, because American student bodies are heterogeneous in ethnic terms, whereas Hong Kong student bodies are homogeneous. Obviously, one must eliminate American subjects who have collectivist cultural backgrounds (especially Hong Kong Chinese!) from the American sample. Given discrimination laws, this step can often be taken only after the study has been run and the subject's ethnicity has been assessed by the experimenter. But assessed it must be, or one is not comparing culturally "pure" groups: Differences will be more difficult to detect.

The Yin-Yang Balance

Readers with an eye for detail and a sense of fun may have already noticed another telling equivalence in this research. Specifically, the work was executed by two foreigners living in each other's country. Each was therefore knowledgeable about the other's culture by virtue of living in and frequently reading about the other's home territory. This mutual background ensured that the study was planned with sufficient background and preparation to avoid the obvious inequivalences discussed above.

In addition, the relationship between myself and my coauthor was (and still is) one of appreciation and respect. These are key elements in any cross-cultural enterprise, scientific or otherwise. They ensure a full give-and-take that allows each cultural party to contribute his or her knowledge to the project, especially during the crucial planning stage. As many others have noted, their absence increases the likelihood that imperialistic, biased research will be imposed on one cultural group by another.

Not in this case. Dr. Leung and I thrashed out these ideas by mail and in person, over lunches, in the office corridor, at the swimming pool, when traveling by car—you name it. We continue to talk openly about our cultures, acknowledging what each of us believes to be their virtues and shortfalls. We observe our own dynamics for possible ideas about cultural differences and freely exchange leadership roles. Ours has been a rich relationship that has enhanced the sensitivity of our cross-cultural research. I recommend such professional friendships for all culture travelers.

The Results?

After all this methodological hand-wringing, the actual results might well seem to occupy a less salient position. Without effective hand-wringing, however, there will be no defensible position for them to occupy at all. So, having paid our dues at the planning stages, Dr. Leung and I were very keen to discover the yield from our labors.

There was good news and bad news awaiting us. The female subjects in our study showed us exactly the interaction pattern we had hypothesized: Chinese women gave more to the high-performance partner but less to the low-performance partner than did American women. This significant interaction was especially encouraging because such an interaction is so rare but so useful in cross-cultural research. As many commentators have noted (e.g., Guthrie in 1979), it is very easy to obtain between-culture differences in one's data, but these general differences are always suspect for the many methodological reasons we have noted. An interaction involving culture, however, cannot be explained away by some plausible rival hypothesis such as response set or inequivalent translations; it must be interpreted in its own right as a real phenomenon. So we were pleased.

As for the men, however, the results reminded us of Huxley's witticism "The great tragedy of science—the slaying of a beautiful hypothesis by an ugly fact." Chinese and American men reversed our hypothesized interaction, with the Chinese men showing more egalitarianism and the American men showing more equity. Well, at least we had found another interaction involving culture, even if its direction was the opposite of our predictions. Back to the scientific drawing board for the next round. This return led us to engage in some serious "what-ifing."

Creative "What-Ifing"

Any cross-cultural study can be improved, and ours is no exception. Guthrie has correctly warned us that "Unfortunately, cultural backgrounds, as complex as they are, can account for all sorts of differences" (p. 351). After all, we did not measure our subjects' personal levels of collectivism directly. What if their levels of collectivism did not in fact differ? What if, despite our care, American male subjects were simply more suspicious of the experimenter's feedback about their test performance relative to their partners' and so chose an approximately equal distribution? What if collectivism, however measured, has no relationship to allocation strategies and our results relate only to some specific, isolated feature of Chinese and American cultures? What if, what if?

These possibilities are intriguing, as are others. Probably no cross-cultural study can withstand such creative "what-ifing" without some loss of apparent certainty. However, it is a matter of degree, with better planned studies suffering less. More positively, such challenges to research suggest new strategies for the future. One should develop and take measures of the subjects' collectivism; one should assess subjects' credibility about the feedback; one should include two collectivist and two individualist cultures to ensure that the common denominator of collectivism rather than other local peculiarities is accounting for the observed difference in allocations, etc., etc. To expand Emerson's maxim, "every wall" in one study "is a door" to another study. The process of scientific refinement continues, especially when one is dealing with a hodgepodge concept such as culture.

CIRCUMNAVIGATION

And the end of all our exploring
Will be to arrive where we started
And know the place for the first time.
——T. S. Eliot, *The Four Quartets*

In our twentieth-century wisdom we know that the world is round. In consequence, a journey to foreign places often leads us back to our original point of departure. For many people this conclusion is good news. Contact with alien cultures is often disturbing. As Conrad acknowledged in *Lord Jim*, "It had the power to drive me out of my conception of existence, out of that shelter each of us makes for himself to creep under in moments of danger. . . ."

Having read this far, some of you may be experiencing exactly this sense of relief: "Thank goodness I have returned home! This culture business is charming in small doses but deadly as a daily diet. Altogether too complex and abstract. How can we ever reach any firm conclusions?" To which I reply, "Right on all counts. But there is one surprising discovery that still awaits many homecomers."

Having left home for a time, one returns from foreign climes to discover that home is not quite the same. Huxley put it this way in *Jesting Pilate:*

When one is travelling, convictions are mislaid as easily as spectacles; but unlike spectacles, they are not so easily replaced.

The shared conventions of language and interaction schemas combine with the constancy of place to give those who do not voyage across cultures a sense of comfort in their worlds. Theirs is a solid place. However, those who are bitten by the culture bug lose this sense of assurance and begin wondering about things.

As young social scientists, some of you may be straining at the bit to return to your familiar laboratories, to get back to an environment where experimenters and subjects have a common understanding about what is happening and how to assess it. But wait. Those subjects you have recruited—is English their first language? Does their gender affect how they respond to the experimental context? Are some of them black, Hispanic, Native American, Asian, or some such ethnic grouping? What social class are they from, and what was their parents' educational background? In many cases we can scrape away the patina of surface sameness in our subjects to reveal a host of differences which may have a powerful impact on our dependent variables.

At present these possible confounds are swept under the rug of our error terms. Alternatively, we limit our subjects to university-educated, white American men and justify our dismissal of diversity by claiming that the processes we investigate are universal. Neither strategy is likely to survive the twentieth century. First, there is going to be more and more cross-cultural interaction as our world contracts into a global village. Second, mounting evidence tells us that culture has a variety of effects on both the processes and the contents of what social psychologists study.

But perhaps I am pushing too hard. There are many problems to explore in social psychology, and culture is only one of them. Nevertheless, some of you will find the topic of culture to be magnetic, as I do, and continue your intellectual travels in this direction. If so, I hope that these reflections on my own journeying will make yours even more rewarding.

Perhaps on some quiet night the tremor of far-off drums, sinking, swelling, a tremor vast, faint; a sound weird, appealing, suggestive, and wild—and perhaps with as profound a meaning as the sound of bells in a Christian country. [Joseph Conrad, *The Heart of Darkness*]

Acknowledgments

I extend my hearty thanks to Mieko Bond, Sunita Bond, and George Guthrie for their help in improving the impact of this chapter. *"Nemo dat quis non habet!"*

*S*UGGESTED READINGS

BRISLIN, R. W., LONNER, W. J., & THORNDIKE, R. M. (1973). *Cross-cultural research methods*. New York: Wiley.

GUTHRIE, G. M. (1979). A cross-cultural odyssey: Some personal reflections. In A. Marsella, R. Tharp, & T. Ciborowski (Eds.), *Perspectives on cross-cultural psychology* (pp. 349–368). New York: Academic Press.

MEDAWAR, P. B. (1979). *Advice to a young scientist*. New York: Basic Books.

SMITH, P. B., & BOND, M. H. (1993). *Social psychology across cultures: Analysis and perspectives*. London: Simon & Schuster.

MROBIN DIMATTEO (Ph.D., Harvard University) is Professor of Psychology at the University of California, Riverside, where she teaches health psychology to undergraduate and graduate students and to students in the health sciences. She is also Resident Consultant in the Social Policy Department of the RAND Corporation in Santa Monica, California, where she conducts research on social science and health policy. She is a fellow of the American Psychological Society and has received fellowship research awards from the W. K. Kellogg Foundation and the James McKeen Cattell Fund. Her research has been supported by the Research Network on Health and Behavior of the John D. & Catherine T. MacArthur Foundation, the Pew Health Professions Program, the National Institutes of Mental Health, the Agency for Health Care Policy and Research, and the University of California, Riverside. She is married, has a young daughter and a new schnauzer puppy, and loves to exercise by doing low-impact aerobics and lap swimming.

12

$\mathcal{H}$ealth $\mathcal{P}$sychology $\mathcal{R}$esearch: $\mathcal{T}$he $\mathcal{I}$nterpersonal $\mathcal{C}$hallenges

❖

*I*t was my first day interviewing patients in the internal medicine clinic of an overwhelmingly busy inner-city hospital. Ten seconds into my explanation of our research interview and of how important her contribution would be, the elderly grandmother bellowed with emphasis.

"*Wait* a minute," she insisted. I looked up from my clipboard, my eyes a bit rounded. "I need another prescription for my diuretics." A moment before I had introduced myself to her as "Doctor" DiMatteo. I thought about telling her right away that I couldn't write the prescription for her because I was a psychologist and psychologists can't write prescriptions. But I was afraid she might walk away, and I wanted her to answer my questions. So I soft-pedaled it.

"Your doctor can give you the prescription when you go in for your visit," I said encouragingly. "May I go on with my interview? Uh, how satisfied are you with the medical care you receive at this clinic? Would you say you are somewhat satisfied, very satisfied, or—"

"Why can't *you* do it?" she asserted.

"Because I'm here to interview you about your medical care," I asserted back.

Our exchange went on for about twenty minutes. I was asking for *her* time, so I felt obligated to give her some of my own. During our conversation I learned that she had come to the clinic that day only because she had run out of her pills.

She didn't want to wait the usual two hours to see the doctor. I also learned about her two daughters who almost never came to visit, about her next-door neighbor who made too much noise, about her cat which tore up the little furniture she had, and about how lonely she really was. After a while I really wished I could help. I think she saw it in my eyes, because she made her original request again.

"Because I can't write prescriptions," I answered honestly but a bit sheepishly.

And then it came—the question I would be asked many, many times throughout my career.

"So, what kind of doctor *are* you, anyway?"

When I explained my true identity to her, she was very gracious and allowed me to interview her. But as I moved on to the next patient, who looked like a good prospect for participating in the research, I decided to dispense with the "doctor" business altogether.

"Hello, my name is Robin DiMatteo," I said cheerily. "I would like to ask you a few questions about—"

"Who are *you*?" he snorted as he looked me up and down with apparent disdain. Then he made eye contact, and a few silent seconds went by before the light of recognition crossed his face. He had figured me out. "Hey," he asked with a bit of excitement, "are you the Avon lady?"

Perhaps I deserved to be seen as a cosmetics representative; I didn't have a white coat on that day. This experience, however, forced me to learn the first rule of conducting research in a hospital: Wear a white coat. If you aren't wearing one (or another kind of uniform) in a hospital, you are, almost by definition, a patient, a family member or friend of a patient, or a "representative" of some sort (such as from admitting or the gift shop). Since I was planning to spend a great deal of my career dealing with patients and hospitals, I decided that I had better wear the correct uniform.

TALKING TO PATIENTS

Donning the white coat was the easy step. Figuring out who I was vis-à-vis patients was the hard one. Throughout my career I have requested all kinds of information from patients: how satisfied they are with their medical care, whether and why they follow (or don't follow) the recommended treatments, whether and how they have adjusted to cancer, how their marriages have withstood the pressures of chemotherapy, how they have coped with pain during childbirth, and what they are experiencing several months after the delivery, to name just a few research topics I have pursued over the years.

My requests for information from patients have often come in the form of interviews. Interviews involve quite a bit more than simply talking to people, although good communication is absolutely necessary. When researchers conduct interviews, they use a format, or set of specific questions, which they have painstakingly developed beforehand. They may allow respondents to answer these questions freely by saying whatever is on their minds or restrict respondents' answers to a set of preestablished choices (for example, "How do you rate your doctor: poor, fair, good, very good, or excellent?"). Regardless of the type of response required, the interviewer must use the interview format with all respondents so that all those participating in the study answer the same questions. Before beginning a study, a researcher must also test the interview format he or she has developed to be sure that those interviewed really understand what they are being asked. Interviewers must practice asking their questions in a very objective manner, without influencing or biasing the responses they receive. Sometimes interview questions can be written out on a paper-and-pencil questionnaire for respondents to fill out on their own.

An excellent example of this type of research is a study of patient satisfaction in a family practice clinic conducted by myself and my colleague Ron Hays. Immediately after leaving a visit with his or her doctor, each patient was asked to spend a few moments answering some questions about that visit. Patients were given the choice of having the questions asked verbally in an interview or answering the same questions on a questionnaire. In response to each of a series of statements, patients were asked to indicate one of five responses in accordance with their reaction to the statement: strongly disagree, disagree, neutral (neither agree nor disagree), agree, and strongly agree. In the following list of ten of the items used, note that some of the statements are worded negatively and responses must be reversed for scoring patient satisfaction to prevent a positive bias in patients' responses: (1) I really like this doctor a great deal. (2) I wish I could stay with this doctor and never have to change to another one. (3) This doctor doesn't give me a chance to say what is on my mind. (4) This doctor always listens to everything I have to say. (5) This doctor doesn't tell me very much about his or her plans to take care of me. (6) I feel this doctor does not spend enough time with me. (7) This doctor is always very kind and considerate of my feelings. (8) This doctor acts like I don't have any feelings. (9) I have some doubts about the ability of this doctor. (10) I have a great deal of confidence in this doctor. Although the entire questionnaire is somewhat longer, this sampling of items illustrates the interview-questionnaire methodology used in our studies on patient satisfaction with the care delivered by their physicians.

Using interviews and questionnaires, my colleagues and I have tried to assess the patient's perspective on all kinds of issues in medical care, such as how to improve the physician-patient relationship, how to promote more positive outcomes of medical treatment, and how to make the medical care system and the health professionals in it more responsive to the psychological needs of patients. We have focused on problems of how best to care for patients as whole human beings whose minds influence their physical well-being and vice versa.

In attempting to improve the outcomes of medical treatment, we have emphasized the complexity of medical and surgical outcomes. That is, we have focused on outcomes that go beyond technical parameters such as lowering blood pressure and speeding the healing of an infection. Broader outcomes are those which have direct meaning for patients' lives, such as whether they are able to be physically active, have satisfying social (including family) relationships, enjoy emotional balance, and participate in the world as productive persons. These outcomes are called "functional outcomes" and go well beyond the purely technical outcomes on which American medicine has tended to focus over the past half century. Our research emphasizes that a human being is more than a bag of chemicals needing an adjustment and that the whole person must be taken into account if medical care is to be successful.

One issue my colleagues and I have examined extensively is patient nonadherence to treatment recommendations. Nonadherence refers to a patient's "failure" to follow the treatment suggested by his or her physician. Because they have misunderstood, have forgotten, or simply don't agree with the recommendations made by their physicians, as many as 75 to 80 percent of patients do not follow through with what they have been told they must do to take care of themselves. In our research we have tried to determine why patients would go through the trouble and expense of seeing a doctor and then ignore what he or she tells them. We have found that patients know what they are doing when they don't adhere and that at least two factors are particularly important. Patients tend not to follow through with treatments that they believe are not worth the trouble. That is, they fail to adhere if they believe that the costs of following the treatment in terms of time, energy, attention, and emotional and/or physical distress outweigh the benefits of doing so. Furthermore, patients tend to ignore a recommendation that is too difficult to follow, one for which there are too few supports and too many practical barriers.

The methodology used in our research on the adherence of cancer patients and those hoping to prevent cancer also involved interview and questionnaire methods. Some of the items which best predicted patient adherence included the following (again using the agree-disagree format described earlier): (1) My treatment plan is too much trouble for what I get out of it. (2) Following my treatment plan will help me be healthy. (3) Because my treatment plan is too difficult, it is not worth following. (4) I am able to deal with any problems in following my treatment plan. (5) Lots of things get in the way of following my treatment plan.

Our research has shown that the physician-patient relationship is at the heart of patient nonadherence and that to solve the problem, communication between doctors and patients must be improved. In our research on physician-patient communication, we have found that too often patients don't understand the potential benefits of a treatment that has been prescribed because their physicians fail to explain the benefits carefully. Furthermore, physicians often prescribe courses of action without checking to see whether patients can in fact carry them out. A very common example is the tendency of physicians to write prescriptions that ask patients to take medication four times a day. Few people can remember to take four pills a day spaced equally over time, particularly if the recommendation involves taking the pill on an empty stomach. We have found that physicians should briefly discuss with the patient his or her daily schedule and how to incorporate the treatment into it. If a suitable schedule cannot be worked out, a more workable treatment, such as a medication that needs to be taken only three times a day, may be chosen. Our research has allowed us to make such simple, practical recommendations to physicians in an attempt to improve the level of patient cooperation with treatment recommendations.

Much of our research has focused on an issue that is at the heart of medical care: patients' satisfaction with the care they receive. Our evidence suggests that patients who are dissatisfied are less likely to cooperate with recommendations made by physicians. They tend to ignore the advice of physicians whom they do not like and whose interpersonal care is inadequate. Patients who are more satisfied with the interpersonal care they receive tend to experience more positive outcomes and to recover faster and more completely. Even if the outcome is less than what they had expected but they are satisfied with the physician's interpersonal care, they are less likely to retaliate against the physician with a malpractice suit.

EMOTIONAL CONNECTIONS TO PATIENTS

I have been gathering data from patients for almost twenty years in an effort to study what I think are important issues for improving medical care. One dilemma has arisen again and again, however. I have never gotten over the feeling that when I am meeting with patients, I should dispense with the interview format and just try to help. Usually these patients have been through illness and a considerable amount of physical and emotional suffering. I ask for their time and their intellectual and emotional focus when, because of all they have been through, they are the ones who should be given time and attention. I feel that I should be helping them directly, not asking them to help me. In many of the hospitals and clinics where I have done research, the patients are old, lonely, and poor. Their care is perfunctory; the doctors are overwhelmed with patients and too busy to listen. I have tried to listen, so much, in fact, that in one study each three-minute interview stretched to an hour or more, jeopardizing the completion of the work I had set out to do. In situations like this the patient's needs have tugged at me emotionally, and I have wondered about the value of what I am trying to accomplish. Research and the publishing of research results seem so remote compared to the immediate needs of patients. If my work eventually contributes to changes in the delivery of medical care, the patients in my studies are not the ones who will benefit. Changes in the system can be made only on the basis of a considerable amount of accumulated data, much of which would be compiled far too late to be of direct benefit to them.

Yet for me two things have militated against giving up on research with medical patients. One is that they usually want very much to contribute to research. By doing so, they feel that they are giving something of themselves to others. I had a small inkling of this feeling when I gave birth to my daughter in a teaching hospital. When I was first admitted in labor, even though I had a private physician, I was interviewed separately by an intern and by two medical students, all of whom repeated the same set of questions. I thought about asking them to leave me alone because I was in a good deal of pain, but I remembered that interviewing is how they learn. And although I was only one of many hundreds of patients in labor whom they would talk to in the next several months, they would learn something from me. I got a glimpse of how patients probably feel when I ask them questions. They believe that they have something to teach me, and they do. The second argument in favor of pressing on with this research is that psychological issues have been very much neglected in late twentieth-century western medicine. In the past fifty years technical developments in medicine have far surpassed any in medical history. Yet more than at any time in history, the mind, psyche, and soul of human beings have been ignored in medical practice. Our goal in research is to modify the focus of advanced technical medicine to include attention to the patient as a person. The more that is known about the social psychology of health, illness, and medical care, the more likely things are to improve for all patients in the long run.

Needless to say, health psychology research sometimes involves subjects who are not at their best. My colleagues and I have interviewed patients the night before a dreaded surgery, soon after radiation treatments and chemotherapy for cancer, during periods of depression after giving birth, and after they have been ill for a long time with a debilitating disease from which they will probably never recover. Sometimes these patients are very tired and weak from being sick or are afraid and confused because they have been given little or no information by health professionals. Often the closest family member, usually the spouse, has been overwhelmingly affected by the illness as well. The couple's life plans have been derailed, and their chances of sharing enjoyment and romance have been seriously diminished. Usually their only trips together are to and from the doctor's office.

The dilemmas that patients face inevitably touch me in very personal ways and force me to face certain issues that I want and need to understand. I often wonder how *I* would feel and what *I* would do under the circumstances that patients face. How would I cope? What would happen to my most treasured relationships? What would happen to my work? These personal questions fuel my research interests.

Several years ago I had an opportunity to conduct research with colleagues at UCLA on the coping and adjustment of women and their spouses as they faced breast cancer. We examined the ways in which these women and their husbands felt they had been affected by cancer, how the relationship had changed as a result, to what extent the issues brought up by cancer were eventually resolved, and the ways cancer had changed them forever. We found, as we had expected, that women who had less disfiguring surgeries for breast cancer had a more positive body image and better sexual adjustment than did those who had more disfiguring surgeries. But the psychological changes faced by all the breast cancer patients were considerable. Forced to confront the possibility of dying, they reevaluated their lives and relationships.

More recently, my students and I have begun to focus our attention on individuals and their spouses as they face serious, debilitating chronic illness. Chronic conditions such as heart disease, diabetes, and rheumatoid arthritis usually can be managed but never cured. Chronically ill patients will never recover in the sense of becoming completely healthy. They may improve for a while, but they and their loved ones can count on living with illness. When marriages begin, it is safe to say, I think, that good health is taken mostly for granted. Despite promises of devotion "in sickness and in health," most people assume and expect that their mates will always be more or less healthy. But as the literature documents and my own observations have certainly borne out, such assumptions are sometimes proved wrong and marriages can be damaged or torn apart by illness. Serious illness can threaten the foundations of loving relationships. The ill person may withdraw into pain and fatigue or react with bitterness at having to be dependent on others. The well partner may feel rejected, lonely in the relationship, restricted from pursuing interests, and unable to depend on social interactions outside the relationship. Resentments on both sides can become destructive to both partners and eventually to the relationship. Chronic illness or disability can require more of a relationship than it can possibly give.

Of course, there is considerable evidence for the opposite outcome as well. Some relationships become much closer in response to the illness of one member. Emotional barriers that once existed between the partners are broken down by their mutual expression of fear and vulnerability. Well spouses find that they can give more than they ever thought was possible. People who are ill sometimes change their lives in ways that, without the illness to jolt their sense of who they are, they might otherwise have never been able to do. As illustrated in recent motion pictures such as *The Doctor* and *Regarding Henry,* sometimes illness helps a person become more of the person his or her spouse has always wished that person would be.

What distinguishes the two possibilities for the effects of illness on a relationship? Does the difference lie in the resources that people bring to solve the dilemmas presented by illness? Does it lie in their commitment to the relationship, or to their own personal optimism about life, or to the characteristics of the disease itself?

In preparation for researching this particular question, we recently conducted a search of the literature and found dozens of articles that approach the very complex question of why, in the face of illness, some marriages become stronger and others become weaker. We are currently planning a several-year longitudinal study to examine patients' and spouses' responses to the challenges of chronic disease.

What I love about health psychology is that the kinds of questions which intrigue me most, such as those mentioned above, are the very stuff of the field. They are questions that a health psychologist can naturally pursue.

STUDYING DOCTORS

I have been studying physicians and their lives and behavior for most of my career. Sometimes, whether I like it or not, however, I can't *stop* studying how physicians do their jobs. Whenever I am a patient, for example, despite any discomfort, fear, and anger I may feel in that role, my consciousness also operates in an attempt to figure out the social psychology of the doctor-patient relationship. I try (both for my own sake and for that of my scientific understanding) to insinuate myself into the decision process of the doctor who is caring for me. I know from the literature as well as my personal and research experiences that two issues regarding medical decision making are of the utmost importance to patients: (1) Good decisions are rarely straightforward, and the patient's psychosocial characteristics and needs must be taken into account if a course of action that is right for that patient is to be decided upon. (2) Patients must have input into the decisions that are made about their lives. Since many physicians are unaccustomed to sharing responsibility for such decision making, however, patients often must be extremely assertive and vigilant in their interactions with physicians, something that may be very difficult when a person is in the patient role. For these reasons, I think the quality of the doctor-patient relationship, particularly its humanistic component, is *the* essential ingredient in the delivery of effective medical care.

My colleagues and I have tried to examine the humanistic aspects of the delivery of medical care in various ways. We have been warned, however, that while everyone might like to have a kind, understanding physician, the *skill* of the surgeon cutting or the internist puzzling out the diagnosis is all that matters. According to this view, physicians who are brusque and unfeeling can still do a good job and talking with patients is superfluous. I don't believe this. Our literature reviews and a major study we conducted on this topic have given me confidence in asserting that physicians who are kind and communicate well with patients get better results in their delivery of medical care. We conducted a major study in several different research hospitals where residents (physicians in training) in internal medicine, family practice, and surgery evaluated each other and themselves and were evaluated by their supervising senior physicians and their patients. Thus, for each physician there were *four* sources of ratings. These ratings involved both their technical skills and their interpersonal skills in interactions with patients. *Technical skill* for the internal medicine and family practice residents consisted of the medical diagnosis and management of disease, and for the surgeons it involved surgical skills. Specifically, the physicians were rated (using a scale from one to five where one is poor and five is excellent) on their intelligence, common sense, medical-scientific knowledge and ability, professional judgment, and technical skill. For all the doctors, *interpersonal skill* involved talking with patients and taking the psychosocial aspects of patient care into account. Specifically, the physicians were rated on their politeness, dedication, sensitivity and perceptiveness, patient rapport, kindness, humaneness, compassion, and empathy. We expected to find that the technical and interpersonal skills of physicians would be independent of each other and that one kind of skill would not affect the other. It was even suggested to us that these skills might be inversely related so that doctors who were skillful in one area would actually be deficient in the other. (In other words, the best surgeons would be the gruff, uncommunicative, uncaring ones.) Instead, we found that there was a *positive* correlation between technical skill and interpersonal skill. This was particularly true of ratings made by the senior physicians (who were very much aware of the skills of the doctors training under them) and the patients (who were the recipients of the care and knew better than anyone how they fared after treatment). In other words, the best surgeons and diagnosticians were *also* the most caring physicians, doctors who talked with their patients and took the psychosocial aspects of patient care into account. The findings suggest that

effective interpersonal skills in medical care are essential to good outcomes.

TALKING TO DOCTORS

Physicians are, I think, the most challenging subjects I have ever tried to
talk to because their cooperation is usually very difficult to obtain. They
are often physically and emotionally exhausted and under considerable
stress. Research tells us that in training and in certain specialties in practice as well, physicians almost never get more than four hours of sleep a
night when on call, and often that sleep is interrupted. They usually
work under considerable time pressure and experience social isolation,
having little time for pursuits apart from medicine. Days and often
nights are spent taking care of people who are ill, have suffered
tragedies, and may be dying. Because so much of patient care is devoted
to treating (managing but never curing) chronic illness, practicing medicine can involve frustration and failed expectations. Another reason why
talking to physicians is so difficult is that they are accustomed to asking,
not answering, questions.

One important challenge I have faced in working with physicians is
time. When I did research with exhausted residents during the first ten
or so years of my career, I quickly realized what a very precious commodity even a few moments was to them. Often I would resort to trading
time with them. ["Please take ten minutes to fill out my questionnaire
(you can sit down) and I will run down and pick up your lab results and
x-rays and buy you a sandwich."] After doing so, I would often return to
a resident asleep in the chair because he had been up all the night before.

Spending a good deal of time with health professionals has taught
me quite a lot about medical practice. When I have joined residents at
lunch, for example, they have spoken of drug dosages and treatment as if
I were part of the patient care team, expecting me to understand and participate. (So that I could, I've spent many evenings reading up on dis-
eases and looking up the medical terms I heard earlier in the day.) I probably have had more exposure to clinical medicine than the average
health psychologist and feel very comfortable working with medical professionals. However, it is always clear to me that I am not one of them.
Sometimes I am caught up short by gaps in my knowledge. More often,
however, my emotional reactions are out of line.

The physician in charge of a department in a hospital where I did
research ten years ago decided one day to show me all the new technical
additions to his department. He guided me through the intensive care
unit, pointing out the newly added equipment, the five new beds, and

the nurses' station. I typically do not have much trouble coping with the sights, sounds, and smells of hospitals because I have spent a good deal of time observing what goes on in them. But all I remember of that tour was the row of unconscious people hooked up to a half dozen monitors, with tubes entering their bodies in four or five places. I remember feigning interest in the newly acquired machinery, little of which I understood, and I congratulated everyone on this up-to-date facility. But as I looked around to where the loved ones of the intubated people were waiting, I tried to catch a glimpse of their faces. My concern was not with the tremendous technical advances in the intensive care unit (ICU). As a psychologist, my focus was on the loved ones of those in the ICU, people who were suddenly forced to have their lives revolve around the ICU, where they waited day after day for some news that their child, spouse, relative, or friend might survive and someday be normal again.

As a health psychologist, I teach medical and premedical students and find myself challenged and tested again and again. Although I emphasize the importance of understanding the trends in empirical data and making judgments on the basis of large sample sizes, my students ask me endless *clinical* questions. They want to hear clinical anecdotes and individual cases that make medicine and psychology real to them. In making a point, one clinical case is often worth a thousand statistics.

Medical students also want to know whether I can handle emotionally what they are handling. I will never know the answer, of course, because my orientation is completely different from theirs. I am not responsible for the physical well-being of patients but rather for their emotional well-being and for understanding what they tell me. However, particularly when I began teaching, the first-year medical students would invite me into their anatomy labs to see if I could cope with the dissection of a cadaver and the overwhelming smell of formaldehyde. "Hey Dr. D.," I remember hearing within a moment of arriving at the lab. "Come on over here and help us cut some of the fat away so we can see the muscle." During my first visit to the anatomy lab, I was enlisted to cut pieces of the body of a deceased sixty-five-year-old woman. I remember thinking that she was probably a grandmother who had knitted and sewn and loved her family. The students watched me intently, wondering if I would faint or experience emotional distress. I searched my mind for the strategies physicians use to distance themselves from the reality of human suffering and death. They use denial, compartmentalization of emotions, and intellectualization, and so did I. While employing them, I realized the short-term effectiveness of these defense mechanisms and turned my attention to scraping away the fat obscuring the muscles and blood vessels I wanted to see. I wondered, however, about the potential maladaptiveness of the long-term use of these strategies and the effect such distancing might have on patient care.

*T*HE LAB AND THE FIELD

Not all health psychologists actually spend time in hospitals. In fact, there are many topics that can be studied without leaving one's office or research laboratory. My colleagues and I have done quite a bit of "laboratory research," which involves conditions of experimentation or observation over which the researcher has a measure of control. The research takes place on the experimenter's "turf." In a few studies I had physicians in training come into a room I had set up in the administration wing of the hospital. This was truly a laboratory in which (for once!) I had considerable control. I gave them a script and filmed them as they tried to convey various emotions. The script involved expressing emotionally neutral verbal communications (such as "The results of your tests are back") while attempting to convey four different emotions: happiness, sadness, anger, and surprise. These expressions were videotaped and shown to students trained as judges, who attempted to determine which emotion was conveyed in each segment. The proportion of the total sample of judges that accurately identified the emotion intended by the physician provided a measure of the accuracy of the physician's expressive communication. This approach provided an assessment of the extent to which the physicians in this research were able to express emotion through nonverbal cues (facial expressions, body movements, and tone of voice). Then I gave them the Profile of Nonverbal Sensitivity (the PONS test), a film test which measured their own sensitivity to the nonverbal cues of other people. (The PONS test is an exciting approach to the reliable and valid measurement of nonverbal sensitivity. It presents 220 two-second-long film and/or audio segments of nonverbal cues of facial expressions, body movements and postures, and tone of voice, without the words. The task of the individual taking the test is to determine which type of emotional expression accurately describes what was conveyed by the minimal information available. This test was developed by Dr. Robert Rosenthal at Harvard University, under whose direction I had the good fortune to study in graduate school.) In this research we found that the doctors who were the most sensitive and expressive through nonverbal cues were those who were best liked by their patients.

Field research on illness, particularly serious illness, usually has to be done in hospitals, clinics, doctors' offices, or people's homes. Field research involves understanding events as they occur naturally, and although the researcher can develop very sophisticated methods for measuring what he or she observes, little control can be exerted. The research takes place on the subjects' turf. Field research can be a considerable challenge, as was described in detail earlier in this chapter.

There is a kind of middle category that involves situations in which the researcher is on his or her own turf and the subjects are definitely on theirs. The telephone interview is a perfect example. Graduate students and I recently carried out a nationwide telephone survey of adults age eighteen and older, asking them to evaluate the medical care system in this country and to rate the amount of confidence they have in physicians, dentists, and nurses. We also asked the respondents to rate (from poor to excellent) their doctors on the ability to accurately diagnose and treat illness, communicate effectively with patients and other health professionals, help patients prevent illness, be sensitive to cultural issues and the cost of treatment to patients, and fulfill high ethical standards in the practice of medicine. In addition, we asked respondents about the importance of these various elements of the role performance of physicians (from "not at all important" to "more important than everything else"). We wanted to know what our respondents found valuable in the job of a physician caring for patients. Our interview lasted only five minutes, and we asked our questions of whomever (age eighteen or older) answered the phone when we dialed a number that was randomly generated by computer. Only 23 percent of the numbers dialed actually connected, since the numbers and area codes were generated randomly and any given ten-digit number did not necessarily exist as a connected telephone number. Our goal was to complete close to 650 interviews. Therefore, my students heard the operator's recording, "I'm sorry, the number you have reached is not in service at this time," over 10,000 times! During the first few days of calling the students would become very excited if they finally reached a working number but would then be disappointed by the respondent's refusal to participate. In fact, only one of ten people who answered the phone agreed to finish the five-minute interview. The rest hung up. They probably assumed that they were receiving a sales pitch or felt they had been surveyed too much already. Then the students hit upon the idea of the personal touch. They revealed to the individual who answered the phone that they were graduate students trying to carry out a research project and requested five minutes of the respondent's time. The respondents were kind and generous and were perfectly willing to help the student at the other end of the line. The participation rate climbed to over 60 percent.

I think there is an overriding theme to the research I have been involved in so far in health psychology. I am trying to understand how human beings come to terms with illness and with requirements to maintain health in their own lives and the lives of their loved ones. Probably because of my early training as a social psychologist, I am most interested in *individuals* (as opposed to the medical care system, for example) and in how they feel, what they think, what they do, and why. My research has examined many ways in which a person's psychology and interpersonal relationships can influence his or her responses to illness and the possibility of avoiding illness through good health habits. My research has also focused on the role physicians and health professionals can play in helping people achieve health and avoid becoming sick.

My research represents my personal and professional orientation to health and illness as very private matters which usually are shared in the deepest sense only with loved ones, family members, and close friends. When someone is seriously ill, the lives of his or her loved ones are very much affected. Illness and illness prevention are individual, intrapsychic, and privately interpersonal experiences. Therefore, the achievement and maintenance of health, coping with illness, and attempts to seek and negotiate medical care are both determinants and expressions of the individual's deepest personal vision. Health psychologists can be privy to this vision of self, learning about and helping another human being develop and maintain it when that person is most vulnerable in the face of the severe challenges brought on by illness.

SUGGESTED READINGS

DiMatteo, M. R. (1991). *The psychology of health, illness, and medical care: An individual perspective*. Pacific Grove, CA: Brooks/Cole.

———— (1993). Expectations in the physician-patient relationship: Implications for patient adherence to medical treatment recommendations. In P. D. Blanck (Ed.), *Interpersonal expectations: Theory, research, and application* (pp. 296–315). Cambridge, UK: Cambridge University Press.

———— & DiNicola, D. D. (1981). Sources of assessment of physician performance: A study of comparative reliability and patterns of intercorrelation. *Medical Care, 19,* 829–842.

———— & DiNicola, D. D. (1982). *Achieving patient compliance: The psychology of the medical practitioner's role*. New York: Pergamon Press.

———— & Friedman, H. S. (Eds.). (1979). Interpersonal relations and health care. Special issue of the *Journal of Social Issues, 35*(1).

———— & Friedman, H. S. (1982). A model course in social psychology and health. *Health Psychology, 1,* 181–193.

———— & Hays, R. D. (1980). The significance of patients' perceptions of physician conduct: A study of patient satisfaction in a family practice center. *Journal of Community Health, 6,* 18–34.

———— Hays, R. D., & Prince, L. M. (1986). Relationship of physicians' nonverbal communication skill to patient satisfaction, appointment noncompliance, and physician workload. *Health Psychology, 5,* 581–594.

———— Hays, R. D., & Sherbourne, C. D. (1992). Adherence to cancer regimens: Implications for treating the older patient. *Oncology, 6,* 50–57.

———— Linn, L. S., Chang, G. L., & Cope, D. W. (1985). Affect and neutrality in physician behavior. *Journal of Behavioral Medicine, 8,* 397–409.

———— Sherbourne, C. D., Hays, R. D., Ordway, L., Kravitz, R. L., McGlynn, E. A., Kaplan, S., & Rogers, W. H. (1993). Physicians' characteristics influence patients' adherence to medical treatment: Results from the Medical Outcomes Study. *Health Psychology, 12,* 93–102.

———— TARANTA, A., FRIEDMAN, H. S., & PRINCE, L. M. (1980). Predicting patient satisfaction from physicians' nonverbal communication skills. *Medical Care, 18,* 376–387.

HAYS, R., & DIMATTEO, M. R. (1987). Key issues and suggestions for patient compliance assessment: Sources of information, focus of measures, and nature of response options. *Journal of Compliance in Health Care, 2,* 37–53. Reprinted in *Diabetes Spectrum, 2,* 55–63.

LINN, L. S., & DIMATTEO, M. R. (1983). Humor and other communication preferences in physician-patient encounters. *Medical Care, 21,* 1223–1231.

————DIMATTEO, M. R., COPE, D. W., & ROBBINS, A. (1987). Measuring physicians' humanistic attitudes, values, and behaviors. *Medical Care, 25,* 504–515.

ROSENTHAL, R., HALL, J. A., DIMATTEO, M. R., ROGERS, P. L., & ARCHER, D. (1979). *Sensitivity to nonverbal communication: The PONS test.* Baltimore: Johns Hopkins University Press.

WELLISCH, D. K., DIMATTEO, M. R., SILVERSTEIN, M., LANDSVERK, J., HOFFMAN, R., WAISMAN, J., HANDEL, N., WAISMAN-SMITH, E., & SCHAIN, W. (1989). Psychosocial outcomes of breast cancer therapies: Lumpectomy versus mastectomy with and without breast reconstruction. *Psychosomatics, 30,* 365–373.

PAUL **B.** **P**AULUS *(Ph.D., University of Iowa) is Professor of Psychology at the University of Texas at Arlington. He is the Editor of* Basic and Applied Social Psychology *and serves on the editorial board of the* Journal *of* Applied Social Psychology. *He has published in the areas of environmental, group, and sports psychology. Recent books include* Psychology of Group Influence *and* Understanding Human Relations *(with Robert A. Baron). The other loves in his life are his family, traveling, and golf.*

13

Have Environment Will Travel: My Life as an Environmental Psychologist

❖

Everyone has images of prisons, often derived from movies. People typically envision large multilevel cell blocks, glowering inmates, and brusque guards. People hear about the violence that often characterizes prison life and the hours at hard labor in prison factories and fields. Most people would rather not spend any of their lives there. I am certainly among this group, but I have spent most of my professional life going into and out of prisons. Fortunately, I was not sentenced to be there but chose to enter as an environmental psychologist. My career as an environmental psychologist specializing in prison design and overcrowding has been an exciting and productive one. It is a career I certainly did not envision as I was training to be an experimental social psychologist at the University of Iowa.

The University of Iowa has a fine tradition of training experimental psychologists who become productive researchers. I was provided with an excellent background in psychology in addition to a strong grounding in methodology and the philosophy of science. When I arrived at the University of Texas at Arlington, I was eager to use my knowledge and skills in developing a program in experimental social psychology. In fact, I have done so for twenty-three years, working mostly to understand the factors that influence the performance of tasks in groups. I very much enjoy the challenge of testing specific hypotheses in carefully controlled laboratory studies. More often than not, my expectations are only partly confirmed, and so I am constantly confronted with new mysteries to solve. There is a sense of intellectual power in this game of experimental science as one tries to devise ways to force nature to reveal some of its secrets. Researchers often get very attached to their discoveries and very protective of their ideas. It can become a very competitive game of trying to be the first to discover a certain phenomenon or getting more support for one's own theory than for someone else's. In one sense this is a bit silly, since all of us are working with the benefits of the insights of those who have gone before. These scholars have greatly influenced our ability to make discoveries and develop ideas. From a broad societal perspective, what is really important is that we increase our understanding of human nature and that this lead to a bettering of the human condition.

THE PRISON ADVENTURE

The Beginnings

If I had done nothing more than live the life of an experimental social psychologist these past twenty-two years, it would have been a most satisfying life. However, fate intervened, and I became engrossed in a twenty-year-long adventure of applied environmental psychology. I was attending a party at the home of my colleague Verne Cox, who is a physiological psychologist. He had been discussing a research program on crowding in humans with another colleague, Garvin McCain, who specialized in animal behavior. They were intrigued by some of the data linking crowding with stress in animals. John Calhoun had done some well-publicized studies with rodents, beginning in the late 1950s, which demonstrated that crowding can have dramatically negative effects. Under crowded conditions, these rodents showed disruption of maternal and sexual behavior and increased violence. There was a high mortality rate, particularly among the young. Calhoun and others attributed these effects to the stressful effects of having too many animals in one area.

The question that intrigued McCain and Cox was whether similar effects might be observed in humans. It was deemed possible that the adaptive capabilities of humans can enable them to cope with highly crowded living conditions. This point of view was championed by Paul Erhlich, Jonathan Freedman, and their colleagues, partly on the basis of the results of studies of urban statistics on health. Some of those studies did not find evidence of negative effects on the health of those living in crowded areas of cities. However, McCain and Cox were not convinced that this research was definitive and decided that they wanted to obtain direct physiological measures of stress. In particular, they wanted to measure urinary catecholamines by making use of recently developed technology. Yet they were faced with a number of problems. First, they had little experience doing research with humans. They decided that my expertise in this area might be useful and asked if I would join the team. Since I was a young, untenured assistant professor, it was probably in my interest to acquiesce to their request. Furthermore, the general issue of crowding was related to my interest in group behavior, and so it seemed to be a natural broadening of my research program. The next problem that had to be solved was locating a population for our research. We wanted to find a population that was experiencing high levels of crowding and would be amenable to our somewhat invasive research procedures. We knew that it would be difficult to obtain such cooperation from families in the crowded areas of cities. We discussed the possibility of doing research in army barracks, which McCain knew from experience could be quite crowded, but there were no convenient army sites nearby. However, there had been much discussion in the news about crowded conditions in prisons and jails, and there were a good number of these facilities in Texas. We had never been in a prison and decided to make some preliminary visits to determine the feasibility of doing research in such an environment. We had no idea whether it was safe or possible to do this type of research in prisons. Even if it was feasible, would we be able to obtain the cooperation of the administration and the inmates? We expected that the inmates might look on our efforts favorably, but we were not clear what benefits the administration would gain from the research.

To our surprise, the responses to our initial inquiries were quite positive. We were welcomed at a number of jails and prisons in and around the Dallas–Fort Worth area. More important, we discovered that it was possible to do meaningful research on crowding in those environments. The housing conditions were quite varied, with some inmates living under very dense conditions while others had rather spacious accommodations. In jails we found cells housing more than seventy inmates with less than fifteen square feet per inmate. This was way below the commonly proposed standard of forty square feet per inmate for multiple-person cells. In prisons we found dormitories that housed about sixty inmates with about thirty square feet per inmate. We were particularly delighted to discover that it was possible to examine the independent contributions of space and number of people, since there was a broad range of housing that varied greatly in terms of the number of people and the amount of space provided. Prison standards generally focused on the amount of space that should be allowed for each inmate and did not consider the importance of the number of inmates in a housing unit.

One potential problem in doing research on prison crowding is that inmates who are assigned to housing that differs in degree of crowding may differ in important characteristics. Inmates who have been good citizens in prison may be assigned to preferred housing, and single cells may be reserved for inmates who are locked up for disciplinary reasons. We did encounter these types of problems in a number of institutions. However, we found a number of institutions where there did not appear to be a problematic housing assignment policy or where it would be possible to assess the role of potential confounding variables such as age and length of confinement. Thus, one of our main tasks as researchers was to locate sites where variations in density within the institution would be informative.

We were excited by our discoveries and decided to tell the world about them by writing a brief note in 1973 on the use of prisons as environments for the investigation of crowding. We felt that this might stimulate other scholars to consider prisons as sites for research. However, there was never a rush of psychology researchers to use prisons for environmental research. Crowding researchers seemed to be drawn to more convenient and less aversive environments, such as college dormitories, grocery stores, subway stations, and playgrounds. There was, however, some critical reaction to our paper. Two psychologists published a paper in the same journal criticizing our suggestions for using prison environments to study crowding. They were concerned about the extent to which inmates had the freedom to participate and about possible experimental manipulations of crowding in prisons. They also felt that we had understated the problem of obtaining meaningful results from prisoners, given the uniqueness of the environments and the residents. These were certainly issues to which we were sensitive. However, we felt that whatever the costs or drawbacks of research on crowding in prisons, they were outweighed by the potential scientific discoveries, which could be of great benefit to both inmates and staff. Such research could provide a scientific basis for prison standards. Arbitrary standards with no factual basis could be discarded and replaced with ones that were consistent with scientific data.

Doing Our Time in Prison

Once we had convinced ourselves that prisons would be great sites for research, we sought permission from the appropriate administrators for such a program. We gained the enthusiastic support of the director of the U.S. Bureau of Prisons. This gave us access to all the units of the federal prison system. We were particularly interested in doing research at the Federal Correctional Institution in Texarkana, Texas, since it was one of the sites we had visited in our initial feasibility survey. We also were interested in the Texas prison system because it was housing four to five inmates in cells designed for two. Although we had been encouraged about our prospects by our initial visits and correspondence, support for our efforts was suddenly withdrawn. The reason was never made clear, but we surmised that various lawsuits involving overcrowding had made the administrators somewhat uncomfortable about supporting research that might produce scientific support for some of the inmates' concerns. We encountered similar resistance from other state prison systems during the course of our research.

With assurance of access to federal prisons, we decided to request funds from the National Institutes of Health for a large-scale project on prison crowding using a broad variety of measures: urinary catecholamines, verbal reports of mood and perceived crowding, performance on a motor task, a test for tolerance of crowding, and illness symptoms reported at visits to the health clinic. Imbued with confidence about the importance and novelty of our proposed research, we asked for $400,000 for a three-year period to study the "effects of different degrees of population concentration on behavior and urine chemistry indices of psychogenic stress." We had solicited the aid of a member of the chemistry department for the urine assays. However, the granting agency was not convinced by our proposal. The review panel was concerned about our lack of experience, the atypical population, and the possibility that the many other stressors of prison life would overwhelm those which might be due to variations in density. Moreover, there were some technical objections to the urine chemistry analyses that were outlined.

We were very disappointed but decided to persist in the grant-seeking process. We submitted a slightly less ambitious proposal to the National Science Foundation. Again we were rejected, this time in part for lack of experience in doing research in prisons. Despite the lack of reinforcement by the granting agencies, we were convinced of the importance of our research plans and decided to request funds from our university and a private foundation to support some initial studies. This way we could gain some experience and data and then make a more convincing case to the granting agencies. So in 1972 we began our first studies of prison crowding at Texarkana. We made some preparatory visits to discuss the project with the warden and other key personnel. We discovered early the importance of gaining the support of the top people. In prisons, the staff often operates along military lines of command, with power definitely coming from the top. With the warden's support, we were able to work out details of the procedures for carrying out research in the institution, but we had to solve a number of problems: Where could we do the interviewing and take the various measurements? How could we get the inmates to volunteer and participate? Would it be safe to bring graduate student volunteers, including women, with us? The prison psychologist turned out to be our main liaison in resolving these issues. We were able to find space in the educational wing of the prison. We were allowed to handpick inmates to be put on call-out sheets. These sheets were distributed on a daily basis to indicate when inmates were to report to various clinics, classes, and programs. We selected inmates who had lived for at least a minimal period in the units of interest. The sheets were posted requesting about ten inmates to report to the educational wing every fifteen minutes. We were also assured that there would be no danger to our students. The inmates in this federal prison were there mostly for nonviolent federal crimes such as income tax evasion and fraud.

We had no trouble obtaining graduate student volunteers. We took along a group of four graduate students on most of the trips. We typically would leave at about six in the morning and arrive shortly after nine at the prison. One member of the team went a day earlier to finalize the arrangements and prepare the call-out sheets. We set up a number of stations at the testing site. One area was used for having inmates fill out questionnaires, while others were used for measures such as blood pressures (systolic and diastolic), crowding tolerance, and motor dexterity. Several members of the team spent the day going through records. We obtained data on inmates' backgrounds, disciplinary infractions, and clinic visits.

Although there was always a certain level of tension while we were working in the prison environment, there were a number of light moments. On one trip a student wore a very short skirt. She was assigned to have inmates do the motor dexterity task, which was a roll-up game that is sold commercially. This game requires a person to roll a ball "uphill" by manipulating two levers. There were actually two stations with this task, with the other one being run by McCain. However, we noted that the lines were considerably longer for the station run by the student. On another visit one inmate who had operated a brothel in Hawaii became infatuated with one of our female students and offered to take her back to Hawaii with him. Although we had been concerned about providing incentives to encourage inmate participation, we had discovered that just interacting with the female members of our staff was a powerful incentive to the residents of this all-male prison. On one of our trips to the Texarkana prison I was greeted by one of the inmates with a bright "Hello, Dr. Paulus." I quickly recognized one of my students from a prior semester. He apparently had been caught smoking the wrong kind of cigarette.

Leaving the prison at the end of a long and arduous testing session was always a euphoric experience. Just being able to leave that rather depressing environment might have been partly responsible for this state. Our trips home were usually filled with animated recounts of the day's experiences and discussions of the possible outcomes of the project. Back at the university we dug eagerly into the data. None of us had expertise in managing large, multivariable data sets, and computer-based data management packages were not yet available. We used the departmental computer to do some simple correlational analyses and t-tests and did some of the other analyses by hand. We quickly discovered some interesting patterns and decided to present our first "cut" of the data at the 1973 meeting of the Southwestern Psychological Association. However, our first results were rather modest. We did not find evidence for effects of crowding on mood or illness complaints, but there were some effects on tolerance and palmar sweating. We found that those living in more dense housing demonstrated less tolerance of crowding on our tolerance test. This test required inmates to place wooden figures into an enclosure that represented a prison dormitory until they felt that placing any more figures would make it too crowded. Also, we found that inmates who had a longer history of confinement had lower tolerance scores. Palmar sweat is a simple measure of arousal. By dabbing the finger with a special solution, one can obtain prints that show the number of open pores. Higher palmar sweat scores were related to higher levels of social density (number of people in a housing unit) but not to spatial density (space per person in a housing unit). The motor coordination, or roll-up, task did not yield meaningful results, but this did not surprise us given the testing circumstances.

We continued to mine the data from three visits over a period of two years and reported the results in the *Journal of Applied Social Psychology* in 1975. By comparing a variety of housing units that differed in spatial density and social density, we found that the most important factor in determining inmate mood is the number of inmates in a housing unit. Further support for the potentially stressful effect of density was provided by the illness complaint data, which revealed that inmates in the dormitories had higher illness rates than did those in single or double cells. This effect was strongest for inmates who had lived at least six weeks in their housing. Apparently, it takes a period of exposure to stressful housing for the effects to become evident in illness complaint rates.

In our visits to prisons and jails we noted that county jails had some of the most crowded conditions. For example, in one jail we found inmates housed in units of two to seventy-three inmates with space per person ranging from 17 to 174 square feet. Inmates in jails are typically confined to their housing units twenty-four hours a day. It appeared rather difficult to conduct our type of research in the jail setting, but at one jail we learned that inmates sent messages or "kites" to the medical clinic to request medical attention. We asked that the messages be collected for us over a period of five weeks. When we compared those who were housed in the most crowded units with those who were housed in less crowded ones, we noted that those in crowded units had a higher rate of requests for medical attention.

One problem with the measures discussed so far (reports of feelings of crowding, mood state, crowding tolerance, and illness complaints) is that they are rather subjective. Although visits to the clinic may involve actual pathology, it is difficult to verify the validity of a particular complaint. The blood pressures did not vary with density. This measure is not considered particularly sensitive to chronic environmental stressors, but a team from Yale University was able to find small increases in blood pressure among dorm residents in a state prison. We did find that higher levels of social density increase palmar sweating, but lack of funds prevented us from utilizing more sophisticated physiological measures until much later in the research program.

ENVIRONMENTAL PSYCHOLOGY OFFSHORE

Our research in prisons had given us confidence that crowded living conditions can have stress-related consequences for humans. However, our efforts were limited by the lack of grant support, and so we began to consider other possibilities. One site that intrigued us was offshore oil rigs, which house workers in two-, four-, or six-person units for seven-days-on and seven-days-off work cycles. The population on these rigs can vary from about 20 to 100 workers. Given the limited space on the rigs, we surmised that the workers could be experiencing some crowding-related stress. Cox called companies listed in the Dallas Yellow Pages under "Oil Drilling" until he finally reached an official in one of the companies who was receptive to the prospect of having three psychologists poke around on his rigs. We received permission from this company to visit two rigs that were located close together. We flew to Louisiana and caught one of the crew boats to rigs about forty miles offshore. We discovered that one of the rigs had been moved about twenty miles away from the first one. So Cox and McCain got off at the first one, while I continued to the second, smaller rig. We were lifted off the boats in a net by a crane. This certainly was an exciting experience on a dark, windy night in the middle of an ocean. When I arrived on my rig, I was treated with great suspicion. They were not expecting a professor to show up at three in the morning. They suspected that I might be a troublemaker from the union. Apparently, the company had failed to inform anyone on the rig of my impending visit. I was kept under "room arrest" until the manager of the rig, called the "toolpusher," appeared and inquired about the reason for my visit. After he checked the veracity of my story over the radio with the company in Dallas, I was released to interview the workers during the breaks in their shifts. I was also encouraged to partake in the Thanksgiving feast that had been prepared for the workers. Although it did not look very appetizing, I decided that it was in my best interest to acquiesce. After putting in a full day, I decided to take a nap and asked to be awakened in time to catch the daily helicopter back to shore. Unfortunately, someone failed to wake me, and I missed the helicopter. The only option left was to take an eight-hour boat trip back to shore in stormy conditions. It turned out to be a less than memorable experience since I managed to get seasick and lose my Thanksgiving dinner in the process.

When we returned, we compared notes and decided that despite the inconvenience of the sites, they represented an interesting opportunity to assess the impact of density in a work environment. We generated another grandiose grant proposal, this time for the U.S. Navy and NASA. We felt that because of the isolation and limited space, the dynamics on the rig would provide some information relevant to workers in a space station. Unfortunately, the officials in charge of grants did not agree. However, that did not diminish our interest in studying a variety of environments. In subsequent years we managed to do research on crowding in junior high schools and homes for aged veterans or domiciliaries. My interest in social stressors also led me to examine the role of spectators on athletic performance in a number of different sports, including gymnastics, baseball, basketball, and bowling.

WORKING FOR JUSTICE

Although the continued rejection of our grant requests was a bit disheartening, some exciting research prospects were developing on the prison front. Prison overcrowding was becoming a serious problem, with the populations having increased greatly without compensatory increases in facilities. Cells designed for one or two inmates now often held four or five, and dormitories were double bunked to accommodate the influx of inmates. Inmates were increasingly seeking relief in the courts from the overcrowding and other prison conditions, arguing that the crowded conditions constituted cruel and unusual punishment. This is of course a subjective judgment, and the courts have always struggled to specify such conditions. Most citizens feel that prisons should be relatively unpleasant places so that they will serve as a deterrent, yet the Constitution specifies that even prisoners have the right to be treated in a humane manner. Our research provided the first objective data that prison overcrowding can have harmful effects on inmates. These data could be used by the courts to justify granting inmates relief from overcrowding and to specify acceptable housing standards.

Legal action in regard to prison overcrowding was occurring in over thirty states. The Civil Rights Division of the U.S. Department of Justice was involved in a number of these cases on behalf of the inmates. Attorneys in this division had come across our work in a prison overcrowding case in New York State and had called to inquire about our willingness to serve as expert witnesses in their cases. We agreed to help but made sure they understood the limitations of our data and realized that we would base our testimony on objective data rather than subjective opinions. In particular, we pointed out that we had not been able to get access to a state prison to see if we could obtain similar results. They obtained court orders allowing us to have access to the Illinois and Oklahoma state prison systems and provided financial support for an intensive effort in Illinois. We visited the ten major units in that system. We obtained blood pressures and brief interview data from inmates in three of the prisons and found that blood pressures increased with an increased number of inmates in the cell at one of the major prisons. We also discovered records on yearly death and psychiatric commitment rates. In a psychiatric prison that held mostly older inmates, death rates increased with increasing prison population and declined when the population declined over a ten-year period. In the Illinois prison system death rates and psychiatric commitment rates were elevated in high-population years. Later we discovered similar patterns for death rates, psychiatric commitments, suicides, and disciplinary infractions in other prison systems. It appears that whenever prison populations increase without an increase in space and facilities to match the higher population level, health and adjustment indicators become more negative. Of course, we could not prove that the crowded conditions were the cause. Some undetected changes in the prisoner-to-guard ratio and prison policy may be associated with more crowded prisons and in some way affect the health indicators. We were able to rule these factors out as possibilities in some instances. Moreover, our data on the health consequences of crowding in prison suggest that crowding stress is an important factor in these findings.

Besides generating compelling data, our visits provided plenty of personal excitement. One of the prisons, Stateville at Joliet, Illinois, was reputed to be the largest prison facility in the United States and housed mostly violent inmates from the Chicago area. The hallway was lined with pictures of guards who had died in the line of duty. One guard had been killed while monitoring an inmate lunch hour a few months before our visit. There were no pictures at all of the inmates who had been killed over the years. However, we heard stories about inmates being pushed off balconies in addition to the more conventional means of being killed. The prison was surrounded by a large wall topped with towers and contained a number of very large cell houses. One of them was a five-story rectangular unit that was used to confine 400 inmates in one- or two-man cells. These were inmates who had violated prison regulations or were too dangerous for the general prison population. They were confined in their cells the entire day, and so we had to interview them and obtain blood pressures through the cell bars. It was here that we came face to face with one of this country's most despicable killers,

Richard Speck, who had killed seven nurses in an apartment in Chicago. Other inmates were housed in large, round four-story cell houses called panopticans. These units housed up to 600 inmates in cells that held 2 to 12 inmates in less than twenty square feet of space per inmate. Inmates were confined to these cells most of the day, except for work details and eating periods. One entire panoptican was used to house inmates who were afraid of other inmates and requested to be confined continuously for their own safety.

Although we had reservations about doing research in that prison, we decided that we could not afford to pass up the rare opportunity to obtain data from such a classic prison. We interviewed the inmates in groups near working stations and in the medical clinic (we avoided the cafeteria!). The interview was limited to asking them to rate the crowding of their housing unit on a four-point scale (not at all crowded, moderately crowded, crowded, very crowded) and obtaining blood pressures. A prison nurse took blood pressures as well, apparently to provide an independent check on the accuracy of our data for the prison officials. We were accompanied on our travels through the prison by several guards and an assistant warden who had the appropriate name Bob Capture. While we were getting volunteers in the medical clinic area, I was handed a note by a large, serious-looking inmate which read, "Watch out, Big Brother is watching you!" I was not sure what it meant. I put it in my pocket and acted as if it didn't phase me. However, I made sure that I was constantly moving and tried to keep myself facing the inmates. I felt a great relief when we finally left the prison a few hours later.

The next day Verne Cox and I stopped at the prison in Pontiac to obtain additional data. Most of the inmates were housed in single cells in this large prison, but population pressures were leading to a change to double celling. Our interviews indicated that the inmates were quite upset by this impending change. Moreover, we noticed that in contrast to Stateville, this prison was run in a very disorganized manner. The guard assigned to us left us alone in a small room at the end of a large cell block with a group of very agitated inmates. We kept assuring them that we were "good guys" who were on their side. Luckily, they did not take out their frustrations on us. However, we alerted the Justice Department to the volatility of this prison and predicted that serious disruptions could occur if attempts were not made to control the situation. Three months later we saw pictures on television of this prison burning as inmates rioted to protest their conditions.

A third prison provided a different set of images. This prison housed inmates who had requested protective custody because they feared violence from other inmates in other prisons. It was one of the few times I have felt tall, since most of these inmates were of rather small stature. This prison was a moderate-security institution that looked more like a college campus than a prison. There was no wall, and there was plenty of open space for outdoor activities, including a go-cart track. There was a relaxed atmosphere in this institution, and the inmates seemed to be much more at ease and less depressed than those in the other two prisons.

THE BIG PRISON PROJECT

Our careers as experts in prison crowding were really beginning to take off. We gained a real sense of competence from our ability to derive meaningful data from prison environments. With this sense of confidence, we approached an agency in the Department of Justice that was funding efforts in law enforcement and corrections. The director of the corrections division was quite supportive of our aims and encouraged us to submit a proposal. Then, after eight years of effort, we were given a large grant to do an extensive study of prison crowding. Most of this research was done in six federal prisons, and the results confirmed and extended the findings we had obtained in earlier studies. We obtained clear evidence of the health consequences of crowding in prisons and discovered that the most important factor in crowding is number of people rather than space. This does not mean that all inmates need to have private rooms. In several prisons we found that simply providing privacy partitions in open dormitories helped reduce much of the negative reaction to this type of housing. Data from several state prison systems indicated that increases in prison populations are associated with increases in disciplinary infractions, suicides, psychiatric commitments, and death rates. In the Texas system psychiatric commitments and death rates were higher in the large prisons than in the small ones.

The report of our findings was published in 1980 and was widely disseminated by the Justice Department. It was eagerly picked up by the media, and we made television newscasts, magazines, and newspapers around the country. We were interviewed by local television stations and CNN. Our findings were cited in many major court decisions, including those by the Supreme Court. We were being sought as expert witnesses in a variety of prison and jail overcrowding cases. The most famous of these was *Ruiz v. Estelle*, involving the Texas prison system. This turned out to be the longest civil rights case in history with 161 days of trial testimony. Our team spent most of a week testifying about our research findings and their relevance to the issues in that case. I summarized for Judge Justice and the court the broad implications of our work for two days. My testimony included a slide show depicting the various prison conditions we had encountered and our major findings. Judge Justice ruled that the prison system violated the civil rights of the inmates in many ways, including confining them in overcrowded cells and dorms. He specified changes in housing design and policy that were consistent with our recommendations. Triple and double celling were to be phased out, and dormitories were to be limited in population. The size of new prisons was to be limited to no more than 500 inmates. Similar rulings have been made in other cases. In fact, our research findings were considered carefully by correctional and public health agencies that were setting new standards for prison housing.

Not all the reactions to our work were positive, however. From the beginning, our publications elicited critical reactions and reviews. A social psychologist who worked with the federal prison system and had collaborated in some of our research wrote a critical review in which he highlighted what he perceived to be the limitations of our work. Since that time he has served as a rebuttal witness in some of the trials at which we have testified. After we summarized our research in the *American Psychologist*, that journal published a paper which argued that our work had limited use for policy makers since we did not provide information on ways to manage large and crowded prisons effectively. One of the most hurtful aspects of that paper was the implication that our type of research reflected a liberal bias in favor of finding negative effects of prison crowding. Ironically, we had always been proud of the fact that we kept our biases out of our work and let the data fall where they might. Moreover, the fact that similar results have been obtained by individuals working for the prison establishment, by a range of other scholars, and in other environments gives us confidence that whatever bias might have lurked in our heads, our research findings reflected realistic effects of crowding. Furthermore, although some of our findings are supportive of inmate claims about the effects of crowding, they also suggest that private rooms may not be necessary. In several prisons, double cells did not lead to negative effects on health, and privacy cubicles in open dorms yielded reactions similar to those in single cells. Thus, inmates do not need "Holiday Inn" accommodations, but some degree of privacy or control over their living environment appears to be important.

We had reached a pinnacle of success. Our research was cited in articles and textbooks and was having a significant impact on prison housing standards. We were in constant demand as expert witnesses. McCain and I received additional funding for a detailed study of jail crowding, and I was awarded a visiting fellowship by the National Institute of Justice. This allowed me to spend an entire year carefully analyzing the mass of data we had gathered with the assistance of Marc Schaeffer, a graduate student who worked with Andrew Baum at the Uniformed Services University of the Health Sciences in Bethesda, Maryland. A number of interesting new findings were uncovered. A detailed analysis of the illness data indicated that illnesses that could be objectively verified by a physician, such as circulatory or upper respiratory problems, and those which were pain-related, such as back or chest pain, were most elevated in dormitories. A group of physicians rated these pain problems as being stress-related. The effects of density appeared to be similar for male and female inmates and for different racial and ethnic groups. However, individuals who grew up in crowded homes or a large city had relatively lower blood pressures in dormitory housing, suggesting that experience with crowded conditions helps one cope with subsequent crowding experiences. This doesn't mean that inmates living in a crowded prison will grow to like it. On the contrary, the longer they are in prison, the more negatively they react to crowded conditions. It certainly makes sense that after a long period of exposure to crowding, inmates increasingly value having some degree of privacy.

What had begun as a grand adventure and had become a success beyond our wildest dreams slowly was becoming a burden. There were the inevitable involvements in lawsuits, the pressures of grant deadlines, and the writing of papers. As a team we had visited over sixty prisons and jails in the United States, Japan, and the Netherlands and had done research in more than twenty of them. We had all spent much time away from friends and family and found it harder to justify the continued deprivations now that we had attained many of our goals. So in retrospect, the most rewarding and special times were the early struggles to gain a handle on the phenomenon. The pressures of success took their toll and took away some of the excitement of having reached our goal. We continued to work together on several summaries of our work but decided to discontinue our efforts as a team of researchers. Cox returned full-time to his first love, physiological psychology, McCain began focusing his efforts on obtaining more archival data on mortality rates in prisons, and I continued to wrap up loose ends from our past research projects. I summarized our work in book form and published it in 1988. I collaborated with Andrew Baum, Marc Schaeffer, and Gerald Gaes on a project to obtain urine chemistry indexes from inmates at a federal prison. As we had predicted many years earlier, we found that prison dormitories were associated with elevations in epinephrine and norepinephrine (urine chemistry measures of stress). I discussed doing a project with personnel in the California state system to examine urine chemistry indexes as newly built cell blocks grew increasingly crowded. However, as with some of the other state systems we had approached, it was vetoed at the highest levels. Apparently, clear data on negative consequences could be politically embarrassing.

MAKING IT TO "PRIME TIME"

In October 1989 I was invited to share my expertise on the popular *Oprah Winfrey* television talk show. I had never had the opportunity to watch a complete edition of that program and was not sure that it would be in my interest to be on it. However, if she plugged my recently published book on prison crowding, it might give its sales a real boost. In any case, my daughter insisted that I be on the show so that she could boast about it to her friends. My initial discussion with the staff indicated that I would be one of the primary guests. They were hoping to interview a young girl who had been raped by an inmate who had been released from jail because of overcrowding. I sent the staff copies of my book and several key papers and spent a day reviewing all the potentially relevant facts and issues.

When I arrived in Chicago, I was picked up by a limousine and taken to a fancy hotel. The following morning I discovered I was sharing the stage with five other guests. In addition to the young girl, the husband of the woman who was raped by Willie Horton (an inmate with a history of violence who had been let out on furlough under the administration of Governor Dukakis of Massachusetts) was present. The first half of the program consisted of interviews with these two guests. The first segment of the second half was taken up mostly by discussions with a lobbyist who was promoting incarceration as a solution to crime and an official from a prison watch group. When my turn finally came, I was asked if confinement to prison could make inmates more dangerous. Unfortunately, this was not a question which we had been able to assess in our research. Obviously, the staff had not bothered to read the material I had sent. I began to answer on the basis of other research studies but was interrupted within about forty seconds by the lobbyist. Oprah and he then got into a brief debate, she took a phone call, and then she interviewed a Chicago official in the audience. Time expired before I was able to find a good opportunity to jump back into the discussion. My brief moment before more than 20 million viewers had been a flop. I was able to get Oprah's autograph for my daughter and had some catharsis in discussions with the lobbyist during our trip back to the airport. Fortunately, I have not been tempted by similar offers to play the role of "expert" on national talk shows.

Although I have continued to do independent research in prison environments, it would have been impossible to have attained the prior accomplishments as a solitary researcher. As a research team we complemented each other in terms of skills and interests. We often played very distinct roles in the enterprise. I was usually in charge of the data management, McCain focused on the acquisition and analysis of archival data, and Cox was involved in all aspects of the project, played the role of motivator, and stayed abreast of the latest developments in health-related areas that were pertinent to our work. Although we had received very different research training, we had no problem applying our skills to the complexities of research in the prison environment. We were able to devise field studies in ways that minimized inferential problems. We were sensitive to alternative interpretations of our data and the need to assess their viability. We also were able to handle the potentially touchy issue of the order of authorship of our papers. We simply rotated the order with each new paper, with a few exceptions. Since I was a new assistant professor concerned with attaining tenure, they let me be the first author on the first two papers we published. We were also able to mesh our different theoretical bents in developing a theoretical model of our work for the *American Psychologist* paper. Most important, we helped motivate each other during the tough times when we were getting very little positive feedback from granting agencies and other funding sources. We kept each other convinced of the importance of the enterprise both pragmatically and theoretically. I doubt if any one of us singly would have been able to persist through the early difficult phases. Moreover, as a team we probably had more impact in persuading the various authorities and agencies to cooperate with the enterprise.

UNCLE SAM CALLS

Although my career in prison research was slowly winding down, another interesting opportunity was lurking. One of my fellow graduate students from the days at Iowa was now at the Walter Reed Army Institute of Research. He was enamored with our prison research and suggested that I might do something of similar scope within the U.S. Army. I did not respond with great enthusiasm, but after giving a talk to his research colleagues, I was formally approached about doing a large-scale environmental study with Army families. The Army was concerned about the morale and well-being of its families. Increasing numbers of servicemen and servicewomen were married and lived with their families in apartment complexes and mobile home parks near the base. There was concern about the low quality of some of those housing areas and the potentially detrimental impact of having Army families live in substandard housing projects. They asked me to do an assessment of this issue. After some preliminary visits to housing areas around the Fort Hood Army Base near Killeen, Texas, I concluded that some interesting and definitive research was possible. Young enlisted families lived in a broad range of housing. Most lived in apartment complexes, while others resided in mobile home parks. Some of the complexes and parks were rather small, and others contained a large number of units. There was also significant variation in housing quality. Some of the apartment complexes and mobile home parks were well maintained and had amenities such as a pool, laundry room, and recreation area. Others had no amenities and were poorly maintained. Although one would expect the better facilities to charge significantly higher rents, there was little difference in the rents charged by the "good" and "bad" facilities. Thus I had discovered a situation where it would be possible to examine the influence of housing quality without confounding it with economic differences between populations. Given the interesting potential of this research site, I signed up for a two-year project during which my salary and research expenses were borne by Walter Reed. Fortunately, a postdoctoral student from India, Dinesh Nagar, arrived during that period to work with me on the issue of crowding. Although we collaborated on several crowding projects, he became a key player in the Army research.

The Army project had some novel challenges. First, Army regulations specified that we could not use incentives to gain volunteers for our study. Given that we wanted to do a longitudinal study that involved three interviews at three-month intervals, this could be a significant problem. Second, institutional regulations also specified that we could not use physiological measures since we were doing the project under the auspices of the Department of Psychiatry. The recruitment of volunteers was handled in a variety of ways. Our preliminary interviews were done with family members who were waiting at a hospital pharmacy or a medical van that visited various housing areas. During the main part of the study we approached people directly at their homes and requested that they fill out a brief questionnaire that we would pick up within an hour. We found that a high percentage of the residents were willing to participate in a project that might lead to improvements in the condition of Army facilities. We did our work mostly on weekends to increase the chances of finding residents at home.

As with the prisons, the first phase involved finding suitable sites for the research. Dinesh and I did an extensive survey of housing areas around the base by interviewing managers or owners of apartment complexes and mobile home parks to obtain their permission for the research. Fortunately, with few exceptions, these individuals were most cooperative. We wanted to find units that housed a high percentage of enlisted Army personnel and that varied in size and quality. We located about sixteen apartment complexes and twenty-two mobile home parks that were feasible as sites. More than 500 families participated in the initial survey, and 170 couples participated in the follow-up interviews. Although we could not use physiological measures, we did employ a wide range of questionnaire measures, including environmental ratings (e.g., attractive, noisy), well-being (e.g., anxiety, depression), morale (e.g., like being in the Army), and self-reported medical symptoms.

Contrary to initial expectations, we did not find a strong negative reaction to mobile home parks. Higher-quality environments were rated more positively, but this effect was rather weak for mobile home residents. The environmental quality of housing was not related to differences in morale, health, or well-being. This outcome was rather surprising given the relatively strong effects we had found in our prison research on the effect of environmental quality. It was not simply that the residents were insensitive to their environment. In accordance with reality, apartment residents did rate their homes as noisier than did residents of mobile homes, and mobile home residents rated their homes as more spacious than did residents of apartments. It occurred to us that the fact that residents were able to choose their housing might have limited the impact of environmental differences. In fact, the greater degree of choice reported by the residents, the greater the satisfaction with their housing.

These findings made me realize the importance of choice and self-selection on the impact of environmental variables. Almost all laboratory research with environmental variables involves random assignment of subjects to different conditions. The subjects in our prison research had no choice in regard to the housing to which they were assigned. Under such conditions individuals may be very sensitive to the negative features of the environment that has been forced on them: Who would choose to live in a negative environment such as a crowded prison cell? However, we found families that chose to live in decrepit-looking housing environments when they could have selected more attractive environments for the same rent. When we interviewed these families, it appeared that they had certain reasons for their choice. Some liked living in a rural area where they could let their dogs roam. Others liked living in a place where they could leave their cars jacked up while working on them. Still others had based their selection on the need to live near friends, work, or shopping. The insights I gained made me wonder whether it might be important to examine the role of choice in some of our laboratory studies. Even though random assignment is important for causal certainty, to what extent are we justified in generalizing the results of experimental studies to real-world settings where individuals have a great degree of choice over the conditions under which they live and work?

Although the Army research provided new empirical insights, it also took its toll emotionally. It required three years of hard work to carry out and analyze the data from this extensive project. It required a lot of time away from home in a rather uninteresting environment. Just as I was always glad to leave a prison, I was always happy to go home after a research visit. On some days the weather was rather unpleasant for going from door to door. I remember well handing out surveys in freezing weather with Dinesh, who had never experienced cold weather before. We had to go to the local discount store to buy gloves, boots, and a hat for him. We also had to contend with the dogs that sometimes roamed the mobile home parks. In one there were packs of dogs mingling with the little children who were playing in the street. In another a large dog ran up to Dinesh, who had a strong fear of such animals. It took him a few days to recover, and I made sure in future visits that the units in which he did surveys did not have roving dogs.

GOING "BACK HOME"

Passing out surveys in inclement weather and contending with hostile dogs were not the sorts of experiences I imagined would be part of a professor's life. While the potential relevance of our work to the lives of thousands of Army families was a gratifying prospect, I started to pine for a return to the more mundane life of the experimental social psychologist. The idea of testing esoteric theories in well-controlled little studies run by graduate and undergraduate students was becoming appealing again. I returned to doing laboratory work on groups, attempting to understand the various factors that influence brainstorming productivity in laboratory groups. Someday I will probably venture into the "real world" again to test the implications of this work in organizations, but until then I will enjoy my sabbatical from the travails of field research in different environments. I will leave it to new young "fools" to rush in to the many new domains that need to be examined. Unfortunately, few outsiders understand the sacrifices involved in doing applied research. Funding is difficult to obtain, and the number of person-hours required to generate a publishable product is infinitely greater than that required in laboratory-based enterprises. Unless one has a strong intellectual and personal commitment to the issues involved, it is difficult for many scholars to justify the personal costs. This is particularly true for young scholars concerned about generating publications so that they can get jobs and keep them. I was fortunate to be in an environment where I was allowed to take the risk of involvement in field research early in my career. Of course, I did not rely solely on the applied research, since I have maintained an active laboratory during most of my academic career and have been able to publish a variety of experimental studies.

It is unfortunate for our society that there is not more encouragement for psychologists who are well trained in experimental research and quantitative techniques to attack important societal problems. They have the requisite intellectual and methodological skills to do high-level applied research. I have found that applied research can in fact stimulate one to think more deeply about the experimental research one is doing. The experimental research may be useful for testing hypotheses generated in the course of this field research. Moreover, applied research is necessary to evaluate the generalizability of findings obtained under very controlled laboratory conditions. Instead of relegating the applied research to one set of scholars and the experimental research to another, I believe that the most exciting and productive model is one that involves the same investigator either simultaneously or sequentially in both types of research. Of course, this reflects a bias in favor of my own career lifestyle. While I have mentioned some drawbacks, I feel that my life has been greatly enriched by the personal and intellectual experiences that have come my way as a result of my involvement in both basic and applied research.

REFLECTIONS OF AN "OLD" APPLIED ENVIRONMENTAL PSYCHOLOGIST

After more than twenty years of research in real-world environments, a few truths have become self-evident.

1. *Take on opportunities when they occur.* We were constantly confronted with interesting opportunities to obtain data and resisted very few of them. We decided to obtain the data and worry about the potential limitations later. In a number of instances the results were rather meager, but in other cases we came across excellent sites for research and "gold mines" of data.

2. *People in many environments are cooperative.* We discovered some of the same dynamics in different environments. In each environment we studied—prison, school, home for aged veterans, housing—we had to obtain the cooperation of key authorities. To our surprise, we encountered very little resistance from those individuals, with the exception of those in state prisons. They seemed to be tolerant of our meddling in their environment and shared some of our intellectual curiosity about the potential outcomes of the research. The inhabitants of these environments were also typically very cooperative. Thus we learned that there is very little justification to limiting research to environments and populations over which one has academic control.

3. *You can't go it alone.* Large-scale environmental research is very labor-intensive and is not feasible for those inclined to solitary pursuits. We needed the assistance of many motivated and good-natured graduate and undergraduate students. As a research team we not only pooled our multiple skills but also provided the mutual support necessary to persist in the arduous process. We were fortunate to have the financial support of enlightened administrators at our university and in a variety of funding agencies.

4. *You get what you don't expect.* Almost every project I've been involved in has yielded results counter to my and other people's initial expectations. Prisons were not expected to yield results because there were too many contaminating factors, such as overall prison stress. I expected strong effects of housing quality but failed to find them. However, regardless of our expectations, the outcomes of our work were often most interesting and eventually made theoretical sense.

5. *If it sticks out, it will draw lightning.* We experienced considerable reaction to the prison work. This is not surprising, in part because such research has important practical as well as theoretical implications. Evidence that prison overcrowding can be harmful can be used to justify spending additional funds to provide better and less crowded prisons. This has occurred in many states in response to prison lawsuits and has cost billions of dollars. Research that justifies such expenditures should not be taken lightly and should be critically analyzed. Although we

would have preferred that all the published responses to our work be focused on its good points, we recognize the importance of the critical approach in science and are ardent practitioners of it ourselves.

6. *Humility is the best policy.* Much of the effort involved in field research is "grunt work." There are many tasks in all phases of the work that have a very small intellectual component, e.g., the extensive travel time and the data gathering, coding, and management. Outside the confines of one's laboratory, one is also typically in a low-power situation, dependent on the cooperation of many parties. Very time-consuming efforts sometimes yield very little in terms of useful data. When interesting data are published, someone will usually find something wrong with them. Moreover, when one presents one's data and opinions in court or another public forum, one is sometimes confronted by hostile challenges by the opposition.

7. *What is "in" today is "out" tomorrow.* We were fortunate to obtain financial support for a variety of projects, yet a change in the national administration led to changes in funding priorities. A harder line on dealing with inmates led to a "drying up" of funds for prison crowding research and a retrenchment of the role of the Justice Department in prison crowding cases. Simultaneously, there was an increase in funding for the Defense Department which allowed for research on the quality of life of Army families. This funding diminished with a change of leadership in the Pentagon and an increased focus on AIDS research. The issue of change in funding priorities by major governmental entities is a particular problem for applied researchers since their work often takes years to complete. I am just now publishing the last of my findings from the Army project, six years after I began the work. The prison book was published ten years after we began the major project. Thus it pays to be intrinsically motivated if one gets involved in large-scale environmental studies.

8. *You must give a little of yourself.* You cannot go into those environments and expect only to take data away. The model of uninterested subjects willingly giving responses to a structured situation in a laboratory for the sake of an experimental credit is not a good one for the real world. When you enter the homes or environments of people, you must be sensitive to their needs. They may need you to listen to their stories. They may see you as someone who might be able to help them with the dilemmas faced by themselves and others. If you will not be able to provide direct feedback or promises of relief, they must be convinced that you are genuinely interested in their dilemma and that your research may play a small role in ameliorating the problems they encounter. This issue was brought home clearly many times. When we requested that inmates at the federal prison at Danbury provide us with urine samples for analysis, they demanded that we send each of them a report of our results. Providing the sample required that they trust our claims of anonymity for their

data. In return for their trust, they felt that we should provide them feedback about the research. We did so about a year later. Similarly, when I was doing an evaluation of individuals working in an underground facility, they made it clear that they would cooperate only if their concerns would be clearly communicated in my report to their superior. The Army families were willing to volunteer for the study because they felt that our results might lead to more benign housing policies. We were not always able to deliver fully what was expected. However, in the case of the prisons, our work obviously had a profound effect on prison policies and judicial decisions in the United States. We did not promise such results, but we did promise that our findings would be broadly disseminated and could be potentially used in court cases to provide relief to inmates. This is one promise that was indeed fulfilled.

9. *The reward is in the process.* Doing research in real-world environments provides many personal and intellectual rewards. We met many interesting people and had many exciting experiences. Although there were no guarantees that our efforts would lead to important theoretical results, the prospects for both theoretical and pragmatic benefits helped motivate us to persist through many difficult phases. Yet the main rewards for us were no different from those which motivate most scientists: the challenge of solving various intellectual and pragmatic problems in order to discover new relationships among significant variables. We were fortunate to be able to solve some of the problems and make some interesting discoveries.

SUGGESTED READINGS

BAUM, A., & PAULUS, P. B. (1987). Crowding. In D. Stokols & I. Altman (Eds.), *Handbook of environmental psychology* (pp. 533–570). New York: Wiley.

COX, V. C., PAULUS, P. B., & McCAIN, G. (1984). Prison crowding research: The relevance for prison housing standards and a general hypothesis regarding the crowding experience. *American Psychologist, 39,* 1148–1160.

————— PAULUS, P. B., McCAIN, G., & SCHKADE, J. K. (1979). Field research on the effects of crowding in prisons and on offshore drilling platforms. In J. R. Aiello and A. Baum (Eds.), *Residential crowding and design* (p. 95–106). New York: Plenum.

McCAIN, G., COX, V. C., PAULUS, P. B., LUKE, A., & ABADZI, H. (1985). The effect of reduction in crowding in a school environment. *Journal of Applied Social Psychology, 15,* 503–515.

PAULUS, P. B. (1987). *Prison crowding: A psychological perspective.* New York: Springer.

————— & DZINDOLET, M. T. (1993). Reactions of male and female inmates to prison confinement: Further evidence for a two-component model. *Criminal Justice and Behavior, 20,* 149–166.

———— & NAGAR, D. (1989). Environmental influences on groups. In P. B. Paulus (Ed.), *Psychology of group influence,* 2d ed. (pp. 111–140). Hillsdale, NJ: Erlbaum.

———— NAGAR, D., & CAMACHO, M. L. (1991). Environmental and psychological factors in reactions to apartments and mobile homes. *Environmental Psychology, 11,* 143–161.

ZILLMAN, D., & PAULUS, P. B. (1993). Spectators: Reactions to sport events and effects on athletic performance. In R. N. Singer, M. Murphey, & L. K. Tennant (Eds.), *Handbook of research in sport psychology* (pp. 600–619). New York: MacMillan.

NORBERT L. KERR (Ph.D., University of Illinois at Urbana–Champaign) is Professor of Psychology at Michigan State University. Most of his research interests focus on behavior in small groups: how groups such as juries reach decisions, how individual and group performance are related (especially how motivation differs in group and individual contexts), and how group members resolve conflicts between their personal interests and the interests of the group. His schoolboy ambition to become a scientist was channeled into a career in social psychology by two chance events: (1) In 1968 he took a social psychology course as an elective toward his undergraduate physics major. The textbook was the first edition of Roger Brown's Social Psychology, and it not only revealed the existence of the field of social psychology but also showed what an exciting scientific field it is. (2) In 1970, as a raw and uncommitted graduate student at the University of Illinois, he had the lucky break of being offered a research assistantship with Jim Davis.

14

Social Psychology in Court: The Case of the Prejudicial Pretrial Publicity

———— ❖ ————

*B*uried in the stacks of university libraries one can find the official record of my story. That official version is a fairly neat and tidy affair which, in a twist, puts courts on trial. Courts are institutions, but institutions created and run by human beings. And those human beings are flawed creatures, subject to prejudices, biases, and shortcomings which social psychologists like me spend much of our professional lives trying to describe and understand. The official version of the story finds the courts guilty of the pervasive human shortcoming of overconfidence, in particular, believing that the remedies they have always relied on to solve an uncommon but irksome problem may fail just when they are needed the most. In this instance the problem is ensuring a fair trial for a defendant when newspapers, radio, and television have been full of unflattering and perhaps wholly inaccurate information before the trial has begun.

As is usually the case, the unofficial story is not nearly so neat and tidy. It is a story of chance events, lucky and unlucky breaks, unexpected delights, and ambiguous, inconclusive evidence.

ONCE UPON A TIME: THE BEGINNINGS OF THE PRETRIAL PUBLICITY PROJECT

The story begins in 1983 in Chicago. At that point in my career I was beginning to drift away from a long-standing interest in decision making by juries (nurtured by my mentor, Jim Davis) and toward another interesting research problem (why group members are often unwilling to contribute their effort, money, and time to the group). I had just given a colloquium at Loyola University and was chatting comfortably with a fellow social psychologist (and old friend), John Carroll. It seems that John and Jim Alfini, a lawyer interested in sociolegal research who was then at the American Judicature Society (AJS) in Chicago, had been discussing doing some research on the effects of prejudicial pretrial publicity. AJS had been approached in 1982 by a foundation interested in journalism and media issues; for reasons that will become clear later, let's call it Foundation X. Foundation X had taken a special interest in pretrial publicity and had invited AJS to develop plans for a research project. It so happened that John and Jim both belonged to a baby-sitting cooperative. One evening in the winter of 1982 John was baby-sitting for Jim, whom he barely knew. At the end of the evening chat, Jim happened to mention the pretrial publicity project. AJS was hoping to involve academic researchers in the project, and Jim eventually talked John into working up a proposal.

During our conversation in 1983 John casually wondered whether I might also be interested in getting involved. His offer was also a bit rash: I knew practically nothing about pretrial publicity. But that's how I had begun most of my research projects, and it had never stopped me before, so I carelessly said something like "Sure, let's talk some more about it." That offhand reply was how I got back into the business of studying jury behavior in a serious way.

Money is the mother's milk not only of politics but also of behavioral research. Although we had some vague, tentative research ideas, we didn't have a single dollar with which to pursue them. Jim and John wrote a brief proposal to Foundation X which outlined an opening strategy: to review relevant law and empirical research; to talk with judges, attorneys, and journalists about pretrial publicity; and to develop a more ambitious research plan. To our delight, in June 1984 Foundation X gave us $45,000 and six months to spend it. Now we really were in business.

FROM VAGUE IDEAS TO A RESEARCH PLAN

I don't know if it is a general rule, but in my experience, behind every successful research program stand talented, hardworking graduate students. They work in a kind of apprenticeship system where the pay is low, the hours are long, and the career prospects are very uncertain. Given these disincentives, it's not surprising that the best students are the ones whose motivations are intrinsic. They need an active curiosity and usually have been bitten by the research bug (i.e., they have discovered the pleasure of doing research as a means of scratching that tormenting itch inflamed for some people by the simple question "Why?"). The opening phase of this project was no exception to the rule: Most of the really hard work (tracking down and summarizing articles, reviewing case law, arranging and conducting interviews) was done by a group of superb students, including Rob MacCoun (from Michigan State), Fran Weaver, and Valerie Feldman (from Loyola).

A big difference between applied and basic social psychology is that for the former you need to be more concerned with persuading nonscientists that your scientific work is valuable. For those of us interested in applying social psychology to the legal system, it is necessary to be concerned with persuading the people who may set the policy for that system (legislators, appellate judges, voters) or work within the system (trial judges, attorneys, court reporters). And in my experience these lay (i.e., nonscientist) audiences are not persuaded by the same things that might persuade a fellow social psychologist (the latter valuing, for example, coherent theory, tight research designs, large samples, and careful statistical analysis). Judges and attorneys are more likely to be persuaded by research that confirms their own (or some respected authority's) experience. Mindful of this, we spent most of our time, effort, and money asking experienced judges, attorneys, and journalists what they thought about the problem of prejudicial pretrial publicity.

The epitome of this strategy was a pair of meetings we held with a blue-ribbon panel of advisers. This panel included a former attorney general of the United States, a former editor in chief of a Chicago newspaper, a dean of a school of journalism, a senior researcher with the American Bar Foundation (the American Bar Association's primary research arm), a leading First Amendment lawyer, and a former United States attorney. At the first meeting we asked for their opinions about what the most interesting research questions on pretrial publicity would be. They told us the same thing most of the other, less renowned people we had talked to had said—that pretrial publicity really wasn't a major problem in American courts. Based on their own considerable experience (punctuated with vivid anecdotes or "war stories"), they asserted that very few cases received very much publicity, that the public ignored or soon forgot the pretrial publicity it had seen, and that in those rare cases which had received unrelenting pretrial publicity, an unbiased jury could always be selected.

Well, we could have just stopped the project there or perhaps made it our goal to provide hard empirical evidence to back up the accumulated wisdom of the legal and journalism professionals we had consulted. There were only two problems. First, there already were a number of good empirical studies that indicated that exposure to prejudicial pretrial publicity certainly *could* affect public opinion about a pending case and hinted that such effects could survive a number of the remedies courts employ and ultimately bias jury verdicts. Second, there was a faint but persistent dissenting voice among our consultants—defense attorneys. They tended to believe that pretrial publicity is a real and unsolved problem. Was it significant that this was the group (or, more precisely, the one representing that group) that stood to lose the most if pretrial publicity turned out to be a genuine but ignored problem? When it occurred, pretrial publicity almost always *strengthened* prosecutors' cases. Trial judges had the responsibility of ensuring that defendants received a fair trial; it could be personally and professionally unsettling even to imagine that they might regularly be unable to fulfill this responsibility. And journalists, zealous in their defense of First Amendment rights, might be expected to be (hyper?) sensitive to any suggestion that news reports may not only inform and serve the public but may also sometimes do real harm.

With all this in mind, John, Jim, and I sat down one afternoon to discuss where our project should head. There seemed to be too much good evidence that pretrial publicity can affect public opinion simply to dismiss the problem as illusory. But there was far less good evidence on whether standard judicial remedies [careful juror selection (voir dire), continuances or delays in beginning the trial, judicial admonitions to disregard pretrial publicity] are effective in neutralizing such biases. This seemed to be a promising and researchable question.

Although Foundation X had expressed interest originally only in supporting a preliminary, planning project, we nevertheless approached them to see if they might be willing to support a full-fledged multimethod and multistudy project focusing on the effectiveness of courts' remedies for pretrial publicity. Foundation X was quick to respond: They were definitely *not* willing to support such a project. The primary problem did not seem to be the projected expense of such a project. Rather, it seemed to be our implicit assumption that pretrial publicity really *could* bias jurors. In our excitement about what seemed to be interesting scientific research questions, we had lost sight of the fact that Foundation X had been created by journalists and shared many of the perspectives and objectives of that profession. Some journalists who were trusted advisers to the foundation had supervised earlier, preliminary reviews of the literature which had concluded that pretrial publicity does not pose a substantial threat to fair trials. Apparently, this was the kind of conclusion Foundation X had anticipated when it funded our seed work. Our proposal not only concluded that pretrial publicity can be biasing but also proposed to conduct research that might even come to the more unpalatable conclusion that existing remedies don't work, which conceivably could *increase* pressures to limit press access to the courts and freedom to report. It had been concern about such attempts to close trials or gag the press which had prompted Foundation X's original interest in the question of pretrial publicity. Foundation X not only declined to fund our full-scale pretrial publicity project but requested that any future reports or publications omit any mention of its past support (hence my circumspect references to Foundation X).

Fortunately, there are a few sources of research support that are relatively indifferent to the political correctness of the findings. We submitted our proposal to the National Science Foundation in early 1985, and it agreed to support a trimmed-down version of our proposal. It had taken us over two years and $45,000 of private foundation money just to plan the project; we now set out to do far more (namely, run one huge jury-simulation experiment and one huge judgment/survey study of attorneys and judges) with only about $68,000 of the American taxpayers' money and two years to spend it.

ON HOUSES OF BRICKS VERSUS HOUSES OF STRAW: FROM RESEARCH PLAN TO RESEARCH REALITY

By that point the base of the project had shifted to Michigan State University (MSU). I had the wherewithal (lab space, access to subjects and the local courts, institutional support) at MSU. More practically, MSU's grant overhead rate was much lower than MIT's (where John had moved). So, largely through a process of elimination, I became the project's principal investigator. However, what I didn't have at that time was graduate student support. Rob MacCoun had just graduated, and none of the other social psychology graduate students at MSU had any background or interest in the topic. A fearsome prospect loomed: *I* might have to assume an apprentice's arduous duties. Just then a miracle occurred—Geoff Kramer walked into my office. Geoff had a master's degree in clinical psychology and had been working as a clinical psychologist in a state prison. He was interested in forensic psychology (broadly defined) and was considering returning to graduate school. Geoff looked like the perfect research assistant for the publicity project; as it turned out, he was even better than he looked. Nominally, I was the project's principal investigator, but over the next few years this became Geoff's project every bit as much as mine.

The centerpiece of the project was to be a jury-simulation experiment. First, mock jurors would be exposed or not exposed to biasing pretrial publicity. Earlier researchers had drawn an interesting distinction between pretrial publicity that suggested the guilt of the defendant (e.g., a news report that a confession had been obtained or that the defendant had previously been convicted of the same offense) and publicity that upset the public but contained no information directly implicating anyone (e.g., gruesome details of a murder or the plight of the parents of a kidnapped child). We called the former type *factual* publicity and the latter type *emotional* publicity. We wanted to look at how well the most commonly used remedies would work for both types of publicity. Our background work suggested that in order of decreasing reliance, those remedies were (1) voir dire (the jury selection process), (2) judicial admonitions, (3) jury deliberation (i.e., jury members preventing one another from considering pretrial publicity), and (4) continuances. The simulation study would directly examine the latter three remedies and would produce materials needed for the follow-up judgment/survey study that would focus on voir dire. (Here I have space only to tell the story of the simulation study; we'll have to save most of the equally interesting story of the follow-up study for another bedtime.)

As was noted earlier, if you want legal practitioners to pay any attention to the results of your study of behavior in a legal setting, you have to keep in mind and, to a certain extent, indulge the preoccupations of those practitioners. In my experience, judges and attorneys are singularly concerned with issues of *realism*, sometimes to the exclusion of all other issues (unfortunately, this is also an obsession of many behavioral scientists, who ought to know better). They want to know whether one's research is based on actual verdicts on real defendants by real jurors in real trials argued by real attorneys before real judges.

For very real practical and ethical reasons, we determined that it was not feasible for us to do a defensible field experiment. We were resigned to doing a simulation study, but how much were we willing to pay to make that simulation realistic? Realism costs. Subjects representative of the population of real jurors are much more difficult and expensive to obtain than, say, college students. It is much more expensive to obtain and edit the videotape of a real trial that would meet our requirements than to produce a fictional audiotape or transcript. But more important, one can spend so much capital on realism that one is left with a worthless study. For example, most juries in criminal trials have twelve persons, but to use twelve-person groups as one's experimental replicates can result in such a small sample of juries (given a fixed subject sample size) that one has insufficient statistical power to detect any effect of interest. Or how can the fact that a stimulus trial is real be compensated for if it produces a floor effect on jury verdicts (i.e., the evidence is too weak to convince any juror that the defendant might be guilty)?

Our response to this ever-present tension between realism and experimental control was willingly to purchase as much realism as we could *as long as it didn't compromise our ability to draw clear inferences on the questions that interested us the most*. So although there was almost no theoretical or empirical reason to believe that students react to extralegal biasing materials such as prejudicial pretrial publicity differently than do older, less well educated people who are more representative of actual jurors, we were willing to make the extra effort (since the National Science Foundation was willing to spend the extra money) to recruit a representative sample from pools of recent ex-venirepersons (people called in for jury duty). Even though direct content analysis of jury deliberation rarely yields information worth the effort, we promised the granting agency to videotape and analyze the content of our mock juries' deliberations. And although there was lots of evidence that judicial admonitions to "disregard what you have seen or heard" are essentially useless or even counterproductive (especially when jurors have seen or heard something attention-grabbing), we included a manipulation of such instructions because doing so cost us little but addressed another "real" remedy of interest to legal practitioners.

But elsewhere the cost of realism was just too steep. If we were a person or two short of the number we needed to make up a jury, we wouldn't trash the session rather than recruit a college student or two to complete the group. (Note that as we had expected, the behavior of such student-jurors turned out to be indistinguishable from that of the ex-venirepersons.) And we declined the idea of spending forever looking for an ideal real trial (with extensive factual and emotional pretrial publicity, videotaped, short enough to be used in the lab, accessible, etc.) which might not even exist when we could modify and augment existing stimulus trials to serve our experimental purposes.

To this end, we contacted everyone we knew to obtain his or her stimulus trial videotapes. We had hoped to find a nice engaging murder case for which we could produce some convincing factual and emotional pretrial publicity. The ideal factual publicity manipulation seemed to be an extensive criminal record. This had already been shown to bias mock jurors' judgments, both when presented at trial and when brought out in pretrial publicity. But there was little point examining the biasing effect of pretrial publicity information which would also be presented during the trial and thus could equally bias jurors who had never seen the publicity. If a defendant testifies in his or her own behalf, his or her past criminal record may well be brought out. Thus, legal procedures put constraints on the kinds of stimuli we could use. Many trial videotapes which were otherwise fine had to be eliminated because the defendant testified. Likewise, we had hoped to vary the emotional impact of pretrial publicity by varying how explicitly the damage done to a victim of a violent crime was described (*New York Times* versus *New York Post* versions of crime reporting). But this raised another dilemma, an ethical one. The stronger such an emotional publicity treatment was, the more upset jurors might become and the greater the risk of harm to the subjects. Besides which, almost all the cases we could find involved victims who showed up in court looking perfectly fine, undercutting the potential impact of the preferred emotional manipulation.

Finally we settled on the videotape of an armed robbery trial lent to us by Reid Hastie. It was based on a real case, the judge and attorneys were real, it was of (or could be edited to) a reasonable length, and it suggested a new way of varying emotional publicity. We came up with the idea of linking the robbery to a second crime, a hit-and-run. What if pretrial publicity (but not trial evidence) indicated that while he or she was driving away from the scene of the robbery, the robber's car hit and killed someone. The trick would be presenting the latter crime in a way that would be emotionally upsetting to jurors but did not increase the apparent guilt of the defendant on the robbery charge. Our solution was to make the victim of the hit-and-run a child known to the jurors. We would first introduce the child in a very attractive, sympathetic light within a television news feature seeking a "Big Sister" for her and then include an interview with her grieving mother after the hit-and-run incident. This avoided relying on unethically gruesome depictions of the physical consequences of a violent crime but still had the potential to carry an emotional punch.

Our next task was to create the required publicity, and this presented me with opportunities to take on a number of completely new and entertaining roles. I had to write the scripts for our bogus TV news reports, cast all the roles (child victim, mother, newscasters), act as both producer and director for the taping of several segments, and edit the final news reports. Of course, I had absolutely no training in any of those areas, no equipment, and only a tiny budget with which to produce realistic TV news clips. But at a large research university such as Michigan State there are all sorts of people and resources one can draw on if one just noses around and begs hard enough. Members of the journalism department served as unpaid consultants and actors, a reporter from the campus radio station agreed to take on the role of the primary TV reporter, a fellow identified through the journalism department who was trying to get established in Detroit TV journalism was hired to be our anchorman, and an old acquaintance and the chair of the communications department, the late Gerald Miller, generously provided access to one of his staff people who was experienced in video production work and with video editing equipment.

As you can imagine, all this involved working on the cheap and at times on the sly. For example, we wanted to shoot an interview with an eyewitness at the scene of the hit-and-run and get some still photos of the child victim bleeding next to her mangled bike. I found a nondescript and relatively quiet intersection in Lansing (it wouldn't do to have jurors from the Lansing, Michigan, area recognize the background when all these events had ostensibly occurred in Cambridge, Massachusetts). Proper procedure would have been to go to the city officials, get their permission and any necessary permits for filming at a public intersection, and so on. Instead, we just grabbed our camera and drove to the site. We quickly got several good takes of the interview. We then did some makeup on our child star (fake bruises, fake blood), loosened enough bolts on her bike to be able to twist it into an unlikely shape, and took photographs of her lying on the curb next to the bike; one of those photos would accompany a bogus newspaper article reporting the hit-and-run. Within a minute or two we had a swelling traffic jam on our hands. Passing cars screeched to a halt, and people jumped out to see if they could help. We found ourselves trying to reassure a growing crowd that there had been no accident and that everything was all right and to wrap it up before the police arrived and justifiably arrested us for creating a public disturbance. I found myself wondering at the time, If Kitty Genovese had lived in this neighborhood, would social psychology have formed its accepted view of unresponsive bystanders?

The most difficult scene was the interview of the child's mother (played by the child actress's actual mother) at the hospital shortly after she has learned that her daughter has died. This would be challenging for seasoned professionals, and (except for the cameraman) we were a bunch of rank amateurs. I suspect that it was more the fatigue of take after take (with an assist to onion-juice eye shadow) than our acting and directing skills that produced the desired effect of numb grief.

Pilot work suggested that this emotional publicity seemed to work: People who saw it got upset and were more likely to convict the robbery defendant as a result. Surprisingly, it turned out to be much more difficult to get an effective factual publicity manipulation. We had to keep adding more and more negative information to get the same impact as the emotional treatment. By the time we were done, the pretrial publicity had painted a very negative image of the defendant: It indicated that he had multiple prior convictions for armed robbery, that he was on release from prison at the time of the crime (not for good behavior but because of prison overcrowding), and that all sorts of incriminating evidence had been found in his girlfriend's apartment (but couldn't be used in court because of a faulty search warrant). Of course, our goal was not to produce *typical* publicity (which seems usually to be absent or not very incriminating); our goal was to see if available remedies would work when they were most needed (when the pretrial publicity was *extremely* prejudicial). In our final check of our manipulations we convinced ourselves that both of our publicity treatments did indeed bias jurors.

We had only one tricky design problem left to solve: We wanted to simulate the granting of a continuance. Half the mock jurors would see the publicity immediately before serving as jurors; that part would be easy. But we wanted the rest of the mock jurors to see the publicity some time before they came to the lab at the university to act as jurors. Ideally, that time interval would be similar to the usual interval between the time a crime (and the initial publicity) occurs and the time the case is brought to trial, but that is often weeks or months. Even if the research grant gave us enough time to wait months between our initial contact with subjects and their ultimate participation (it didn't), how could we contact them, expose them to the publicity, and ensure that they showed up on a specified date months down the line?

As Joe McGrath has pointed out, when you're doing research, you're constantly on the horns of a dilemma. In the present instance, the more realistic we made the continuance (or delay) treatment, the harder it would be to get long-delay subjects. McGrath suggests that the best you can do is pick which horn you want to avoid and accept the fact that you're going to be impaled on the other; it's the nature of most dilemmas that you can't avoid both horns altogether. As our earlier biases might indicate, we chose to sacrifice realism rather than risk not being able to examine the effects of delay at all. So we opted for a much briefer delay; it turned out on average to be about twelve days. We also took advantage of a technological innovation, the home VCR. For most of our high-delay subjects (those with VCRs), we just mailed them a videocassette containing pretrial publicity and asked them to view at home the background information it contained. This was simple and relatively inexpensive, helped stimulate subject interest, and thus encouraged people to show up at the lab.

ON THE RESEARCH ASSEMBLY LINE: RUNNING THE STUDY

For me, thinking up research ideas and translating them into actual research procedures is the fun part of the research process (writing is the most difficult). It allows you to be creative and solve puzzles and, best of all, lets you live blithely waiting for clean, unequivocal, and exciting findings. But after the novelty has worn off, the actual task of collecting the data can become a laborious chore. It must be a lot like acting in a long-running play, except that you get no applause at the end of each day's work.

Irv Altman and Joe McGrath have described how a successful social psychologist (or, for that matter, nearly any academic researcher) tends to spend less and less time in the lab and more and more time in other roles (fund seeker, project manager, empire builder). It is the graduate apprentices who usually end up doing the really hard work in the lab. In the present case it was Geoff Kramer, assisted by dozens of capable undergraduate volunteers (whom we hoped to infect with the research bug), who provided the many months of diligent effort needed to complete the study.

However, I usually try to come to a few sessions of every study just to get a feel for what's going on. And in this study I was very nervous about how the subjects would react to the publicity I had dreamed up and spent so many hours producing. I distinctly remember sitting with a group of no-delay jurors watching the high-emotion pretrial publicity version. Would they react to the story of the little girl and her mother as involving and tragic or as hokey and unbelievable? Would what they saw really touch their emotions? The last image on the monitor was of the tearstained face of the mother at the hospital. I stopped the tape and looked at the group. The room was eerily silent, and every face looked grim and tense. Although outwardly I was appropriately sober, inside I was exultant—it was working!

*T*RIAL BY DATA: ANALYSIS AND FINDINGS

Of course, what really mattered was not my beliefs about how people were reacting to the situation we had created for them but how they actually behaved. After more months of coding their responses and the content of their jury deliberations, we were finally in a position to address directly the questions we had first posed five years earlier.

Early in the process of data analysis I encountered an unexpected obstacle. My Scots ancestry seems to incline me toward thriftiness (some of my blunter friends would say miserliness). I suggested early on that we could save a little money by dropping one condition. Why, I argued, include a control condition (i.e., exposed to neither the factual nor the emotional publicity but just to some fairly neutral publicity) with a delay? It was costly to preexpose delay subjects, and since what they would see should be nonprejudicial anyway, we could simply rely on the no-delay controls to tell us how jurors would decide the case in the complete absence of prejudicial pretrial publicity. This was not logically unreasonable, but it set a statistical bear trap. It turns out that all the usual methods of analyzing a multifactored experiment will not work properly when just one cell is missing. I trudged from one statistically sophisticated colleague to another and read through several statistics textbooks to find a solution to this unanticipated problem. We finally came up with (i.e., had to concoct) a workable solution. Although we had saved a few lab hours and dollars at the front end, that "savings" ended up costing several times as much in time and effort at the data analysis stage.

What did the data show? An initial and distressing finding was that the predeliberation verdict preferences of individual jurors were affected only slightly by the prejudicial pretrial publicity. How could this be? Our pilot study had produced very reliable effects on jurors, and we had much bigger samples now. More to the point, how could we study the effects of remedies for pretrial publicity–produced bias if there was no such bias to remedy? Fortunately, when we looked at *jury* verdicts (which are practically all that really matters), we found that both the emotional and the factual pretrial publicity significantly increased conviction rates. Rather than attenuating publicity-induced bias, jury deliberation had *exacerbated* it. Further, giving jurors strong judicial admonitions to ignore any publicity they had seen did not affect jury verdicts at all. In fact, under certain conditions receiving such an admonition actually made jurors exposed to biasing pretrial publicity even more negative toward the defendant than they would have been if they had received no such admonition. The only remedy that seemed to do any good at all was creating a delay (continuance) between the exposure and the trial. However, that remedy worked only for the factual publicity; it had no beneficial effect for the emotionally biasing publicity.

Just to round out the story, I'll briefly summarize our other study. During the simulation study we videotaped mock jurors' replies to what our legal consultants said were the questions typically posed to prospective jurors during voir dire in a high-publicity case. We then sent those tapes to a national sample of volunteer prosecutors, defense attorneys, and judges and asked them to make their usual jury selection decisions. To make a long story short, the net effect of their choices was nil. Jurors who were exposed to biasing publicity and who passed the screening of those experienced attorneys and judges were just as likely to convict as were the exposed jurors who had been rejected as biased, but both groups of jurors were more likely to convict than were jurors who never had been exposed to the publicity. Such findings tend to undermine confidence in jury selection as an effective remedy in high-publicity cases.

OUR STORY'S MORALS

Stories often have a moral, and in looking back over this project, I see several.

Moral 1: Research, Like Life, Is Chancy

The path our project took was partly a result of careful thought and planning but at least as much a result of dumb luck. Both John and I would never have become involved at all except for chance conversations. The project would not have been completed nearly as well (or perhaps at all) if fate had not brought Geoff Kramer into my office at just the right time. Many other examples could be given. I suppose the trick is to do what you can to be prepared to take advantage of the lucky breaks and to cope with the unlucky ones.

Moral 2: There's Nothing so Theoretically Useful as a Practical Question

Most students of social psychology are taught Kurt Lewin's famous dictum, "There's nothing so practical as a good theory." A fuller quotation is as follows:

> Many psychologists working today in an applied field are keenly aware of the need for close cooperation between theoretical and applied psychology. This can be accomplished in psychology, as it has been accomplished in physics, if the theorist does not look toward applied problems with highbrow aversion or with a fear of social problems, and if the applied psychologist realizes that there is nothing so practical as a good theory. [p. 169]

One reason to do *applied* social psychology is to shed some light on interesting, practical problems. But my own experience is also congruent with the less widely quoted part of Lewin's statement (and with much of his career as a scientist): Social psychologists interested in developing a broad, powerful theory should not show aversion to applied research; quite the contrary. Focusing on a practical problem almost always ends up raising and illuminating questions of much broader theoretical interest than the practical problem with which one began. We began this project by focusing on a very practical question: What can courts do to reduce the impact of prejudicial pretrial publicity? The project did, we think, shed some light on that practical question, but by the end of the project I was even more intrigued with some new theoretical questions, such as, What is the special role of affect or emotion in the courtroom? I haven't been able to pursue that question yet; I'm waiting for another Rob MacCoun or Geoff Kramer with an interest in such questions to walk into my professional life. But Rob, Geoff, and I have since been pursuing another equally fascinating theoretical question: When will groups be more biased than individuals, and when will they be less biased? Our curiosity about this question and some lines of attack on it were direct results of certain findings in the pretrial publicity project—namely, the way publicity did not affect jurors' behavior but did affect juries' behavior.

Moral 3: Research Producers Must Both Remember and Forget Research Consumers

In planning and executing our project, we had to be mindful of the people who would be consuming our products: the foundation officials, the grant panel members, the judges of the local court, the people who decide whether to do anything different about the way pretrial publicity is dealt with in the courts. There was little use in planning to do what in our eyes was the most rigorous and informative research if no one would support, read, or be persuaded by our findings. So at many points—the choice of trial stimuli, subjects, and even research questions—we were influenced by the values and preoccupations of those significant consumers. But at many other points—designing the delay treatment, choosing jury size, settling on publicity content—we made choices which we could safely assume would rub many of those consumers the wrong way. Research routinely entails such choices and compromises; the trick is to neither ignore nor pander to your consumers but to accommodate where you must, pick your controversies well with an eye to what's central and what's peripheral in the research, and then be ready to educate your consumers and explain why you've made those choices.

Moral 4: Many of Research's Rewards Are Hidden

When I was a graduate student, one of my professors, Joe McGrath, said (paraphrasing freely) that if one's motivation for doing social psychology is to solve the world's problems, one is destined for frustration and disappointment. The world's problems are complex and often intractable, and individual behavioral scientists can at best only shed flickering light on parts of their solutions. But if one's primary motivation for being a social psychologist is more prosaic—because it is fun to do research—then one will always have a good reason to come to work (and, incidentally, will probably do more and better work).

A number of the judges and attorneys to whom I have described our work have dismissed it as too limited and artificial to be relevant to their concerns. And our necessarily equivocal and inconclusive findings certainly have not stimulated concerted efforts to change what courts routinely do in high-pretrial-publicity cases. I hope our work will be noticed, stimulate new and better research, and ultimately contribute in a small way to the solution of a real problem. But even if it is ignored completely, I've profited a lot from the project and in ways that are not evident from the official record of publications. I've had a chance to work with old friends and make very interesting new acquaintances (including some leaders in their professions). Much of this contact occurred in new and to me exotic disciplines (television journalism, courtroom trial tactics). I've been able to turn my statistical blunders into a deeper understanding of certain statistical issues that should help me in future work. And I've had a chance to have all sorts of new and captivating experiences: writing a mini-"screenplay," sitting in the director's chair, gauging an audience's reaction on "opening night." Working in a profession that regularly gives one such opportunities for new challenges and experiences—that is, being a research social psychologist—keeps providing me with lots of good reasons to come to work.

Acknowledgments

Preparation of this chapter was supported by NSF Grants SES#8419944 and BNS#8818952. I'd like to thank Jim Alfini, John Carroll, Geoff Kramer, and Rob MacCoun for their comments on an earlier draft.

SUGGESTED READINGS

ALTMAN, I., & MCGRATH, J. E. (1966). *Small group research: A synthesis and critique of the field.* New York: Holt.

BRAY, R. M., & KERR, N. L. (1982). Methodological issues in the study of the psychology of the courtroom. In N. L. Kerr & R. M. Bray (Eds.), *The psychology of the courtroom* (pp. 287–323). New York: Academic Press.

CARROLL, J., KERR, N. L., ALFINI, J., WEAVER, F., MACCOUN, R., & FELDMAN, V. (1986). Free press and fair trial: The role of behavioral research. *Law and Human Behavior, 10,* 187–202.

FRASCA, R. (1988). Estimating the occurrence of trials prejudiced by press coverage. *Judicature, 72,* 162–169.

HANS, V. P., & DOOB, A. N. (1976). Section 12 of the Canada Evidence Act and the deliberations of simulated juries. *Criminal Law Quarterly, 18,* 235–253.

HOIBERG, B. C., & STIRES, L. K. (1973). The effect of several types of pretrial publicity on the guilt attributions of simulated juries. *Journal of Applied Social Psychology, 3,* 267–271.

HVISTENDAHL, J. K. (1979). The effect of placement of biasing information. *Journalism Quarterly, 56,* 863–865.

KERR, N. L. (1992). Behavioral research on the effects of pretrial publicity. *From the Mind's Eye: Behavioral Research News for Trial Attorneys, 1*(3), 1–11 (published by Sierra Trial & Opinion, Reno, Nevada).

———— & BRAY, R. M. (1979). Use of the simulation method in the study of jury behavior. *Law and Human Behavior, 3,* 107–119.

———— & BRAY, R. M. (Eds.). (1982). *The psychology of the courtroom.* New York: Academic Press.

———— KRAMER, G. P., CARROLL, J. S., & ALFINI, J. (1991). On the effectiveness of voir dire in criminal cases with prejudicial pretrial publicity: An empirical study. *American University Law Review, 40,* 665–701.

———— & MACCOUN, R. (1983). Pretrial publicity and juror judgment: A review of empirical research. Unpublished manuscript, Michigan State University.

KRAMER, G. P., & KERR, N. L. (1989). Laboratory simulation and bias in the study of juror behavior: A methodological note. *Law and Human Behavior, 13,* 89–100.

———— KERR, N. L., & CARROLL, J. S. (1990). Pretrial publicity, judicial remedies, and jury bias. *Law and Human Behavior* (special issue on law and media), *14,* 409–438.

LEWIN, K. (1951). Problems of research in social psychology. In K. Lewin, *Field theory in social science: Selected theoretical papers* (pp. 155–169). New York: Harper & Brothers.

McGRATH, J. E. (1982). Dilemmatics: The study of research choices and dilemmas. In J. E. McGrath, J. Martin, & R. Kulka (Eds.), *Judgment calls in research* (pp. 69–102). Beverly Hills, CA: Sage.

PROCEEDINGS OF THE SYMPOSIUM ON THE SELECTION AND FUNCTION OF THE MODERN JURY. (1991). *American University Law Review, 40,* 541–630.

SIMON, R. (1966). Murder, juries and the press. *Trans-Action, 3,* 40–42.

STAW, B. (1982). Some judgments on the judgment call approach. In J. E. McGrath, J. Martin, & R. Kulka (Eds.), *Judgment calls in research* (pp. 119–127). Beverly Hills, CA: Sage.

THOMPSON, W. C., FONG, G. T., & ROSENHAN, D. C. (1981). Inadmissible evidence and juror verdicts. *Journal of Personality and Social Psychology, 40,* 453–463.

PHILIP **E.** TETLOCK *(Ph.D., Yale University) is Distinguished Professor and Director of the Institute of Personality and Social Research at the University of California, Berkeley. He serves on several editorial boards of scientific journals and has received several awards, including the Behavioral Science Research Prize of the American Association for the Advancement of Science, the Erik Erikson Prize of the International Society of Political Psychology, the Early Career Award for Distinguished Scientific Contribution to Social Psychology from the American Psychological Association, and the Woodrow Wilson Foundation Book Prize from the American Political Science Association. He is married, has a teenage son, and is a hopeless news junkie.*

15

Complex Answers to a Simple Question: Is Integrative Complexity "Politically Correct"?

❖

Writing an autobiography is a tricky business under the best of circumstances, and explaining how one came to be a political psychologist is fraught with more than the usual amount of peril. My professional mind-set—the product of years of indoctrination in graduate school and many more years of teaching and research—predisposes me to be skeptical of what people say about the reasons and motives behind their actions. Politicians, as everyone knows, often use words to achieve political objectives. They may claim to be guided by principle when they are guided by expediency; they may claim to be altruistic when their motives are selfish.

Why should what I say about the reasons behind my actions be granted more credibility than the pronouncements of politicians? The standard answer is, "Because I am a scientist." Scientists are supposed to be dedicated to the truth. If the dispassionate and rigorous pursuit of the truth leads them in directions they find distasteful, they are still supposed to continue the pursuit. I might prefer for a personal or moral or religious reason to believe that the planets orbit the sun in perfect circles, that the Book of Genesis accurately describes the origins of the human species, or that racism is the sole "politically correct" explanation for the existence of racial inequality in the United States today. In principle, however, I should be willing to abandon all those beliefs and many more if the weight of scientific evidence shifts against them.

Doing political psychology well is exceptionally difficult. The root of the difficulty does not lie in the technical or mathematical complexity of the subject matter. Let's face it: Political psychology is not subatomic physics. Nonetheless, political psychology can sorely test the character and intellect of its practitioners. Political psychology requires an openness to evidence that may overturn assumptions quite dear to us, assumptions about the causes of war between nations or the causes of inequality within nations. Conceding that one might have been wrong is never easy; making this concession on emotionally and politically charged issues is impossible for many people.

A useful place to begin is by acknowledging that the tabula rasa model of the political psychologist is dead wrong; political psychologists do not approach their subject devoid of preconceptions and prejudices. Political psychologists tend to be politically liberal (in this regard, surveys tell us that they are like most social scientists). They prefer egalitarian social policies that reduce the gap between rich and poor. They detest racism and support policies to reduce prejudice in the present and eliminate the residual effects of past discrimination. They are deeply skeptical of the use of force in international relations. Most political psychologists may not be principled pacifists, but they are very suspicious of justifications for going to war. In short, political psychologists are not just scientists who study human behavior; they are human beings who subscribe, sometimes passionately, to certain moral and political values.

Throughout my career in social and political psychology I have wondered whether there is a contradiction here. Is it possible to do rigorous scientific research on topics that touch one's deepest moral and political feelings? There are all sorts of ways in which one's political point of view may contaminate the research findings one obtains or bias the theoretical explanations one offers. Let's consider some concrete examples drawn from what I know best: my own work.

INTEGRATIVE COMPLEXITY

For the last fifteen years I have had a special interest in social and political reasoning. In graduate school I liked to listen to people as they talked about their opinions on such controversial issues of the day as abortion, capital punishment, and affirmative action. I was interested, however, in more than whether they came down on the positive or negative end of a simple attitude scale. I wanted to know why they took the positions they held. What do people say in their own words about the reasons behind their positions? Social psychologists were, I thought, too quick to assume that they could successfully anticipate everything of interest that subjects might say. We needed to get beyond all those rating scales and go with the flow of natural language.

There was, however, a big problem with this plan. Natural language is not "data." Before becoming data, it has to be coded, analyzed, and processed by independent observers who are preferably "double-blind," or blind to both the source of the material and the hypotheses being tested. All this coding and processing is an expensive, labor-intensive process, far beyond the means of a humble graduate student.

So I confronted a dilemma. I was surrounded by a mass of interesting potential data but lacked the means of analyzing it and turning it into "real" data. Then I discovered content analysis. In particular, with the help of Peter Suedfeld, I discovered the integrative complexity coding system.

In reading political arguments, I had noticed that people differ not only in the positions they stake out for themselves but also in the styles of reasoning they use to justify those positions. When I read some justifications, there was a rigid, self-righteous ring to the language: There is only one right way to think about this problem, and that is my way of thinking. Other people were more flexible and open-minded. They were willing to acknowledge that they did not have a monopoly on good arguments. They were aware that the other side might have at least a few good counters. They saw taking a stand as a matter of weighing conflicting values and making trade-offs. There was room for reasonable people to disagree.

The integrative complexity coding system—the product of earlier work by Harold Schroder, Siegfried Streufert, Michael Driver, and Peter Suedfeld—gave me a precise, well-calibrated means of translating these crude intuitions about styles of thinking into a measurement scale. The key to the coding is to ignore *what* people say and focus on *how* they say it. Consider the topic of abortion. At the lowest level of the integrative complexity scale (scores of 1), we observe responses that show no tolerance for other ways of looking at the world (low evaluative differentiation):

> Abortion is about freedom of choice. Women won't stand any longer for a bunch of shriveled up old men telling them what they can and cannot do with their bodies and their lives. Outlawing abortion will simply drive women into the hands of back-alley butchers.

One can be equally integratively simple at the other end of the political spectrum:

> Abortion is infanticide. The mass killing of unborn babies since *Roe v. Wade* in 1973 is a sin on par with Hitler's genocide of the Jews. The so-called pro-choice movement consists of nothing more than selfish apologists for promiscuity and murder.

As we move up the integrative complexity ladder to score levels 2 and 3, we see greater tolerance for alternative ways of looking at the world. An example of score level 3 would be as follows:

> I am pro-choice, but I don't see it as an easy choice to make. I find abortion personally and morally repugnant. But I recognize everyone doesn't agree with me. I don't have a right to impose my personal religious and moral philosophy on other people.

As we move to score levels 4 and 5, we not only see evidence that reasonable people may disagree on an issue, we see active attempts to explain how such disagreements might have arisen or to specify how the conflicting perspectives of reasonable people may be reconciled. For example,

> Some people see abortion as murder; some people see it as a fundamental civil liberty. Which position people take depends on how they look at the fetus. At what point should we grant the fetus the rights we grant to human beings? A reasonable compromise is at the point of viability outside the womb.

As we move to the highest score levels in integrative complexity coding (levels 6 and 7), we see not only the emergence of efforts to integrate conflicting values and points of view but also the emergence of flexible and complex combinatorial principles. For example,

> Some people see abortion as murder; some people see it as a fundamental civil liberty. Which position you take depends on a host of issues, including biological-medical (at what point does the fetus become viable?), ethical (at what point should we grant the fetus the rights we grant to human beings?), and legal-constitutional (did the Supreme Court overreach itself when it declared a right to abortion to be inherent in the U.S. Constitution? Should legislators or judges make these decisions?). Reasonable people can disagree not only over the legal and ethical status of abortion but also over who should be making such decisions. It is possible, for example, to favor continued access to abortion but to deny that abortion is a constitutionally protected right and to accept that legislators may limit access to the procedure under certain conditions. Abortion is not an all-or-nothing issue.

Training people to assess integrative complexity usually requires a weeklong workshop in which coders learn to recognize the telltale linguistic indicators of differentiation (e.g., *but, however, although*) and integration (e.g., *mutual, joint, balancing, trade-offs*). It also entails disabusing people of the notion that the "good guys" are always more integratively complex than the "bad guys." Most of our coders have been liberals. I needed to ensure that there was no political bias in the integrative complexity codes that people assigned. For this purpose, we created a set of practice materials in which we eliminated any correlation between the integrative simplicity-complexity of arguments and the liberalism-conservatism of positions taken. We dug up (from the archives) or conjured up (from our imaginations) simple and complex arguments for both liberal and conservative policies. I remember a long training session about ten years ago in which we were discussing the score to be given to a "law and order" Republican speech that also acknowledged the need to protect people from unreasonable search and seizure. As we looked at the text, there was overwhelming evidence of evaluative differentiation. One coder, however, refused to be "duped." The man, in her view, was nothing more than a "sophisticated racist," and she wasn't going to "reward" sophisticated racists with high integrative complexity scores. This would-be coder made two mistakes. First, she thought she could read beyond the text to the state of mind of the speaker. She may or may not have been right, but if we allow coders to project their own biases into texts in this manner, we foreclose a lot of possibilities. Only people who agree with our coders could be rated complex—hardly an interesting or compelling result. And research teams that harbor different political prejudices will be unable to replicate our findings—hardly the basis for a cumulative science. The coder's second mistake was her notion that she was rewarding somebody by assigning a high complexity score. There is nothing inherently good about complexity (one can be an integratively complex planner of mass murder) or inherently bad about simplicity (one can be a simpleminded advocate of love of humanity). The enormous difficulty people have in thinking about integrative simplicity-complexity (or, for that matter, any form of political behavior) in a value-neutral way is a leitmotif of this chapter.

My early work on integrative complexity illustrates the law of the hammer. Give a child a hammer, and everything becomes a nail. After having been given the integrative complexity coding system, I soon was coding the integrative complexity of everything I saw and heard. This habit can become tiresome for one's friends. The next time a friend goes off into a passionate political harangue, explain to that friend that his or her response was "integratively simple—only a 1." It sounds more than a trifle condescending, even insulting, but I made an interesting discovery. Although most people did not take kindly to my characterizing their opinions as "integratively simple," a few people accepted the label with pride: "Yes, that is indeed the way I like to think. No pussyfooting around. I get to the point, and quickly. Like Harry Truman (who once begged for a one-armed economist), I don't have much patience with 'on the one hand' and 'on the other' thinking." At first this reaction struck me as a perverse and willful defense of dogmatism. Later I changed my mind.

I didn't have much time, however, in my pretenure days to contemplate "normative questions" about how people *should* think. I wanted to describe and explain how people do think, and for that purpose I had to collect data, data, and more data. In collaboration with many others, I applied the integrative complexity coding system to a wide range of documents. Sometimes we coded the thoughts college students had on contemporary issues. Sometimes we coded diplomatic communications that heads of state exchanged during crises that either did or did not result in war. Sometimes we coded the speeches of revolutionary leaders or presidential candidates or British parliamentarians or members of the Soviet Politburo. Sometimes we coded quarrels between husbands and wives over how to divide family responsibilities after a baby was born. In short, there was virtually no limit to the range of applications of integrative complexity coding.

We discovered a variety of things about integrative complexity. We learned about the types of situations that can motivate people to become more or less integratively complex. We learned about the types of people who are more likely to be integratively complex on average. And we learned about the consequences of integrative complexity. Are integratively complex thinkers more "accurate" judges of others or "better" decision makers?

One discovery I made in formally presenting my work on integrative complexity to audiences around the country was that, like my coders, academics tend to agree that integrative complexity is a good thing. How, after all, can one be too open-minded and tolerant? And what can possibly be good about being closed-minded and intolerant? This tendency to place a positive value on integrative complexity and to devalue simplicity was reinforced by many of the early findings that came out of the research program:

1.   We found that national leaders who spoke or wrote in integratively complex ways were less likely to go to war than were leaders who spoke or wrote in integratively simple ways. Integrative simplicity tended to be the language of war: "Our side is completely right; your side, completely wrong; do what we say or else." Indeed, we found a sharp decline in integrative complexity to be a useful "lead indicator" of the intention to resort to violence. Complexity tended to plunge in the months, sometimes weeks, before a war.

2.   Integrative complexity tended to be associated with reaching major international agreements or treaties. Integrative complexity was the language of conciliation and compromise: "We understand your legitimate interest in X; try to understand our legitimate interest in Y; perhaps we can work out a reasonable agreement that reconciles these interests and leaves us both better off than we were before." In short, integratively complex negotiators try to strike a balance between deterrence (be strong

enough to resist exploitation) and reassurance (convince the other side you are not out to destroy them). Increases in integrative complexity by both sides are "lead indicators" of treaty signing in the next three to six months.

3. We found that Presidents were much more integratively cómplex after coming to power than they had been during election campaigns. As campaigners, they relied on simplistic slogans; the prevailing assumption among elites is that the public knows little about politics, has a limited attention span, and can be most effectively swayed by vivid images (of crime, unemployment, etc.) and by short, snappy one-liners. Actually coming to power is, however, a sobering experience. Now politicians have to explain to people why all those simple promises on the campaign trail will be extremely difficult to honor: "I'd love to increase price supports for your crops, but . . ." or "I hate to increase taxes; however, . . ."

The implication that integrative complexity is highly adaptive did not receive support only from the archival and library research. It also received support from laboratory experiments in which there are reasonably clear-cut criteria for what constitutes good or poor performance (negotiating partners succeed or fail in identifying a mutually beneficial compromise solution to their conflict of interest; observers of other people's behavior are or are not too quick to draw strong conclusions about the personalities of other people and are or are not too slow to change their first impressions in response to contradictory evidence). Because the experimenters know the "right answer"—they created the problems that subjects work on—they are in a relatively strong position to judge the quality of subjects' performance.

Consider the following examples of what we have learned from such experiments: (1) Simulation studies of international crises (in which students role-played national leaders) showed that subjects who were classified as integratively complex were much more likely to find peaceful solutions to disputes and correspondingly less likely to go to "war" with each other than were subjects who were classified as integratively simple (this finding parallels quite precisely the archival work on actual heads of state). (2) Experimental studies of negotiators showed that complex negotiators better understood the priorities of the other side and were often better able to reach viable compromises that left everyone better off. (3) Studies of person perception and social cognition showed that integratively complex subjects were less susceptible to many biases in thinking compared with integratively simple subjects. Integratively simple subjects were more prone to the primacy effect (the tendency to jump to conclusions based on evidence that has been presented early and refuse to revise those impressions in response to later evidence), the fundamental attribution error (the tendency to jump to conclusions about other people on the basis of a single incident even when there are alternative situational explanations for the behavior), and overconfidence (the tendency to think that one knows more than one actually does). Integratively simple thinkers were also poorer predictors of the behavior of others. Complex thinkers were less likely to make sweeping trait judgments of others (total workaholic, social butterfly, etc.) and to recognize that different situations activate different aspects of people's personalities.

In short, the evidence steadily mounted that the prevailing wisdom might be right. Maybe integrative complexity was an unalloyed 100 percent blessing; maybe there was no "down side." That conclusion increasingly, however, rubbed me the wrong way. Ironically, it struck me as far too simplistic to conclude that complexity is always beneficial. I had met too many people who held integratively complex opinions that I found to be confused, poorly reasoned, or downright immoral. Thus integrative complexity could not be a sufficient condition for wisdom. And I'd come across a number of integratively simple opinions that impressed me with their clarity, rigor, and adherence to principle. Thus integrative complexity could not be a necessary condition for wisdom. I don't expect you, however, to be persuaded by ex cathedra pronouncements about what constitutes wisdom. You want (or should want) evidence. What can be counted as reasonably good evidence that integrative complexity leads to conclusions that we judge as cognitively inferior (thinking this way leads to judgments that deviate from widely held prescriptions concerning how people should think) or morally inferior (thinking that way leads to judgments that, given our ethical and political values, we disapprove of)? Let's first examine the morality of integrative complexity, focusing on how integrative complexity correlates with political ideology, and then turn to the issue of cognitive efficiency.

THE MORALITY OF COMPLEXITY

To illustrate the two-edged moral quality of integrative complexity, it is instructive to compare a 1984 study we carried out on British parliamentarians with a 1992 study we have just finished on politicians in the pre–Civil War United States. In the study of British politicians we had access to in-depth interviews conducted by the political scientist Robert Putnam. The politicians talked about a wide range of problems confronting Britain, including the difficulty of simultaneously helping the poor, restoring confidence in the economy, controlling government spending, and encouraging individual initiative. We found that politicians were most likely to be integratively complex if they took moderate liberal or social-democratic positions that recognized trade-offs between economic efficiency and social equality and between encouraging individual effort and taking care of the poor. They wanted taxes to be high enough to transfer wealth from the well off to the poor but not so high as to discourage the well off from working and contributing to economic growth. They wanted to help the poor, but not so much as to encourage chronic dependency on government aid. By contrast, politicians on the "far left" (radical socialists who favored very generous welfare schemes and high levels of taxation to redistribute wealth) were less integratively complex. For them, most policy questions had easy answers. Wealth was illegitimate and should be redistributed; capitalism was evil and should give way to socialism.

When we move away from the social democrats in a rightward direction, we again see a gradual and then a dramatic decline in integrative complexity. For extreme conservatives, the answers were again easy. Free-market capitalism provides the surest path to the efficient allocation of resources and the generation of wealth in the long term; welfare schemes only exacerbate poverty in the long run by enervating the poor. Although the hard-line (Tony Benn) wing of the Labor party and the hard-line (Thatcher) wing of the Conservative party could hardly be farther apart in the types of social and economic policies they endorsed, there was a remarkable similarity in the underlying structure or style of their reasoning. Both sides tended to deny value trade-offs. Both sides argued that if only people had the good sense to adopt the politically correct policies, everyone would be much better off in the long term. From the point of view of cognitive style, the extremists resembled each other in their underlying style of reasoning but differed dramatically from the moderates.

Most social psychologists tend to be moderate liberals and favor redistributive schemes similar to those endorsed by the social democrats in the Putnam sample. In the mid-1980s, I remember presenting these data and hearing a number of colleagues comment on either the moral or cognitive superiority of the integratively complex social democrats: reasonable people trying to strike reasonable balances under difficult circumstances.

In the Civil War study we again looked at the integrative complexity of politicians across the political spectrum. This time, however, the political spectrum was anchored on the left-wing end by abolitionists (who regarded slavery as a moral abomination that must end immediately no matter what the consequences), free-soil Republicans (who regarded slavery with deep distaste but were prepared to tolerate it in states where it already existed for the sake of preserving the Union), Buchanan Democrats (who were more tolerant of slavery and were willing to allow it to spread to additional territories within the Union as long as local majorities favored it), and advocates of slavery (who defended the practice and were willing to endorse even southern secession to preserve that traditional way of life). The point of maximum integrative complexity in this study emerged around the free-soil Republicans, the group that was most emotionally and politically torn between the desire to preserve the Union and moral objections to slavery. Integrative complexity fell off as we moved to the left toward the abolitionists (for whom the issue was fundamentally simple: eliminate the evil of human beings owning human beings). Integrative complexity also fell off as we moved toward the right to Buchanan Democrats and finally to southern secessionists (who were the least integratively complex of all the political groups). Defenders of the moral or cognitive superiority of integrative complexity now find themselves in the awkward position of preferring two political factions that favored preserving slavery over a political faction that favored its immediate abolition. Were these reluctant defenders of slavery, once again, just reasonable people trying to strike reasonable balances under difficult circumstances? Or was integrative complexity merely a mask for moral inertia or even cowardice?

There are many other junctures in history at which the integratively simple side in major debates looks more farsighted or more morally principled than the integratively complex side. To offer but one more example, consider the sharp debate in Great Britain in the late 1930s over the intentions of Nazi Germany. The prime minister, Neville Chamberlain, believed that it was possible to appease Nazi Germany, that Hitler was a reasonable man, and that once legitimate German demands were taken into account, there would be "peace in our time." This policy led Chamberlain to do nothing when Hitler annexed territory after territory in central Europe. Chamberlain's sharpest critic within the Conservative party was Winston Churchill. Churchill argued that Nazi Germany was no more than an organized criminal conspiracy (a state of thugs) which would be satisfied with nothing less than the complete domination of Europe. He argued that integratively complex efforts to reconcile British and German national interests were fated to ignoble failure. Not surprisingly, when we code the political rhetoric of Churchill and Chamberlain in this period, we find that Chamberlain held a much more integratively complex view of Nazi Germany and of British policy toward that country than did Churchill.

THE EFFICACY OF COMPLEXITY

Up to now I have shown that integrative complexity can be associated with political positions that most observers in the late twentieth-century United States regard as deeply misguided or morally repugnant. There is another, very different way of making the anticomplexity case: by showing that complexity thinkers are more likely than simple thinkers to deviate from widely accepted standards of "rationality" in judgment and decision making.

Consider the following experimental study of the dilution effect. When we ask subjects to predict the grade point average (GPA) of a student and give those subjects only one item of information (that the student studies either three or thirty-one hours a week), we find that the subjects make confident predictions about grade point average. They expect the diligent student to have a GPA in the vicinity of 3.5 and the lazy student to have a GPA in the vicinity of 2.3. The subjects agree that the number of hours a student studies per week is "diagnostic" of future grades. When we present subjects with diluted information about the student (we not only tell them how many hours a week the student studies but also provide information about dating habits, the furniture in the apartment, and other "irrelevant facts"), we find that the subjects become much less confident in their predictions of GPA. This erosion of confidence is called dilution, and the effect does not make a lot of sense from a strictly statistical point of view. Why should predictively useful information suddenly become much less useful merely because it is accompanied by useless information? In a study with Richard Boettger, we showed that people who think in integratively complex ways are especially prone to the dilution effect and look for relevance even in irrelevance. As a result, they frequently go off on inferential wild-goose chases, turning their imaginations loose and constructing sometimes fanciful stories around evidence of dubious usefulness. For example, on learning that the student had never dated anyone longer than two to three months, one integratively complex subject concluded that the student had to be emotionally unstable. From that, the subject concluded the student was likely to be doing relatively poorly in school. Another subject, focusing on the fact that the student played tennis three or four times a month, drew the conclusion that the student had a high activity level and therefore was doing well in school. Integratively complex thinkers try "to do the right thing" and weave all the information presented into a coherent account of the student's life. The result, however, is often predictions that are inferior to those which would have been reached if the subjects had simply focused on the relevant information and ignored the irrelevant.

This example is revealing. The same habits of thinking that reduce bias and improve accuracy in some settings can do exactly the opposite in other settings. Integrative complexity can eliminate overconfidence, but it can also produce underconfidence.

A final example comes from an experiment that examines a common problem confronting society. When should we accept a new drug into the U.S. pharmaceutical market? The Food and Drug Administration of the federal government is formally charged with this task, and in principle it is not supposed to admit drugs into the market that are not both "safe and effective." Unfortunately, if we took this test literally, virtually no drug would be permitted on the market: Even aspirin can be dangerous. "Reasonable" people must balance the costs and benefits of particular drugs against each other. There is often the risk that a drug that will save many lives will endanger at least some. We asked subjects to make a series of judgments about the acceptability of a drug for breaking up blood clots that can cause fatal heart attacks. We experimentally manipulated the number of lives likely to be saved and lost from introducing the drug into the U.S. market. In the process, we learned something interesting about integrative complexity. When the drug had not yet been accepted into the market, integratively complex thinkers were more likely to require a higher standard of proof than were integratively simple thinkers. For simple thinkers, it was often enough that the drug would save twice as many people as it would endanger (a reasonable—albeit still highly conservative—standard given that the only people who would receive the drug would already be in serious danger of dying from heart failure). For integratively complex thinkers it was necessary that the drug save between *six and nine times* more people than it endangered. It is important to understand the implications of this decision. It means that many people whose lives could have been saved if the drug had been permitted into the market will now die. Moreover, the number of people who will die as the result of this failure to act far exceeds the number of people who would die from side effects of the drug. Lives lost from omission are valued much less than lives lost from commission (especially if one thinks in integratively complex ways). There was also a strong tendency for integratively complex thinkers to buck-pass and procrastinate when confronted with difficult cost-benefit decisions. Whenever possible, they were more likely to try to transfer responsibility for making decisions to others or try to delay making a decision until further evidence came in (although they realized the likelihood of new evidence coming in any time soon was extremely low). It is reasonable to ask: How many people are we willing to allow to die as the complex decision makers painfully and slowly weigh the pros and cons of action and inaction?

Where does this leave us? It underscores the importance of looking at integrative complexity in an integratively complex way. In the eyes of many people, integrative simplicity represents rigidity, dogmatism, and self righteousness, whereas integrative complexity represents flexibility, open-mindedness, and tolerance for diverse viewpoints. In the eyes of others, integrative simplicity represents a willingness to stick by one's principles, a willingness to persevere, and the ability to distinguish the irrelevant from the relevant, whereas integrative complexity represents wishy-washiness, moral confusion, and even paralysis.

There is, of course, a double irony here. I started off as a believer in the benefits of integratively complex reasoning. My doubts grew, and I abandoned that belief. Now, as I look back and try to make sense of this research program, I find myself returning to my original conviction, although in modified form. Good judgment in social and political life does not always require that one think in integratively complex ways. It does require, however, that one have the capacity to think that way and the wisdom to know when to use that capacity.

This broad overview of my research on integrative complexity brings us full circle back to the title of this chapter. Political psychologists must continually grapple with the temptation to design studies in ways that make the side one prefers look more psychologically "attractive" than the side one rejects. The story of integrative complexity research serves as a useful reminder that it is possible to have "too much" of a psychological variable that at first glance looks like a good thing. Political psychologists need to ask themselves excruciatingly difficult and soul-searching questions: Am I allowing my fear and hatred of war to influence my judgment about the effectiveness of policies of deterrence in achieving a nation's goals? Am I allowing my abhorrence of racism and poverty to influence my psychological characterizations of people who disagree with me about welfare policy or affirmative action? Has my desire to protect children from sexual abuse blinded me to the ways in which interviews generate false accusations? The list is potentially a long one indeed. Moreover, and this point should be emphasized, there is nothing wrong with entering political psychology with the hope of making the world a better place. Research can be long and hard work, and researchers often need the extra motivational push that idealism can provide. The problem arises when our political passions direct us toward one conclusion and the rules of fair and rigorous scientific procedure direct us not to draw any conclusion at all or even to draw the opposite conclusion. Many thoughtful people see this choice as an integratively complex dilemma with no satisfactory solution. Speaking for myself, however, I think there is a good integratively simple answer. Stick with the scientific method and don't play political favorites.

Why do I close with such a dogmatic and emphatically simplistic answer? It comes back to personal experience. I've been asked a number of times in the last decade to consult with officials in the legislative and executive branches of the government. These people have typically been very smart and quite suspicious. They are smart in the sense that they understand, respect, and respond to evidence that bears directly on their concern of the moment. They are suspicious in the sense that they are on the lookout both for hired guns (who, for a fee, will argue that smoking does not cause lung cancer) and for zealots (who, for a cause, will twist evidence to render it consistent with the prevailing "politically correct" orthodoxy on the left or right). The lesson I've drawn from my encounters with the world of power is that credibility is our most important asset. When we lose our credibility, we become just one more activist group clamoring for public attention.

Heartless though it may sound, we must resist seduction by good causes. If we overstate the evidence in one case, the overstatements will ultimately come back to haunt us. Indeed, this has already begun to happen to the American Psychological Association, which has submitted friend-of-the-court briefings to the Supreme Court (on two separate cases) that simultaneously argued that (1) the psychological evidence supports the view that adolescents are as capable as adults of making decisions in "rational" and deliberative ways (therefore, parental permission for adolescent abortions cannot be justified on the ground that teenagers lack the competence to foresee consequences and balance counterarguments) and (2) the psychological evidence suggests that adolescents are much more likely than adults to make decisions in impulsive and shortsighted ways (therefore, capital punishment for minors should be prohibited). I would guess that most psychologists would sympathize with the moral objectives behind these two interventions in the legal process. It is hard to imagine, however, that the long-term credibility of psychology as science is well served by selectively highlighting or downplaying evidence as a function of the values at stake. And if we lose our credibility, we won't be in a position to help any cause. It is as simple as that!

SUGGESTED READINGS

Breslauer, G., & Tetlock, P. E. (1991). *Learning in U.S. and Soviet foreign policy.* Boulder, CO: Westview.

Schroder, H. M., Driver, M., & Streufert, S. (1967). *Human information processing.* New York: Holt.

Sniderman, P., Brody, R., & Tetlock, P. E. (1991). *Reasoning and choice: Explorations in political psychology.* New York: Cambridge University Press.

Suedfeld, P., & Tetlock, P. E. (1991). *Psychology and social advocacy.* Washington, DC: Hemisphere.

Tetlock, P. E. (1984). Cognitive style and political belief systems in the British House of Commons. *Journal of Personality and Social Psychology: Personality Processes and Individual Differences, 46,* 365–375.

———— (1992). The impact of accountability on judgment and choice: Toward a social contingency model. In M. Zanna (Ed.), *Advances in experimental social psychology* (vol. 25, pp. 331–376). New York: Academic Press.

———— Armor, D., & Peterson, R. (1994). The slavery debate in antebellum America: Cognitive style, value conflict, and the limits of compromise. *Journal of Personality and Social Psychology, 66,* 115–126.

———— & Boettger, R. (1989). Social and cognitive strategies of coping with accountability: Conformity, complexity, and bolstering. *Journal of Personality and Social Psychology: Interpersonal Relations and Group Dynamics, 57,* 632–641.

———— & Kim, J. (1987). Accountability and overconfidence in a personality prediction task. *Journal of Personality and Social Psychology: Attitudes and Social Cognition, 52,* 700–709.

———— McGuire, C., Peterson, R., Feld, P., & Chang, S. (1992). Assessing political group dynamics: A test of the groupthink model. *Journal of Personality and Social Psychology, 63,* 402–423.

Epilogue

———— ❖ ————

*A*fter reading *The Social Psychologists: Research Adventures,* we hope that you feel the excitement that characterizes the exploration of important issues in social behavior. More important, though, we trust that you have gained insight into the social psychological research process and the people who engage in that process.

We have devoted a great deal of energy to the preparation of this book and would appreciate your feedback. If you have any comments or suggestions for improvement, we would like to hear from you. Please forward your comments to us at the Department of Psychology, State University of New York at Plattsburgh, Plattsburgh, NY 12901.

Thanks.
Gary G. Brannigan
Matthew R. Merrens